THE EVOLUTION OF MODERN ITALY

ARTHUR JAMES WHYTE

The Norton Library

W · W · NORTON & COMPANY · INC ·

NEW YORK

PREFACE

THE outstanding events and personalities of nineteenth-century Italy have been the subject of numerous books by English writers. The classic volumes on Garibaldi by Professor Trevelyan, now Master of Trinity, Mr. and Mrs. Berkeley's study of Pius IX and the events of 1848, my own two volumes on Cavour, Mr. Griffith's portrait of Mazzini and various other books have recorded the dominant features of Italian history between 1815 and 1870. In the last quarter of a century, however, Italian historians have concentrated mainly on other aspects of this period: on the origins of the movement: on the work of Charles Albert: on the light thrown by documents and other sources on hitherto accepted verdicts and interpretations, as well as the publication of many memoirs, diaries and letters. As to events after 1870 they have as yet scarcely begun to consider them critically, Croce's *History of Italy from 1870 to 1914* and Rosi's *Storia Contemporanea* dealing very gently with the political life compared with Miss Hentze's indictment in her volume on Pre-Fascist Italy or the strictures of Mr. Sprigge in his recent volume on the Development of Modern Italy.

The present volume, written mainly from Italian sources, has kept a double purpose in view: to link the more or less familiar story of the Risorgimento to what preceded and followed it, and to bring into greater prominence those aspects of the movement upon which more light has been recently thrown. The rapid survey of Italian history in the opening chapter seemed necessary to throw into relief the task of the Risorgimento and to emphasize the importance of the Napoleonic period, which some Italian writers tend to underrate, maintaining that the movement was purely Italian and, in essence, independent of French influence, which merely retarded a process begun with the reforms of the eighteenth century: a point of view which the present writer does not accept. At what point to close the story was also difficult, since Fascism was in action before the Peace Treaty was signed. But the Treaty of Rapallo seemed the point where the claims of Italy appeared definitely settled and from which the two paths of Italian history, linked to the past and to the unknown future, most clearly diverged.

Italy had but sixty years of parliamentary government, which was, moreover, an alien importation unsupported by tradition, strongly opposed by the Church, and planted in a soil corrupted by absolutism. Based on a wide conception of liberty, uncontrolled by the necessary corrective of political education and self-discipline, it produced a state of political weakness and a social condition akin to anarchy. The twenty years of dragooning into greatness which followed was no more successful, imposed as it was upon a reluctant people, too intelligent to mistake appearance for reality and too innately sceptical to accept at its face value either the rhetoric of the balcony or the panegyrics of a subservient Press. These two successive failures of liberty and compulsion have been a bitter lesson, and it remains now for Italy to devise a *tertium quid*.

.   .   .   .   .

War-time conditions have necessitated the elimination of footnotes and references, which is, however, not without its compensations, for, though of value to the student, this appearance of erudition is apt to alarm the ordinary reading public to whom it is hoped that this work will appeal.

ARTHUR J. WHYTE

LATIMER ROAD
OXFORD

CONTENTS

MAPS

AUSTRIAN EMPIRE

PIEDMONT

LOMBARDY

1859

VENETIA

1866

OTTOMAN

EMPIRE

KINGDOM

PARMA

1860

MODENA

1860

STATES

OF

TUSCANY

THE

CHURCH

1860

1870

PAPAL

°Rome

STATE

OF

SARDINIA

THE TWO SICILIES

1860

Miles 50   0   50   100   150 Miles

ITALY IN 1920
NEW BOUNDARY 1920

THE EVOLUTION OF
MODERN ITALY

CHAPTER ONE

THE PREPARATION, 1715-1814

THE history of Italy in the nineteenth century is the story of a national resurrection, a Risorgimento, and before considering it, it will be well to cast a rapid glance across the past and recall the debt which the world owes to Italy, for her contribution to civilization has been incalculable. Her language, her law, her culture and her religion, were the formative elements of human progress for a period of nearly a thousand years. Emerging under Kings, she won her Empire as a republic and held it under Emperors. When she could no longer conquer with the sword she conquered with the Cross, and built up the marvellous fabric of the Catholic Church. Terrible in war, she civilized in peace, and whilst her legions kept watch upon the boundaries of her empire, her gracious villas spread culture and refinement from York to the Euxine. When at last the bastions gave way and the empire was overrun by barbarians, she absorbed, civilized and christianized her rude masters, and led captivity captive. Throughout the dark ages she kept alight the flickering lamp of learning until the leaven of Christianity and Roman Law had done its work and stability returned to Europe. She gathered up the religion, the ideals and the learning of the new age in Dante's immortal Vision, and then, with unexhausted vitality, set herself to recover the treasures of the forgotten past. Her passion for the classical world and the learning of the ancients inspired the Humanist movement and her wealth and generosity saved the remains of classical culture from the exterminating Turk. The flowering of her literary and artistic genius in the fifteenth and sixteenth centuries is an epoch to itself and needs no comment, for wherever European culture has spread the work of the Italian painters and poets, sculptors and builders in the Renaissance is known and treasured.

But Italy drank too deep of the heady wine of pagan thought and beauty, and corruption followed. Though herself barely touched by the Reformation, the stern spirit of the counter movement, while it purified the Papacy, killed the Renaissance. Her last great poet, Tasso, was educated by the Jesuits and wrote under the shadow of the Inquisition. Before the close of the sixteenth century Italy ceased to laugh, joy died, and her genius fled. She bequeathed to Europe the wealth of her political experience, the glories of her art and literature, and the rigid devotion of her historic faith, and sank into impotence. Her military spirit was decayed: unity she had none: and the little states into which she was divided, so fertile in genius in the Renaissance, were a fatal weakness in the face of the great Powers now taking shape beyond the Alps. For a century and a half she lay inert while France and Spain fought for possession of her unprotesting body. While Italy slept a new world came into being. One might almost date it from the year 1564 when Michelangelo died and Galileo was born. For the new world was one of scientific thought, of relentless criticism, and experimental methods. Even in this, Italy was among the pioneers, for the 'new men' as Bacon called them included Telesio, and Giordano Bruno, burnt as a heretic, and Tommaso Campanella who rewrote his works from memory in prison after they too had shared the fate of Bruno. But throughout the seventeenth century there was no sign of life in Italy and not until the eighteenth century does she at last show signs of waking.

The long struggle against the ascendancy of France came to an end at last with the Treaty of Utrecht (1713) and the death of Louis XIV two years later. It made great changes in Italy. Naples and the Milanese or Lombardy, as it now came to be called, passed from Spain to Austria and the deadening weight of Spanish Viceroys was at length lifted. The Duke of Savoy received the island of Sicily and took his title of King from his new acquisition. But this settlement did not last long. In 1717 Spain attacked Sicily. Charles Emanuel, unable to defend the island, offered no opposition and three years later accepted a new arrangement by which Sicily passed to Austria and in exchange he received the island of Sardinia. Thus the Dukes of Savoy became Kings of Sardinia, a title they held until in 1860 they became Kings of Italy. The next change took place in 1735. Elizabeth Farnese, heiress to the Duchy of Parma, the masterful wife of Philip V of Spain, resolved to attempt the recovery of Naples and the Milanese from Austria. She despatched an army for this purpose to Italy under her son Don Carlos. Frustrated in the north, he turned southward, and without difficulty took possession of Naples and Sicily. As Charles III of Naples, he and his descendants of the line ruled the Kingdom of Naples until in 1860 it was surrendered to Garibaldi and Victor Emanuel II. Three years later the last of the Medici, Giovanni Gastone, Grand-duke of Tuscany, died, and the Duchy then passed to Francis of Habsburg-Lorraine, the husband of Maria Theresa, who became Archduchess of Austria on the death of her father Charles VI in 1740. In 1745 Francis was elected Emperor and Tuscany passed to his son Leopold. The final change was that of the Treaty of Aquisgrana in 1748, by which Sardinia, on withdrawal from the War of the Austrian Succession, advanced her boundary to the river Ticino and received back Nice and Savoy. Italy was now settled on the general lines which were to last until the formation of the united kingdom in 1860, for although these rulers or their successors were destined to be driven out by Napoleon, they were all restored in 1815. Henceforth, until the French invasion of Piedmont in 1793, Italy was at peace.

The eighteenth century was a period of great social contrasts. There was a crust of great wealth at the top and underneath a mass of poverty. This was, perhaps, more marked in Italy than in other countries owing to the absence of any considerable middle class, and the rich seemed richer and the poor poorer than elsewhere. Italy at this time was almost entirely an agricultural country in which the political and intellectual life was largely confined to a few big towns, Milan and Naples, Venice, Florence and Rome. The great majority of the people, living in villages and small towns, took little interest in politics. Governments, to the peasantry, were merely organs of taxation and oppression from whom no benefit was to be expected. Very few could read. From long experience sceptical of promises, practical in their attitude to life, they took their opinions from their parish priest to whom they turned for everything. There were great contrasts also in the temperaments of the natives in different regions of Italy. The easy-going Tuscan, with a natural leaning to art and poetry, was a very different individual from the hot-blooded, quick-tempered Romagnuol; as the pleasure-loving Venetian was of another type to the superstitious, suspicious Neapolitan, sun-loving and lazy, but secretive, quick at revenge and dangerous when roused. Regionalism was very strong and the degree of jealousy between states or districts was in inverse ratio to the distance between them, as we can see by the chronic suspicion of Lombards and Genoese towards their neighbours in Piedmont. All this must be borne in mind in dealing with the Risorgimento, for it helps to explain why the peasantry as a whole stood aloof from the movement and why there was so little genuine co-operation, so that the true motive force consisted of a minority who bore the whole burden.

A glowing picture has been drawn of Italian city life in this period. Its most famous panegyrist was Goethe. Rome was the artistic and religious centre of Europe. The gorgeous pomp of the Papacy, the sumptuous banquets and receptions of the Cardinals and Roman nobility, the treasures of the Libraries and Museums and the new interest in archaeology, attracted to Rome not only the wealthy aristocracy and the cosmopolitan element from all over Europe, but poets and painters, sculptors and writers. All who could travel came to Italy and Italy meant Rome. Venice too, where Goldoni's comedies and the Carnival were a special attraction, welcomed many visitors. Florence was, then as now, a centre for all who loved Renaissance architecture and painting, and in spite of bad inns and dangerous roads many visitors found their way to Naples. But there was another side to Italian life which the visitors did not see. Crime in Italy was rampant. In Rome during the Pontificate of Clement XIII (1759-1769) 13,000 homicides were registered in the Papal States, of which 4,000 were in Rome itself, with a population of 160,000. The wealthy city of Milan, which could boast of its two thousand smart equipages in the afternoon parade on the Corso, was even worse. In the twenty years from 1741 to 1762 the executions or life sentences to the Venetian galleys amounted to 73,000. So widespread were crimes of violence that the municipality provided an itinerant Court of Justice, with a judge, a criminal lawyer, a confessor and an executioner, together with a posse of police, who patrolled the city on horseback, with power to arrest, try and execute any malefactor whom they caught. The conditions of things in Venice and Naples, with their dark, narrow streets and overcrowded quarters, was quite possibly even worse, but neither the Council of Ten nor the Neapolitan police kept any record. Yet it is necessary to remember that the criminal law throughout Europe in those days was of terrible severity, to which England was no exception. As late as 1818 in the Assizes held at Lincoln, out of twenty-four cases in which the most serious charges were burglary and larceny, no less than fifteen sentences of death were passed, and a distinguished English judge has written that even in the early forties 'offences which would now be treated as not even deserving of a day's imprisonment in many cases, were then invariably punished with death'.

The social condition of Italy in the second half of the century, brilliant on the surface and tragic beneath, produced a considerable intellectual movement, especially in Lombardy and Naples. The writers of this period reflect the general tendencies of the age: the spirit of criticism, dissatisfaction with existing conditions, and the demand for reform. The unaccustomed degree of liberty of expression allowed them, was due to the fact that their views coincided in general with those of their rulers; for this was the age of the 'Benevolent Despots', of Frederic the Great and Catherine of Russia and the Emperor Joseph II. These monarchs, though no less despotic than their predecessors, took an interest in the welfare of their subjects, and according to their lights, endeavoured to promote improvement in their conditions of life. Three states in Italy benefited from their activities: Lombardy, under Maria Theresa and later under Joseph II; Tuscany under Leopold I, Joseph's brother; and Naples, under Charles III, a disciple of the same school of thought, whose work, after his translation to Spain as King in 1759, was continued by his Minister the Marquis Tannucci.

The golden age of Austrian government in Italy was the reign of Maria Theresa, when except for the Viceroy and a few high officials the administration was in the hands of the Italians themselves. The most beneficial reform in Lombardy was the censimento, a fixed tax on land made after an exhaustive survey in 1757. The assessment was moderate and led to the development of an intensive form of cultivation which made Lombardy the most prosperous part of Italy. The reform of the communal administration which preceded it, simplified the system of rural government, replacing the ancient councils and congregations by three responsible officials. The abolition of privileges and exemptions equalized taxation and improved the lot of the smaller proprietors. With the Church, Joseph was more severe. He suppressed more than a hundred convents and monasteries, though even this left some three hundred untouched, and by a Concordat with the Papacy brought all ecclesiastical possessions acquired since the sixteenth century under taxation. The proceeds from the sale of the suppressed religious houses were devoted to hospitals and the development of the University of Pavia. The Lombards were exempted from all military service, and except for a few regiments kept to maintain the imperial dignity, military rule was absent. In his later years Joseph developed a mania for centralization, to the great detriment of Lombardy. The senate was abolished, Austrian judges and officials replaced Italians, and the province was bound close to the general Austrian system and treated as an integral part of the Empire.

The reforms of Leopold in Tuscany were even more thorough-going. He established free trade, abolishing all restrictions on imports and exports; swept away the whole mediaeval system of trade guilds and replaced it with a Chamber of Commerce. In 1770 he imposed equality of taxation on all citizens including the Royal Family. He introduced vaccination, reformed the prisons, abolished secret pro-cedure, torture and the death penalty, exposing implements of torture found in the prisons in the courtyard of the Bargello. He restricted appeals to Rome, suppressed useless convents and monasteries, and used for public purposes the income accruing from vacant benefices. Leopold had no use for the army or navy. The former he disbanded, keeping only a garrison for the radical city of Leghorn, and replaced it with a civic guard, the latter he sold to Russia; there were only two corvettes. In his last years Leopold tried to reform the Church, under the inspiration of Scipione Ricci, Bishop of Pistoia. In this he failed after the Bishop's submission to Rome and subsequent resignation. The effect of this work was to make Tuscany one of the best governed states in Europe.

A far more difficult task awaited the reforming zeal of Charles III in Naples. The soil of the country was owned by the Church, the Barons and the King. 'If we divide all the families of the kingdom into sixty parts', wrote the economist Antonio Genovesi in 1765, 'one of these owns land, the rest have not enough to be buried in. Half the soil of Naples is held by the Church and may not be sold, a mortal wound, I know not if it is remediable.' For a population well under five millions the Church provided twenty-one Archbishops, one hundred and sixty-five Bishops and Abbots, fifty thousand Priests and more than the same number of monks and nuns. She drew an income from all sources estimated at not less than twelve millions of ducats. The Church lived in ease and often luxury, amidst poverty and squalor unequalled in Europe. No less a problem was presented by the baronage, who owned vast tracts of land, often wild and uncultivated, but which included great numbers of villages and small townships. All were held in feu. On the condition of the peasantry the verdict of contemporaries is unanimous. Abject and utterly ignor-ant, living in hovels and caves, tied to the soil, without rights or defenders, they were like beasts of burden that cannot eat the food they carry on their backs. 'The earth, the water, the minerals, the forests', writes the most recent historian of Naples at this time, 'the very souls and bodies of the inhabitants were regarded as part and parcel of the feu. Up to the second French invasion the *Jus feminarum*, the *Jus stercoris* (manure), the *Jus aquae pluviae* (rain water), were in force, though the first could be commuted for a money payment.'

With a country in such a condition reform was a labour of Hercules, but something was done. By a Concordat with the Papacy the clergy were rendered liable for half the amount of taxation paid by the laity, though with a long list of exemptions. The ratio of clergy to population was fixed at ten per thousand, and after nearly half a century of effort their numbers were reduced from a hundred thousand to eighty-one thousand. After the King's departure for Spain, Tannucci the Viceroy continued the same policy. He persistently asserted the rights of the throne against the Church, abolishing privileges, insisting on the royal consent before the publication of Bulls and Papal ordinances, and extracting money from the Church whenever possible. The Pope retorted by refusing to fill episcopal vacancies. Then Tannucci expelled the Jesuits, and two years later refused to pay the *Chinea*, an annual gift to the Pope of a white horse and seven thousand ducats, which had been paid from Norman times as a recognition of Papal overlordship, a claim which had long since become an anachronism.

The attempt to suppress feudalism was even less successful, owing to the fact that the judges who had to apply the law were appointed by the barons themselves. Charles endeavoured to attract the nobility to Court and relieve the tenants of their presence. He issued an edict permitting the peasantry to sell their produce in the open market and not to their feudal lords only. He admitted the right of appeal from the Baronial to the Royal Courts, but distance and expense rendered it nugatory, apart from the risk of unpleasant reprisals from an indignant feudal lord. Another edict limited the number of armed retainers, chiefly brigands, protected by the barons and used indiscriminately against exasperated peasants or the royal power, and he abolished a number of degrading personal services which tenants were called upon to render without payment. Tannucci continued to harass the baronage with new ordinances and restrictions, but, in practice, they had little effect, for the evil required a far stronger hand and much more drastic methods, and he never touched the root of the difficulty.[1]

Both in Lombardy and in Naples, the efforts at reform had the support of the liberal and progressive elements. At Milan, the Marquis Beccaria, whose work on Crimes and Punishments was to be a landmark in criminal legislation, was a strong advocate of every forward movement. The brothers Alessandro and Pietro Verri, senators like Beccaria and both economists, wrote freely on current needs and methods of improving them. It was the same in Naples, where a group of economists and social reformers did their best to stimulate the government towards reform. Probably the most influential of these men was Antonio Genovesi, for whom the first Chair of Political Economy in Europe was founded at the University. His lectures as well as his numerous writings helped greatly to create that spirit of liberalism which promoted the reaction of 1799 which came to a tragic end with the restoration of the King from his exile in Sicily. Besides Genovesi, the fine work of Filangieri on the History of Legislation, the Political Essays of Mario Pagano and the writings of Melchiorre Delfico, Galanti and the Abbé Galiani, all reflect the new spirit of economic freedom and social amelioration characteristic of the age.

The rest of Italy was untouched by the spirit of reform. Venice, still under its Doge and Council of Ten, silent and decadent, with no policy but neutrality and no life but frivolity, lay torpid amidst her lagoons. The states of the Church rivalled Naples in misery and misgovernment under the rule of priests, where every bishop had his private prison and every literary work was subject to a triple censure, police, bishops and Inquisition; where the hopeless overlapping of authorities brought all improvement to a standstill and made reform, even had it been suggested, impossible. In the northwest corner of the peninsula lay the Kingdom of Sardinia, the least Italian but the most virile of all her states.

This little kingdom, destined to be the motive force in the making of united Italy, which was to provide the soldiers and statesmen of the Risorgimento and to seat on the throne of the new nation its own House of Savoy, was the only state in Italy which had an army with a fighting tradition. As a buffer state between France and Austria, geography conditioned her policy, and her readiness to defend her frontiers alone safeguarded her existence. Surrounded on three sides by her Alpine barrier and on the other facing Austria across the Ticino, without access to the sea except for the inadequate port of Nice, Piedmont was almost cut off from the rest of Italy. Her King was an absolute monarch. Her nobility was feudal, but of a patriarchal type very different from the Neapolitan barons, and under them lived a poor and hard-working peasantry, who rallied to the standard of their King with a readiness and an unswerving loyalty born of long tradition and an innate sense of self-preservation. The Piedmontese were a devout and simple people whose religion was close woven into their lives, and loyalty to throne and altar was an outstanding quality in all classes. If her mountains provided Piedmont with a hardy race of soldiers they cut her off from Europe, and it is scarcely surprising that the reform movement passed her by; for her Kings were quite content with the existing system and had small sympathy with literature and none with political innovation. The severity of the double censorship of Church and State crushed all freedom of thought and the activity of the Holy Office ensured a rigid orthodoxy. Under such conditions writers chose voluntary exile. Baretti, the friend of Dr. Johnson, went to England, Denina wrote his *Italian Revolutions* abroad, and Alfieri the tragic poet, who has left us in his autobiography a vivid picture of the lamentable state of Piedmontese education, left the country as soon as was possible, for royal permission was necessary to do so. But Victor Amadeus III who came to the throne in 1773 was a keen soldier determined to defend his country. He strengthened the fortifications on his Alpine boundary, increased both the active army and the reserves, and drilled them incessantly. It was well he did so, for it enabled him to defend his country for three years when war broke out with France in 1793 and he succumbed only to the genius of Napoleon.

Such in outline was the state of Italy in the second half of the eighteenth century. But neither in its political nor its literary aspects can the period of reforms be regarded as in any sense 'national'. There was no demand for them, they were not the result of popular agitation, expressed by demonstrations or deputations. They were imposed on their respective subjects by the three foreign rulers who governed the greater part of Italy. The 'native' rulers made no reforms. Joseph had a mania for centralization and desired to make Lombardy an integral part of his empire. He would, no doubt, have liked the Lombards, as his nephew Francis II expressed it in 1815, 'to forget they were Italians'. Leopold was a real reformer who wanted to make Tuscany a model state. In Naples, to curb the wealth and power of the Church, to weaken the feudal barons and increase that of the state, was the objective. Neither rulers nor subjects as yet dreamed of a united Italy. This is also true of the writers. They were the men of their time, tolerant and sceptical, humanitarian and cosmopolitan, keenly interested in reform in the abstract, and in the concrete so far as it concerned their own state, but no thought of an Italian kingdom entered their minds. The inspiration of their thought was French. There were three editions of Diderot's Encyclopaedia printed in Italy. We may be sure it was studied. It was, in fact, French thought and action combined which gave birth eventually to the idea of unity as the only way to rid Italy of French and Austrian oppressors.

As French revolutionary thought developed, the more subversive brand of the 'Liberty, Equality and Fraternity' type reached Italy through other channels than learned books and academic lectures. It came through political agents, and the organization through which it penetrated was the Masonic Lodges. English Freemasonry had been reorganized in 1717 and with the appointment of the Duke of Montague as Grand Master four years later, had become definitely aristocratic. It was the travelling proclivities of the English nobility which carried it to the Continent. Lord Derwentwater founded the first French Lodge at Paris in 1725, and others followed. It soon spread to Italy where the Duke of Middlesex founded a Lodge at Florence in 1733. From here under Grand-ducal patronage it spread to Verona, Vicenza, Milan and as far as Venice. In the south of Italy it is not, however, until 1749 that we get definite information of the craft at Naples. This was partly due no doubt to its condemnation by Pope Clement XII in 1733. In 1749 the patronage of the Duca di Sangro made Freemasonry popular with the aristocracy. He resigned, however, two years later, and after a second condemnation by Benedict XIV the King prohibited the society. Nevertheless, ten years later it revived, this time aided by the Queen, Maria Carolina. A quarrel ensued between the Queen and Tannucci, who opposed Freemasonry, and in 1775 it was again suppressed by the King. The society was then reformed on the lines of the 'strict observance', with the result that the aristocracy left it and it became middle class, less social and more political.. It was at this point that Freemasonry became permeated with French revolutionary thought. It dropped out of sight and became dangerous. The Lodges were turned into clubs on the French model and served as propaganda centres for the Revolution. Freemasonry in Italy was never patriotic. It was non-Catholic, francophil and non-nationalist. It was this fact which led to the foundation of Carboneria and its many derivatives. Carbonarism was professedly Christian if not Catholic, anti-French and pro-Italian. Its earliest appearance would be in 1796, if Botta's allusion in his *History of Italy* to 'the Black League more feared by the French than were the Austrians' refers to Carbonarism as its name suggests. On the eve of the Revolution, however, only Freemasonry existed in Italy.

The four years that elapsed between the outbreak of the Revolution in 1789 and the declaration of war on Austria and Sardinia in 1793 were a period of active penetration and propaganda by French agents, official and non-official, throughout Italy, but chiefly in Piedmont and Naples. The ground was already prepared. Strange figures flitted about Italy at this time. One such was Antonio Jerocades, poet and lecturer, who under the soutane of priesthood nurtured the most subversive and anti-clerical views. Expelled, for corruption and immorality, from his post of schoolmaster he found a position in a Jesuit seminary for priests. Dismissed by the Bishop, he joined Freemasonry and became a professor at the University of Naples. An enthusiast for the new ideas of liberty, he seems to have spent his time touring the Lodges of Calabria, the stronghold of Massoneria, spreading revolutionary ideas and keeping in touch with French thought by periodic visits to Marseilles. As the poet of Freemasonry his *Lira Focense* and *Paolo o L'humanitá liberata* clothed dangerous doctrines in smooth metastasian verse and spread abroad the fervid Jacobinism of his thought. Such were the precursors. Genoa was full of French agents, who thence obtained easy access to Piedmont and Lombardy, where they collaborated with the restless elements. There were arrests in Genoa and Pavia, Brescia and Milan. At Turin three Jacobin clubs were discovered and a plot to seize the citadel and murder the Royal House. Sections of the intellectuals and upper classes also, following the example of the French aristocracy, gave evidence of an academic enthusiasm for liberty and equality, but the real support came from groups of extremists scattered throughout the country who were only waiting for a favourable opportunity to take action.

Then in 1793 France declared war on Sardinia and Austria. For three years the Allied armies kept the struggle on the Alpine border, until Bonaparte took over his first command. He led his ragged and famished army to speedy victory. Striking at the junction of the two armies, he crushed the Sardinians and forced them to sign the disastrous Treaty of Cherasco which put Piedmont into French hands. Advancing into Lombardy he defeated in succession three Austrian armies and became master of northern Italy. Then, in October 1797 he signed the Treaty of Campoformio, handing over Venice to Austria and retaining the rest of northern Italy for France. Before the close of the year Bonaparte left Italy for Paris, en route for Egypt. In the wake of the French armies republics sprang up like mushrooms. Genoa became the Ligurian; Reggio, Bologna, Modena, Ferrara formed themselves into the Cispadane; Milan, Brescia and other towns into the Transpadane. At the suggestion of Bonaparte these two latter combined and Bonaparte raised his first political structure when he gave them a constitution under the title of the Cisalpine Republic.

Italy was unarmed. There were no troops in either Tuscany or the Papal States and the effectives available in Naples were scarcely twenty thousand men. In the four years which had passed since the outbreak of war the Italian governments had done nothing. The attempt of Victor Amadeus to form a league and present a common front to the enemy was a complete failure. In 1792 a French fleet had sailed into the Bay of Naples and under threat of bombardment had demanded the immediate despatch of a Neapolitan representative to Paris, strict neutrality, and the acceptance of the citizen Mackau, as the representative of the French Republic. While the terrified government negotiated, the French officers landed, fraternized with the citizens, accepted a banquet offered by the Jacobin elements and in return gave a reception on the flagship at which the admiral sketched out a plan for a club on the usual French lines. From Naples two French agents, Flotte and Bassville, went on to Rome, where their conduct so exasperated the populace that the mob sacked their residence and killed Bassville. All over Italy there were disturbances. In Sicily, at Naples and Bologna, there were plots followed by executions and imprisonments. All this played into the hands of the French. Berthier, left in command after Bonaparte's departure, seized the opportunity, after the killing of General Duphot in Rome, to occupy the city. The Pope fled to Tuscany and once again Rome became a Republic. The presence of the Pope in Tuscany soon brought trouble, General Miollis was ordered to occupy Florence and the Grand-duchy became the Etruscan Republic.

While these events were taking place Ferdinand of Naples was collecting an army under the Austrian general Mack, urged on by his wife and the English, whose fleet was keeping open Sicily as an asylum in case of disaster. Ferdinand was a feeble creature, without military training or capacity, devoted only to hunting and women, and completely dominated by his Austrian wife Maria Carolina, who, in the intervals of bearing him twelve children, governed the Kingdom. In December 1798, when the French troops were dispersed in winter quarters, Ferdinand marched unopposed to Rome. The expedition has been picturesquely summed up by Alfredo Oriani in these words, 'Ferdinand entered the Eternal City as a conqueror; he recalled the Pope, and from the summit of the Campidoglio, with the voice of a rabbit, proclaimed to Europe that "the Kings are awake".' His triumph was brief. Hastily collecting his troops, Championnet attacked, and the Neapolitan army beaten and demoralized fled back in disorder to Naples. No one ran quicker than the King, who arrived in his capital in time to collect the Queen, his Minister Acton and all the treasure he could lay his hands on and embark on a waiting British warship which took him to safety in Sicily. On the approach of Championnet the condition within the city was chaotic. The nobility thought only of compromise, fearing spoliation either from the French or from the masses, and suggested immediate additional taxation (since the King had looted the public treasury) to bribe the French not to enter the city. The Liberals on the other hand were prepared to welcome them. The decision was, however, made by the *lazzaroni*, who, though disgusted with the cowardly flight of the King and Court, were roused to frenzy against the heretic French. They defended the city with desperation and though French discipline triumphed in the end they paid heavily for their victory. When order was at last restored Naples was transformed into the Parthenopean Republic. Thus in a little over eighteen months, what was left of Italy (for Piedmont was now French with the King in exile in Sardinia, and Venice was Austrian) was a group of Republics held in being by French bayonets.

The new republican system was hardly established when the power that sustained it was suddenly withdrawn. The allies had won over Russia, and in March 1799 an Austro-Russian army under Suvorov crossed the Adige and swept the French from north Italy. The southern army, now under Macdonald, was hastily recalled from Naples and, after narrowly escaping disaster at the Trebbia, joined Massena at Genoa, the only corner of Italy left in French hands. The conduct of the French armies had quickly disabused the Italians of their earlier dream as to the nature of French liberty and equality. The brutality and irreligion of the soldiery, the systematic looting by the *savants* attached to the armies, only equalled in thoroughness by the rapacity of the 'financial experts' who descended like vultures upon each prostrate government in turn, had outraged all classes of the nation. Italy had been treated as a conquered country, looted, plundered and trampled on, with a greed and cynicism which roused bitter hatred against their so-called 'liberators'. No sooner were the armies withdrawn than the infuriated peasantry, under whatever leaders and with whatever weapons they could find, rose against the scattered garrisons and outposts still remaining. Thousands flocked to the standard of the 'Army of the Christian Mass' led by an obscure individual who called himself Brandaluccio. The Bishops of Asti, Albi and Acqui, in Piedmont, led their flocks in warfare against the remains of the invaders. At Arezzo in Tuscany, under the inspiration of two peasants, believed to be S. Donato and the Madonna of Comfort, the peasantry formed themselves into the Aretine army under the 'pious Buglione' and the 'Maid of the Valdarno', and looted and sacked and murdered; from whose fanatic zeal Florence itself escaped with difficulty. In Lombardy and Emilia the Austrians, not content with driving out the French, arrested, imprisoned and shot the supporters of the Cisalpine Republic wherever they could be found. But it was in Naples that the reaction assumed its most tragic and horrifying aspect.

The aims of the Parthenopean Republic were inspired by a group of cultured Liberals, impractical and idealist, perhaps, but with the highest aims and the best intentions. Men of the stamp of Mario Pagano, Domenico Cirillo and Francesco Conforti and women like Lucia Sanfelice and Eleonora Pimentel. The sudden retreat of the French army cut the ground from under their feet while they were yet struggling to bring order out of chaos. The moment was seized by King Ferdinand to despatch Cardinal Ruffo from Sicily to the mainlaind, to collect an army and recover Naples. The nucleus of his force was detachments of English, Austrian and Turkish troops, to all of whose governments the King had appealed for help. Around these Ruffo gathered an army of peasants and outlaws and bandits, including the famous Fra Diavolo and his crew of cut-throats, numbering altogether some forty thousand. An imposing Altar, at which Mass was said daily, accompanied the army, for this was the 'Army of the Holy Faith'. Arrived at Naples the attack began. After two days of slaughter, looting and incendiarism, Ruffo called a halt to save the city from further destruction. The republican government and garrison, who had seized and occupied the strong Castel S. Elmo, finally surrendered on terms, which included a safe conduct and transport to Marseilles. The King's representative signed the capitulation, as well as Ruffo ánd the commanders of the foreign contingents. At this moment Nelson sailed into the bay. When he learnt what had been arranged, prompted or perhaps ordered by the King, he repudiated the terms of the capitulation, handed over those who had surrendered to the royal vengeance and hanged Admiral Caracciolo, who had deserted the royal cause and taken command of the republican forces, from the yardarm of his own flagship.[2] The vengeance of Ferdinand and his Queen was savage. More than a hundred of the leaders, 'the flower of Neapolitan virtue and intellect' as Benedetto Croce calls them, were hanged or shot: two hundred and twenty were sent to the galleys for life: three hundred and twelve for definite periods and some hundreds exiled. Thus did the King's brutality crown the victory of the Army of the Holy Faith.

Once more the wheel of fortune turned with surprising rapidity. In October of this year (1799) Bonaparte escaped from Egypt and landed in France. By the spring he had an army organized for the reconquest of Italy. In June, while Massena still struggled with Austria on the Alpine border, he crossed the S. Bernard Pass and descended into Lombardy behind the Austrians and crushed them at Marengo. Eight months later by the Treaty of Lunéville (Feb. 1801) France received the north of Italy to the Adige leaving Western Venetia in Austrian hands. There were no more great battles in Italy. In the ensuing years the country was gradually organized into three areas, the Kingdom of Naples; the Kingdom of Italy; and Piedmont, Tuscany and the Papal States west of the Apennines, including the city of Rome, which were incorporated in imperial France. Bonaparte was now First Consul, and after Marengo he reorganized the Cisalpine Republic, which emerged from the Council of Lyons, to which four hundred and fifty Italian delegates were summoned, as 'The Italian Republic', a title changed to 'The Kingdom of Italy' (Regno d'Italia) when Bonaparte became Emperor. At its first formation the Cisalpine had adopted the *tricolore*, the Papal red and white of Bologna and the green of Liberty, which was to be the future Italian flag, and thereby became endeared to the Italians who have always regarded it as Italy's first child of liberty. Napoleon had also a genuine interest in this his first political creation. In 1806 Venice was added to it, and two years later the Italian Tyrol, and in 1810 the Marches of Ancona; it had then seven million inhabitants with an army of a hundred thousand men. Its Viceroy was Eugene Beauharnais, the Emperor's brother-in-law. In 1806 Napoleon settled accounts with Naples. On the approach of the French army Ferdinand fled once more to Sicily and his place and title were bestowed on the Emperor's brother Joseph. After two years employed in reforms, Joseph went to be King of Spain, and Marshal Murat became King Joachim of Naples, where he remained until the fall of the Empire. Except in the south where there was a constant undercurrent of war between the French and the banditti amongst the mountains, Italy settled down quickly under French rule and remained quiet until the last disturbed period which heralded the fall of the Empire. To Napoleon, Italy was a reservoir of manpower and a useful financial support. It was heavily taxed and steadily drained of its youth, who fought well and followed the Napoleonic eagles from Madrid to Moscow. But French rule had one concealed and relentless enemy, who fought her by a sustained and ever-spreading system of propaganda, this was the Secret Societies.

These offshoots from Freemasonry were purely political. The first article of their creed was the suppression of 'tyrants', which meant primarily the French, or Napoleon, the 'grosso lupo' as they called him, but included the Austrians, in fact all foreigners on Italian soil. The second article was 'a constitution'. They were never a fighting organization; as a means of expelling the hated foreigners they were a complete failure. They could neither inspire an heroic insurrection like the Tyrolese nor instigate a bitter guerilla ·warfare like the Spaniards. They never produced a popular leader or an effective body of troops, but they penetrated everywhere, they undermined and destroyed confidence, so that in the last phase of the Empire neither Murat in the south nor Beauharnais in the north could rely on the trustworthiness of his subordinates. Besides this the one valuable work they performed was to hold fast to the idea of independence and to spread it unceasingly amongst all classes of the community. No one who joined a secret society, especially the Carboneria, with all its paraphernalia of oaths and daggers, was ever likely to forget that he had sworn to achieve his country's independence, however little he was prepared to implement it. This idea of independence under a constitution was so incessantly reiterated and with such dramatic emphasis that it worked its way into the very fabric of the national consciousness and formed the foundation upon which the subsequent realization was built.

During the Russian campaign of 1812, in which both Murat and Eugene Beauharnais took part, the secret societies increased with great rapidity all over Italy, in the south especially. The civil service was honeycombed with disaffection and many of the Italian generals wanted a constitution. After his return from Russia, pressure was brought to bear upon Murat to grant a constitution. This he refused, and the subsequent opposition of the Carboneria rendered his final appeal to Italy useless. But Italian opinion had neither leadership nor organization nor even a candidate of its own for the throne of Italy. Neither Murat nor Beauharnais was acceptable. The Regno d'Italia made a weak effort to remain in being, one party supporting the Viceroy and another opposing him. His candidature led to riots in Milan and the brutal murder of the capable but much hated Minister of Finance, Prina. This gave Austria her opportunity, Marshal Bellegarde occupied Milan and Italy's chance of expressing her wishes vanished. In fact, the fate of Italy was being settled elsewhere. Metternich and Castlereagh had their own solution ready for the Congress in which Italian desires were neither consulted nor taken into consideration.

The work of the Napoleonic period, when considered with reference to Italy's future development, is both extremely interesting and of genuine importance. For although Napoleon and the secret societies were in bitter opposition, they were, as we can now see, in reality working together and supplementing each other in a joint work of laying the foundations for a future united and constitutional Kingdom; Napoleon clearing the site and Carboneria providing the programme. The work of Napoleon has been accused of being more destructive than constructive, but it was the destruction of the skilled housebreaker who pulls down and prepares the ground for others to build. Over two-thirds of Italy he broke down the old boundaries, swept away local prejudices and threw the people together, giving them a wider outlook, an excellent administrative system and the boon of a uniform system of law in the Code Napoleon. Out of this came the first glimmer of national consciousness for they began to think of themselves as Italians rather than Piedmontese or Tuscans. In the south of Italy the application of the same principles extending over a number of years, swept away the worst features of feudalism, made rich and poor equal before the law, and cleared away the mosaic of the Neapolitan codes dating back to Norman times, upon whose intricacies and contradictions, it was said, no less than twenty-six thousand lawyers flourished in Naples alone. His treatment of the Church, though rude in its methods, freed the Papal States for a time from corruption and the futility of government by priests, and made it clear that the possession of temporal power was not necessary for the adequate performance of the Church's spiritual function. Under the Emperor's firm rule and pressing financial needs, privileges and exemptions disappeared whether of nobility or ecclesiastics, and all had to contribute. He opened a career to talent, many Italians prominent later receiving their training outside Italy in the service of the Empire. He taught the youth of the country to fight, widened their views, and gave them a new pride in the profession of arms. Above all, it was Napoleon who at last shook Italy from the long torpor in which she had lain, since, exhausted by the overflowering of her genius in the Renaissance, she had fallen back under the deadening rule of Spanish and Austrian Viceroys.

To this work of Napoleon, fundamental for the future development of Italy, the secret societies added the outline of the future programme, Independence, Constitutional Government and Unity, though this last conception was never stressed with the same force as the other two. When all hopes of any immediate realization of their aims were dissipated by the settlement of 1815, the secret societies remained the hidden repository where the hopes of Italy were still kept untarnished, until through constant repetition they passed into the common heritage of the national thought. Italy had a long and difficult road to travel before these aims were fulfilled, but the thought was born and the old Italy of placid acceptance of foreign domination was gone for ever.

CHAPTER TWO

THE AGE OF CONSPIRACIES, 1815-1831

IN relation to the wider framework of European reconstruction, the settlement of Italy at the Congress of Vienna was a matter of secondary importance. Italy was destined to be the area of compensation for Austria. As the wise old Sardinian ambassador Giuseppe de Maistre put it, Italy was 'just money with which to pay for other things'. It was necessary, of course, that Italy should be prevented from again falling into the hands of France, and to give Austria a strong bridgehead in North Italy was therefore desirable. Metternich had made Austria's interpretation of this general principle unmistakably clear in the secret Treaty of Prague, which he signed with England in 1813, by which Austria was to have the Regno d'Italia, that is, Lombardy, Venetia and the Papal States east of the Apennines down to the Umbrian border, and a control over the rest of the Peninsula.[3] When the deputations from Lombardy, relying on the promises of liberty and independence, proclaimed so loudly by English and Austrian generals, Lord William Bentinck and Marshal Bellegarde amongst them, came to the Emperor and Castlereagh to urge their claims, their reception was frigid. The Marquis Alfieri, Sardinian Minister in Paris, reported the Emperor's reply as follows: 'Gentlemen, Lombardy is to be added to my hereditary dominions by right of conquest and previous possession. The Lombards would have done better had they understood that my victorious troops having conquered Italy there can be no further question of independence and constitutional government.' Castlereagh, in his reply, blandly assured them: 'You have nothing to fear from the paternal government of Austria. I am intimately convinced that your interests will be adequately safeguarded'; and the Count San Marzano, Sardinian representative at the Congress, summed up the attitude of the Emperor thus: 'He is determined to stamp out Italian Jacobinism and to assure quiet in the Peninsula, and to extinguish all ideas of constitutions and national unification. He will not take the title of King of Italy. He has already disbanded the Italian troops and suppressed all those organizations likely to serve as a preparation for a great national kingdom'; and the Emperor added: 'It is necessary for the Lombards to forget they are Italians. Obedience to my will is the

chain that will unite my Italian provinces to the rest of my states.'
'Chain' was the right word.

Austria, however, did not get all she expected. In spite of what she termed her 'incontestable rights' over the Papal Legations, the states of the Church were returned intact to the Papacy. Nor was she more successful in her attempt to procure the High Novarese from Piedmont, across which Napoleon had built a military road from France to Italy. The protests of Sardinia were strongly supported by Russia, and Austria withdrew her claim. The rest of the Peninsula was handed back to its previous rulers, Tuscany to Ferdinand of Habsburg-Lorraine, Sardinia and Piedmont to the House of Savoy, enlarged by union with the republic of Genoa, and Naples, now known as the Kingdom of the Two Sicilies, to Ferdinand. The Duchy of Parma was to be the domicile of Napoleon's wife Marie Louise. The Archduke Francis, the most ambitious and astute of the Austrian princelings, became Duke of Modena. His previous history is a curious sidelight on the last years of the Napoleonic régime. As governor of Galicia he had wanted to marry Marie Louise. On her marriage with Napoleon, Francis resigned his position, took a violent antipathy to Metternich, and left Austria for Dalmatia. He was accompanied by two companions who later filled important positions: Count De la Tour, for many years Foreign Secretary of Sardinia, and Count Ficquelmont, the successor of Metternich at the Foreign Office in 1848. At Scutari, he planned an Albanian-Montenegrin rising for the expulsion of the French from Dalmatia, undertaking to pay the insurgent army and promising a long list of presents to the organizers, including such curiosities as airguns for the Basa of Scutari, and canaries and goldfish for his mother. We hear nothing more of it. He then travelled to Malta via Salonica, Constantinople and Smyrna, and set to work to raise an army to expel the French, induce the English government to transfer the Peninsular army to Italy, and make himself King of Italy. Lord William Bentinck, in Sicily, was one of his sponsors with the English government. However, the small force which he raised was shipped by England to Spain, and seeing his kingdom vanish, he went to Sardinia and married his niece Beatrice, eldest daughter of Victor Emanuel, thus setting up a claim to the throne of Sardinia, as there were no direct male heirs. His claim was a thorn in the side of the house of Savoy until the safe accession of Charles Albert in 1831.

The welcome accorded to the returning rulers was enthusiastic. The Pope was received with a delirium of rejoicing. 'Never shall I forget my reception by the good people of Turin,' exclaimed Victor Emanuel in a letter to his wife. Even the egregious Ferdinand of Naples was given a gratifying welcome, whilst illuminations and an outburst of adulatory verse hailed the arrival at Modena of Francis, who was to prove the most bigoted and tyrannical little despot in the Peninsula. With one accord the returned rulers began to put back the clock. The Pope, surrounded by devoted but greedy Cardinals, clamouring for place and power, hastily restored the rule of priests and relegated the laity to subordinate positions. Tuscany was little disturbed, for the Grand-duke was no reactionary and he had a wise minister in Fossombroni. Victor Emanuel of Sardinia, in his hatred of Napoleon, threw the whole country into confusion with a single edict, which refused recognition to any law passed since the Constitutions of 1770. In Naples, Ferdinand had a difficult path to tread. There were two parties, the Murattisti who were governing the country and were in command of the army, whom he hated and distrusted, and the 'Federlone', the faithful, who had followed him to the safety of Sicily, the Court officials and the army officers who had commanded the garrisons in the island. There was, however, a large body of Austrian troops in the kingdom, expensive but effective, and while he could afford to pay them, lodge them and feed them, as was always required by Austria, there was small fear of trouble. For the present he held his hand.

In the meanwhile Metternich had lost no time in carrying out his policy for Italy. In its wider aspect he appears to have planned the creation of a Mittel-Europa with Austria as the radiating centre of power and influence, having the states of Germany in the north and Italy in the south bound to her by treaty, based on the common bond of Absolutism, and prepared to support her with arms in times of crisis. In pursuance of this policy he first approached Naples, with whom he found no difficulty, for although his throne had already cost him dear, Ferdinand having lavished money on all receptive quarters at the Congress, including a dukedom and a handsome annuity to Metternich himself, he owed his throne to Austria, and he signed the proposed treaty without demur. By this, after a mutual guarantee of their respective states, Ferdinand undertook not to alter the constitution of Naples without first consulting Vienna, and in case of war to furnish twenty-five thousand men to the common cause. Equally easy, because unable to resist, was a similar arrangement with Tuscany, whose military contribution was to be six thousand. Here, however, his success ended. At Rome, neither pressure nor blandishments served to move the Pope from his declaration that the policy of the Vatican could in no way favour the proposed alliance with a single Power, since through the nature of her government she must live at peace with all countries alike. An equally definite refusal came from Turin, for Sardinian policy was based upon never binding herself to either of her great neighbours, for this was the only path of safety. Thus the attempt to link each Italian state individually to Austria fell through.

Metternich was no more successful in his scheme for a Confederation of Italian States, in which Austria, as holding Lombardy and Venetia, would be a member; for Victor Emanuel refused to surrender his position as an independent sovereign to become a cipher in a federation controlled by Austria and her subservient Italian Archdukes. Not only so, but Victor Emanuel even attempted to form a league of small states, to oppose Austrian aggression, of which Bavaria and Naples, the Papal States and Sardinia, were to be the principals. Naples, however, too deeply pledged to Austria, refused, and the Pope returned the same answer as he had given to Metternich, and so the scheme came to nothing.

In these negotiations the Austrian Chancellor invariably added an innocent-looking request for a postal convention, by which the states' foreign correspondence should pass through Austria. Acquiring information of all kinds and from all sources was an obsession with Metternich, and this was one of his most effective methods; for he had set up at Vienna a special bureau for opening, decoding, copying, and then resealing, all correspondence that came through the post. Everything deemed of interest was copied and forwarded to the Chancellery. This was the source by which Metternich so often astonished foreign ambassadors by displaying the most intimate knowledge of all that went on in the inner circle of their governments, and gave him that belief in his own omniscience, so conspicuous in his memoirs. It was of course supplemented by reports from his spies, secret agents and police. However, in this case, the existence of his special bureau and its purpose being well known, both Rome and Sardinia refused. Occasionally Metternich was hoisted with his own petard. Here is the way in which Della Margherita, Charles Albert's Foreign Secretary, procured the recall of an uncongenial Austrian Minister at Turin.

Not wishing to complain of him officially nor to ask the Chancellor to recall him, but knowing that all diplomatic despatches entrusted to the post were opened, I decided to make use of this fact. In a private letter to the

Sardinian Minister, Count di Sambuy, I gave vent to my anger at the conduct of Count Brunetti, adding that I distrusted the communications he
made to me, but that it was not a matter to be mentioned to the Prince.
The letter was opened, and some time after, Metternich, forgetting the
source of his information, spoke about it to Count di Sambuy, who expressed his great surprise that the Chancellor knew about a matter of which
he had said nothing and which he had received in a diplomatic despatch
from his Foreign Minister. Metternich, much confused, got out of the
predicament as best he could. Shortly afterwards Count Brunetti asked
for leave of absence and did not return.

In 1819 the Emperor and Empress of Austria, with Metternich in
their train, paid a visit to Italy, journeying through Milan and
Florence to Rome and then to Naples. Metternich found Italy 'perfectly tranquil' and unless, he wrote, some great event took place in
Europe, he anticipated no movement whatever in Italy. It was a
superficial judgement as he was soon to discover. Italy was full of
discontent. In Piedmont, the tactless policy of Victor Emanuel was
alienating the officers of the army and rendering the middle classes
resentful and uneasy. His refusal to allow French decorations to be
worn, his preference for those who had followed him to Sardinia,
the frequent lowering of the grades of officers to make room for the
favourites, quickly bred symptoms of trouble in the army; while his
revival of reactionary legislation and long-forgotten ordinances made
business uncertain and difficult. In the Papal States the forced resignation of officials to make way for priests, and the return of all the
worst abuses of the former Papal régime exasperated large sections of
the population, stimulated the work of the secret societies, and filled
the Lodges and Vendite with new recruits, for the hatred of priestly
rule was deep seated. It was here that the first outbreak took place,
in 1817; a plot to seize the town of Macerata was to be the signal for
a general rising and a demand for the abolition of priestly government.
It was an utter failure. At the critical moment the leaders failed to
arrive, a few shots were fired and the handful of conspirators then
dispersed. But the plot had been betrayed, and the government reacted with a ferocious repression. Large numbers were arrested and
after eighteen months of imprisonment, ten sentences of death and
twenty sentences to the galleys for periods from five years upwards,
were pronounced. The sentences of death were commuted for life
imprisonment. It was the brutality of such punishments, out of all
proportion to the crime, delivered by a court of priests with a
Cardinal as President, which made the whole Papal system hateful
to those who lived under it.

The condition of Naples was far worse. The whole country was infested with brigands. These wretched creatures, the *disjecta membra* of all the armies, camp followers, deserters and stragglers, sometimes singly or in small groups, occasionally in large and formidable bands, roved the countryside, living by every kind of pillage and terrorism. Many of them had been criminals of the lowest class, released, armed, and landed on the mainland from the prison settlement on the island of Ponza to make trouble for King Joachim. How real was the danger from these banditti can be seen in the memoirs of General Pepe. In 1817 he paid a visit to his father at his country house on the Gulf of Squillace. 'My visit was a great expense to my father', he writes, 'for besides having to keep open house for all who came to see me, he had also to board a detachment of cavalry and another of infantry. The latter was for the defence of the house, and the former escorted me whenever I went abroad. This was not for show but for my personal safety.' It was the same everywhere, between Capua and Terracina the highroad was picketed with troops to protect travellers, and an escort of a thousand men was required to protect the mail that ran twice weekly from Naples to Calabria.

To deal with this pest, after the withdrawal of the Austrian troops in 1818, the government formed a militia, and this proved the cause of the first serious rising in Italy, the revolution of 1820 in Naples. General Pepe, in command of the third military Division of Avellino and Foggia, was responsible for raising ten thousand men in his two districts. He soon discovered that the only suitable material for the new force were all Carbonari, feared far more than the brigands by the King and the government. In spite of this he proceeded to recruit them, refusing to allow membership of a Carbonarist Lodge to be any detriment to a suitable candidate for the militia. By his personal interest and obvious sympathy with Carbonarism, though he was not himself a member, he won their confidence, and before long had a fully-equipped contingent of ten thousand men at his command. Assured of his power, Pepe decided to use his militia to force the government to grant a constitution. This new avenue to power and influence was not lost on the Carbonari, who began to enroll at once in the militia throughout the kingdom, undermining thereby the loyalty of the army. In January 1820 the Spanish revolution broke out, the government was overthrown and the single chamber constitution of 1812 established. News of the events in Spain reached Naples in March, and threw government and people into a ferment. To overawe any attempt at insurrection, the Ministry formed an imposing military camp at Sesso and induced the King to take up his residence with his army. The troops were demobilized shortly before the revolution broke out.

In the meanwhile Pepe, anxious not to miss the favourable moment, planned to raise the standard of rebellion on June 24th. But, as at Macerata in 1817, the attempt misfired. The bonfires which were to be the signal were not lit, and Colonel Russo, his chief confidant, failed to put in an appearance. Afraid that his plans were known he hastened to Naples, but found the Ministers quite unsuspicious. He remained some days in the capital and while still there the rebellion broke out. Two lieutenants, Morelli and Salvati, raised the flag of revolt at Nola, in Pepe's district, independently of Pepe altogether. His presence at Naples averted all suspicion of Pepe's complicity and General Nugent, the Minister for War, consulted him as to what steps to take. Pepe promptly suggested that the militia should be called under arms. This was approved, Nugent believing that the purpose of it was to suppress the rebellion, whereas, in reality, Pepe's motive was exactly the opposite. A few days later he slipped away from Naples, accompanied by General Napolitano and some squadrons of disloyal dragoons, put himself at the head of his militia, and after issuing a proclamation demanding a constitution, marched on the capital.

There were three generals in command of troops who might have barred his progress, but none could trust their men, and all alike were paralysed by the extent of the movement. In Naples the Ministers were helpless, the King, who lived in terror of the Carbonari, and was haunted by the fate of Louis XVI, took to his bed, appointed his heir Francis, Duke of Calabria, Vicar General, and prepared to submit abjectly to all demands. On July 9th Pepe and his army of disloyal regulars, militia, and a crowd of armed but unorganized Carbonari, defiled before the Vicar General and the Royal Family, all of whom wore Carbonari rosettes. The Constitution, the Spanish of 1812, was granted almost before it was asked for, a Junta was appointed, and Parliament was summoned for the first of October. Four days after Pepe's triumphal entry, Ferdinand took the oath to the Constitution in his private chapel, in the presence of the Court and the fifteen members of the Junta. After taking it in a firm and convincing tone, he turned to Pepe and said: 'Believe me, General, I have sworn from the very bottom of my heart'. Pepe was so moved that he wept; he then made a short speech in praise of the King, who, equally moved, wept also.

The reaction of Metternich, when the news from Naples reached him, was one of anger and disgust: 'Two squadrons of cavalry', he wrote bitterly, 'overturn a throne and expose the whole world to incalculable dangers. Things will not go at Naples as they have in Spain. Blood will be shed in torrents. A half barbarous people, utterly ignorant, superstitious beyond limit, whose final argument is always the dagger—offer a promising material for the application of Constitutional principles!' But he was wrong as to the bloodshed. The Carbonari, having got what they wanted, simply gave themselves up to an orgy of celebration. Except for a single outburst of ferocity, the murder of the hated Minister of Police, Giampietro, the event passed off peacefully, though, but for the intervention of Pepe, one or two unpopular Ministers might have fared badly. The one cause of anxiety to Metternich was the attitude of the Czar, upon whose reputed liberalism the Neapolitans were relying to mitigate the punitive instincts of Austria, for Metternich was bent on force. He hastened the preparations for the Congress of Troppau, called to consider the situation in Spain, and took the necessary steps to have a military force available.

The Revolution quickly spread to Sicily. Palermo revolted, drove the aged General Naselli, sent as Viceroy, back to Naples, decapitated two reactionary nobles, and pillaged and burnt as usual. They then formed a Junta to choose a constitution. Pepe's brother, General Florestano Pepe, was sent to restore order, which he did more by tact than force, assuring their loyalty, but permitting them to choose their own form of government. Eventually a separate constitution was abandoned and Sicily sent twenty-four members to the Parliament at Naples. During the months which passed before the assembly of Parliament, Pepe kept order, and as long as he did so, nothing was too good for him in the eyes of the King. Honours were showered upon him. It must, however, be said that Pepe, though a poor man, came through the Revolution with clean hands. He refused the great position of Grand Master of the Order of S. George, and though he might have made a fortune with ease, did not do so even returning the handsome gratuity given him by the Council of Ministers. So unusual was this in Neapolitan political or any other circles, that it deserves to be recorded.

The King opened Parliament in person and again took the oath to uphold the Constitution. The solitary session which it held was a complete fiasco. Ignorant of parliamentary practice or procedure, the Cabinet had to be selected from amongst the least objectionable or most subservient of the Royal Ministers. The debates were reduced to chaos by the behaviour in the public galleries, from which the speakers were shouted down, threatened or clamorously applauded, according to the violent partisanship of the audience. But this form of intimidation was less effective than that of the Carbonari, who, meeting in their own assembly, dictated the national policy. The work of the Parliament may be passed over in silence, for the centre of significance of the Revolution did not lie amongst the deputies sitting in the church of Santo Spirito, but at Laibach, to which the Congress of Troppau was about to move. Ferdinand had, of course, applied to Austria for help. His professed loyalty to the Constitution was mere double dealing, as was the enthusiasm evinced by the Vicar General. The reply came in November in the form of three autograph letters from the Emperors of Austria and Russia and the King of Prussia, inviting him to attend the Congress at Laibach. As the consent of Parliament was necessary to leave the Kingdom, he applied for permission, repeating his determination to support the new constitution before the Powers. Parliament weakly consented and Ferdinand, with gratitude on his lips and vengeance in his heart, departed for Laibach.

It might fairly be argued that the deepest quality in the Italian character is its love of colour. Obvious in its national dress and its display of gorgeous pomp and ritual in Catholic worship, as well as in its art and literature, in the word-pictures of Ariosto and the canvases of Titian and Giorgione, it is no less conspicuous in the Italian love of rhetoric. To bring colour into the drab debates of Parliament by the splendour of words, to conjure up visions of moral perfection and colourful pictures of imperial greatness both past and future, has been a feature of Italian parliamentary life throughout its half century of existence. It was so in Naples. Pepe records how one day, one of the most eloquent of the deputies said to him with intense conviction: 'The discourse I shall deliver to-morrow will produce a revolution in Europe'. True to this fond illusion, the permanent Commission, which, by the terms of the Constitution, was appointed to watch the executive when the Chamber was not sitting, marked its assumption of office, when the parliamentary session closed on the first of January, with a proclamation, which ended with these words:

'Fame will avouch to these monarchs of the north, the firmness of our calm and noble bearing. They will say: "This is a nation worthy of its high destiny". Our good King Ferdinand will listen, his heart thrilling with joy, to the well-merited applause of his people.'

The reality was far different. The Czar had been won over; neither France nor England protested; Metternich had had his way and once again the hated Croats and Hungarians marched south for the extinction of incipient Italian self-government. The blow fell in February.

A copy of General Frimont's address to his troops was the first indication, followed by a letter from the King to the Vicar General, revealing the determination of the Congress to replace him unconditionally on his throne and to abolish the Constitution. At the same time he advised his people to accept the inevitable, and submit unconditionally. The conduct of the Viceroy was irreproachable. Aware of his danger from an exasperated populace, he became more ardently patriotic than ever, and until the arrival of the Austrians should enable him to remove his mask, identified himself with the Constitution. Parliament was hastily summoned and the deputies, far more fearful of the crowd in the piazza than of the still distant Austrian army, accepted the ultimatum of the Carbonarists and declared for war. A Commission of Generals drew up a most elaborate plan of campaign. Two armies, one to defend the line of the Garigliano under Carascosa, the other in the Abruzzi under Pepe, and each as large as the Austrians, were put under arms. The plans of defence, under the direction of General Colletta, established three concentric lines. Naples was to be defended, the archives removed, and a great camp formed on the Faro, from where the remnants of the heroic armies were to be transported across to Sicily for a last stand. It was all on paper. Only one clash occurred, at Rieti, on March 7th. The militia fought well for a few hours, Pepe tells us, but when the action went against them they were seized with panic and fled. The débacle was absolute. In twenty-four hours the whole army simply disappeared. Pepe fled to Naples and escaped to France. As to Carascosa, what he might have done is unknown, for his army disappeared as rapidly as that of Pepe, and both he and General Colletta sought safety in exile. The Austrians occupied Naples unopposed. Behind them, at a safe distance, came King Ferdinand, bringing with him as Minister of Vengeance the infamous Prince of Canosa. An orgy of revenge, floggings and executions, imprisonments and banishments, followed, which was the King's interpretation of the intentions of the allied monarchs, which he wrote to his son in these words:

They sincerely desire that surrounded by the most honourable and wise of my subjects, I should consult the real and permanent interests of my people, without, however, losing sight of what is necessary for the maintenance of general peace, and that the result of my solicitude and efforts may be a system of government calculated to guarantee for ever the repose and prosperity of my kingdom.

The lofty sentiments and nauseating complacency of this letter, which breathes the very verbiage of Metternich, for the ignorant Ferdinand could never have composed it, though he held the pen, are scarcely less contemptible than the cowardice, duplicity and cruelty of Ferdinand himself. Thus ended the first attempt in Italy to undo the settlement of 1815, an effort which was to continue for fifty years until in 1870 it was finally attained.[4]

The Austrians had scarcely occupied Naples when a similar rebellion broke out in Piedmont. It was the work of a group of highly placed army officers under the leadership of Count Santorre di Santarosa, who occupied an important post at the Ministry for War. The Marquis di Caraglio, son of the Foreign Minister, the Marquis di Collegno, Equerry to Prince Charles Albert, the Cavaliere Perrone di San Martino, and the Marquis di Priero, formed the inner circle of the conspiracy. Their programme was war with Austria under the flag of constitutional government. There was no animus against the King, who, it was believed, would look with favour upon war with Austria and would not, under pressure, be averse to granting a constitution. For some time Ministers had been uneasy and aware that something was on foot. A mysterious order for the provisioning of the citadel at Alessandria, a war measure, the origin of which could not be traced; a plan signed by the King for the organization of a militia, which was unknown to the new Secretary for War, Count Saluzzo; inflammatory posters and anonymous letters: all were indications of coming trouble. The first tangible evidence, however, came, following a hint from the French police, when the examination of the travelling carriage of the Prince della Cisterna revealed letters and documents having affiliations with both Lombardy and France, including the late French Minister at Genoa, the Duke Dalberg, who had been recalled at the request of the King for his liberal intrigues. Letters to Luigi Angeloni, a celebrated leader of Carbonarism and founder of the sect of the Filadelfi, widened the possible scope of the organization. All this should have prompted action from the authorities, for the suspected leaders were well known, but the evidence was vague, the Ministry weak, and nothing was done.

In the meantime, subversive propaganda among the troops had undermined the loyalty of considerable sections of the army, especially at Alessandria, where there was also an active civilian

Carbonarist movement headed by a lawyer, Urbano Rattazzi, the uncle of Cavour's colleague and would-be rival of the same name. The departure from Lombardy of the large body of troops sent to Naples precipitated matters, and on March 21, 1821, the garrisons at Vercelli, Alessandria and other places mutinied, demanding a constitution and war with Austria. When this news came through to Turin the Ministers were petrified, no one knew what to do. The King, hastily recalled from his country seat at Moncalieri, summoned a council, which debated the question of a constitution, but came to no decision and took no steps to suppress the rebellion. Half the army was in revolt, half of it remained still loyal. While they debated, the garrison of the citadel at Turin mutinied, shot their commandant, and threatened to bombard the city unless a constitution was proclaimed. Then to add to the confusion, the Sardinian delegate at the Congress of Laibach, the Count of San Marzano, father of one of the leading conspirators, arrived at Turin with the ultimatum of the Powers, forbidding under threat of armed invasion the promulgation of any constitution. Faced with the alternatives of civil war or foreign intervention, Victor Emanuel, first declared his intention to leave Turin, rally the loyal troops, and suppress the rebellion by force. Changing his mind he abdicated in favour of his brother Charles Felix, then at Modena; appointed the Prince Charles Albert as Regent, and left the capital for Nice.

The sudden and unforeseen abdication of the King completely dislocated the plans of the conspirators, for they well knew that they would get no mercy from the narrow absolutist temperament of Charles Felix. After the departure of the King all the Ministers resigned, and no one would take their place. With one accord all began to make excuse, one unconscious humorist even pleading the death of his grandmother. At last after great difficulty, the Prince filled the vacant posts and the new Ministers met to discuss the situation. By now the Carbonari, who had hitherto held aloof, began to agitate. Crowds surrounded the palace shouting for the Spanish Constitution of 1812. To a deputation making the same demand Charles Albert replied that he could not alter the Constitution without the consent of the new King. A similar demand in writing, signed by the Municipal Council, the Decurioni, met with a like answer, and it was not until it was unanimously supported by a hastily convened council of Notables, Generals, ex-Ministers and leading citizens, that the Regent gave way and proclaimed the Spanish Constitution from the palace balcony. At Modena, Charles

Felix, who had little desire to ascend the throne, exasperated by his brother's abdication, and more so by the conduct of Charles Albert (who was now his heir, and who he was convinced was a Carbonaro), urged by his host the Duke Francis, appealed to the Austrians to crush the rebellion, an appeal at once granted. At the same time he ordered Charles Albert, 'if he had a drop of royal blood in his veins', to collect what loyal troops he could, leave Turin, and put himself under the orders of General de la Tour at Novara. The Prince obeyed, and from Novara, with an escort of Austrian dragoons, was despatched into exile with his father-in-law the Grand-duke, at Florence. After this the end soon came. Austrian troops under General Bubna scattered the insurgents without much difficulty and occupied Alessandria, sending the keys of the city, with the usual tactless arrogance so often displayed by the Austrians towards Italy, not to the King, but to the Emperor, which Charles Felix noted with annoyance when writing to his brother. Not until September did the new King appear at Turin. In the meanwhile a special commission drew up a terrifying list of death sentences and banishments, but by the time it was published the victims had all safely escaped abroad. Only two suffered capital punishment.[5] The almost simultaneous success of Austria in the suppression of the two revolts gave great satisfaction to Metternich. At the close of the Congress he summoned the Italian delegates and addressed them. After commenting on the successful issue of these unhappy events, he pointed out that 'protective intervention' was clearly not sufficient to prevent their possible repetition, and closed by saying that 'never, perhaps, had the spirit of the allied sovereigns been manifested under an aspect more consoling for the human race and more reassuring for the Italian courts', adding that all they asked in return was for 'a pledge of common felicity'.

These fine sentiments were followed by the practical measures deemed necessary to supplement the 'protective intervention'. Forty thousand troops were quartered on Naples, twelve thousand over-awed Piedmont by the occupation of Alessandria, and in spite of their protests, the Pope had to admit and pay for an Austrian garrison at Ancona, and the Grand-duke of Tuscany for one at Florence, while Duke Francis at Modena combed his little duchy for sectaries and succeeded in hanging the unfortunate priest Andreoli and imprisoning others. Even so, Metternich was not satisfied. In 1820 there had been arrests of suspects in Lombardy and after the events in Piedmont in 1821, the police were urged to greater efforts. The arrest of Count Confalonieri and his trial resulted. Metternich had two primary objectives: to discover evidence of the complicity of Prince Charles Albert, and to unearth that central directing body of Carbonarism, which he always believed to exist. Although the trial was prolonged for nearly two years, no evidence of either was forthcoming, and in the end the unfortunate victims were sent to the Spielberg without his principal object being attained.[6]

The exile of some hundreds of the most active, or as Austria considered, the most dangerous, political agitators from Italy, with the armed occupation of the peninsula, produced a two-fold result. For ten years, until the outbreak of 1831, Italy was quiet and the centre of political agitation was transferred to France. Henceforth it was Paris that became the home of Europe's exiled liberals where in an international committee they plotted the overthrow of tyranny and all its works, and it was this body which sponsored Italy's next effort, the rising of 1831. The after-effects of 1821 upon the rulers in Italy consisted mainly in increased vigilance. The Italians had now to live under a régime of secret police and spies. Not only was the police system of the legitimate ruler a constant source of danger to all free speech, but the Austrian Minister at every court had his spies and informers from whose unwelcome attention no class of the community was free. The wretched class of paid police-informers haunted every café and street corner and the endless denunciations intensified the hatred of Austria and the system which she represented. Metternich himself was indefatigable. He revived and pressed his postal conventions. 'The intrigues of the Court of Vienna', wrote the Sardinian representative at Laibach, 'make it clear that she is trying to bring there the whole foreign post of the Italian states, so as to be able to use her influence in Italy as she wishes'. Not yet content with the ubiquity of the police and spy system, he now proposed to co-ordinate it with a kind of super-police, with representatives from all the states, who would collate reports and direct the entire complex of activities. Once again it was Tuscany and the Papal States who refused their co-operation, and Metternich had to be content with police interaction between such states as were amenable.

The Congress of Laibach was followed by that of Verona. Although there was no Italian question on the agenda, a matter of considerable importance was settled unofficially before it closed. Charles Felix, brooding over the iniquities of Prince Charles Albert, suddenly decided to disinherit him in favour of his infant son. 'Count della Valle', wrote Mr. Hill, the English Minister at Turin on February 23, 1822, 'only two days since, informed me in the strictest confidence that H.M. has at last, rather suddenly, resolved to make an appeal to his august allies against the succession of the Prince Carignano to the throne.' To convert Metternich to his views, Count Pralormo, the Sardinian Minister at Paris, was sent to Vienna. The Austrian Chancellor's reply, when he opened his case, must have been disconcerting, for he told Count Pralormo bluntly that the first step was to produce evidence, which must be based 'neither on prejudices nor suspicion, nor even isolated facts, but on a mass of proofs capable of carrying conviction not only to the Sovereigns but to the whole of Europe'. The plain truth was that such evidence did not exist. The diplomatic exchanges continued and were finally closed by a long memorial from Metternich. In this, after a severe indictment of Charles Albert, he overruled the King's wish to disinherit him on the sacred ground of legitimacy. The Chancellor's fear was that, if thwarted, the King would abdicate, which would leave a most awkward situation, with the heir under suspicion and in exile. To avoid this, while he rejected the King's appeal for disinheritance, his judgement on the Prince was so severe that it must have left Charles Felix with the conviction that, after all, he was morally right. This satisfied him, and he undertook not to disinherit the Prince, and sent him to fight the liberals in Spain with the French army under the Duke of Angoulême. It was a clever piece of diplomacy.

In 1825 Ferdinand of Naples died, leaving the throne to his son Francis. He had been King for sixty-six years and he left behind him a record of cowardice, treachery and self-indulgence seldom equalled. His brutal repression of the liberal movement of 1799 left an indelible stain upon his character, and his abject behaviour in the revolution of 1820 and his subsequent cruel revenge were in keeping with a character which had neither courage nor kingliness. In the States of the Church, the pontificate of Leo XII (1823-1829) saw little improvement in conditions. A chronic state of sectarian warfare existed and the ferocities of Cardinal Rivarola, sent in 1825 to restore order, only made matters worse. For many years yet the unfortunate people governed by the Pope were doomed to live under a government whose readiness to suppress disorder was only equalled by its capacity to provoke it. By way of contrast the mild rule in Tuscany was earning for the Grand-duchy the title of the Earthly Paradise.

There is a striking contrast between the spirit of Italy after 1815 and that of the eighteenth century. It is no longer a question of humanitarian reforms advocated in books and lectures. Italy is seething with suppressed conspiracy, and the Austrian policy, backed by the Church, is merely intensifying it and driving it deeper underground. Its aims are confused and it is not yet national, but it is becoming so, and the next effort, that of 1831, was the first to embrace the conception of the union of separate states under a single ruler. It was the culminating effort of the secret societies formed on the Carbonarist model, and was largely the work of a single conspirator, Enrico Misley, a well-to-do young lawyer of Modena. Early in 1826 Misley left Modena 'to travel' with a passport to Milan, the Modenese police refusing to extend it further. At Milan the liberals procured him a passport to France and England. At Geneva he got in touch with the Russian agent Capodistria to whom he opened his plan.

A constitutional kingdom of Central Italy was to be established by a concerted rising in the duchies and legations, which was to be extended as opportunity offered to the whole peninsula. It was the old Maltese plan of 1811-1812 revived, this time from within. To prevent its immediate suppression by Austria, Misley looked to Russia, now preparing for war with Turkey and anxious to embarrass Austria and prevent her support of Turkey. To this end sympathetic risings in Hungary, Bohemia, and if possible Lombardy, were suggested. The ruler of this new kingdom was, as before, to be Duke Francis IV of Modena. He was rich, determined and thirsting for a real throne, and in Misley's opinion the only prince in Italy strong enough to hold so precarious a position. From Geneva Misley went to Paris, where, having got in touch with the leaders of the International Committee, the Comitato Cosmopolita, he unfolded his scheme once more. He found intense repugnance to accept Francis as sovereign, for both in Paris and Italy the hatred and distrust which he inspired was profound. After three months' effort he returned to Modena with sufficient encouragement to warrant revealing the scheme to the Duke in person. Here he remained for a year, winning the confidence of the Duke, maturing his plans with Paris, and making the necessary contacts throughout the duchies and legations.

The attitude of the Duke was far from satisfactory. He was enigmatic and non-committal. He was, in fact, prepared to double-cross Metternich and accept a constitutional throne—if it materialized. He was equally prepared to double-cross Misley, suppress the rising and hang the leaders, if his personal safety made it advisable. For three years Misley worked incessantly, touring Europe from France to the Balkans via Germany and Austria, knitting together the threads of conspiracy, and keeping in touch at once with London, Paris and Modena. The supreme obstacle was the repugnance to accept the

Duke. At last, in January 1829, Misley triumphed. The London Committee had demanded a pledge of the Duke's sincerity. On this Committee was a certain Modenese, Camillo Manzini, condemned to death, *in contumaciam,* by Francis for his implication in the events of 1821. Misley offered to procure a full pardon and a safe conduct, together with a personal interview, for Manzini from the Duke, to prove his sincerity. He did so, and when it arrived, the Committee finally accepted him as Sovereign of the new State. How deep, nevertheless, was the distrust, is revealed in the minutes of the Committee under the date February 18, 1829, when after stating that the 'great Italian Society intends to make Italy one single, free and independent State', it adds, that to announce the name of the 'Personage' selected as the future King would at the present stage be inadvisable 'considering the general repugnance existing towards him'. After the receipt of the safe conduct, however, they change, and record that 'after long consideration they have decided that the personage proposed—Francesco IV—is the only person capable of undertaking the work of Italian liberty and independence'.

All now seemed ready for the outbreak. In Italy, while Misley was in Paris, the arrangements were being perfected by Ciro Menotti, his friend and confidant at Modena. But in September, Russia made peace with Turkey and resumed friendly relations with Austria. At once, the Duke, terrified lest his political activities should be revealed to Metternich by Russia, drew back hastily and severed all relations with the liberals, and the original plan of the conspiracy came to an abrupt end. Bitterly disappointed, Misley returned to Paris to reconstruct the ruined fabric of his designs while Francis hastened to Vienna to assure himself that the voice of truth (he published a paper with that title in his duchy) had not reached Metternich.

The new plan was to be a simultaneous rising in France, Italy and Spain. A constituent assembly would choose the new Italian ruler, who, Misley assured the Duke, would be himself. Here the Italians coalesced with the French party, working for Louis Philippe and the overthrow of Charles X, who were, of course, fully conversant with their plans. Misley departed for England where he interviewed the Spanish generals, Mina and Quiroga, returning four days before the July revolution. The advent of Louis Philippe upon the French throne and the appointment of a cabinet which included the most prominent members of the Comitato Cosmopolita raised high the hopes of the conspirators, and Misley, full of enthusiasm, left Paris for Modena in a final effort to induce Francis to take the lead. All hopes faded, how-

ever, when the Duke told him that Metternich was already suspicious
of him, for Louis Philippe had betrayed the Italians' plans to Austria.
He could not believe it, and the announcement of the doctrine of non-
intervention by the Foreign Secretary, Sebastiani, in September, again
raised Italian hopes, for it was a direct challenge to Austria, proclaiming that if she sent troops to suppress an internal movement in states
which did not belong to her, France would oppose her by force.
Everything now depended on France's loyalty to her own declared
principles. Marshal Soult in the Chamber of Peers, and the Premier
Lafitte in that of the Deputies, officially declared their determination
to support it. Sebastiani, Lafayette, Dupin and others, adhered to it;
and satisfied of their sincerity, the Italian Committee, in the words of
Misley, 'having taken all possible precautions, and having obtained
both personal and public assurances from the Ministry of Louis
Philippe, as well as that of the principal members of the Chamber of
Deputies, proclaimed the insurrection of Central Italy'.

The conspirators, however, had not allowed sufficiently for the
craftiness of Louis Philippe, the determination of Metternich or the
capacity for treachery in the Duke. The latter, fully informed of
everything, gave Menotti a free hand until the last minute. On
February 2nd when all the leading conspirators were assembled
to make the final arrangements, he surrounded the house with troops,
and after a brief resistance captured them all. When, in spite of this,
the rising broke out at Bologna, he retired at once, surrounded
by his soldiers and dragging Menotti with him, to the safety of the
Austrian garrison at Mantua. The rising spread with great rapidity.
As the liberal troops under Sercognani marched south, all the towns
from Rimini and Bologna to Perugia, threw off the Papal yoke with
unanimity. Their delegates met at Bologna and declared themselves
the United Italian Provinces. Metternich, haunted by the fear of a
sympathetic movement in Lombardy-Venetia, openly defied France
and marched in troops. Faced with implementing the declaration of
non-intervention, which meant war, Louis Philippe took French
policy into his own hands, reassured Metternich privately that France
would not interfere, dismissed Lafitte, and reorganized the Cabinet
under Casimir-Périer. Austria occupied Bologna, hunted Zucchi's
levies as far as Ancona, where they dispersed, and stamped out the
whole movement. So ended the last attempt of the secret societies to
bring about a revolution in Italy by a popular movement. When all
was quiet again, Francis of Modena returned, hanged Ciro Menotti,
and resumed his role of a loyal Archduke of Austria.[7]

The suppression of the rising of 1831 brought the first stage of the Risorgimento to a close, and opened another whose characteristics and personalities were different. It ended the work of the old type of secret society. Their work was not without value. They had kept alive the ideal of independence under a constitution, despite the avowed intention of Austria to permit neither the one nor the other. But if these old organizations with their oaths and symbols, their fantastic ritual and incomprehensible passwords, disappeared, the spirit of conspiracy remained, nourished by bad governments, poverty and repression. Young Italy, Mazzini's offspring, was a secret society but of another kind, combining political conspiracy with a high moral code, and for the first time using the Press as a political weapon. At the same time there were changes on the thrones of Italy. Francis I, King of Naples, less brutal but quite as despicable as his father, died in 1830, giving place to Ferdinand II, who, if he earned the title of 'Bomba' from bombarding his own country, and permitted a type of rule that Gladstone called the negation of God, had a certain vulgar *bonhomie* that endeared him to the *lazzaroni*. In the next year Pope Gregory XVI succeeded Leo XII. An obscurantist in his views, a vulgarian in his habits, his long pontificate of sixteen years was marked chiefly by his refusal to introduce the least modern improvement in his States. Of far more importance was the accession of Prince Charles Albert to the throne of Sardinia on the death of Charles Felix in April 1831. Silent and enigmatic, distrustful and distrusted, he was destined to lead Italy in the first War of Independence, to be defeated, to abdicate and die in exile, and to receive the posthumous honour of the title Il Re Magnanimo. But the most significant fact of all was the July Revolution and the appearance of Louis Philippe. For fifteen years Austria had had no opposition in dealing with Italy; from now onwards the old competitor was back again and the possibility of French support of Italy had always to be reckoned with. It was not long before this new factor made itself felt. Thus with new men at the helm, and new ideas in men's minds, Italy opened the second phase of her struggle for liberty and independence.

CHAPTER THREE

CONSPIRACY ON PAPER, 1831-1848

LOUIS Philippe had saved France from war at the price of repudiating the declared policy of his own government, betraying the Italian liberals, and yielding before the open defiance of Austria. France was humiliated, and Casimir Périer felt called upon to warn Metternich that a repetition of Austria's occupation of Papal territory would force France to act. He then circularized the Powers, suggesting that, as the revolt was clearly the result of Papal misgovernment, the ambassadors in Rome should be authorized to meet and draw up a statement of necessary reforms to be recommended for adoption by the Pope. This was done, and thereby the whole question slipped out of the narrow confines of the States of the Church and became a matter of European interest. The meeting of the ambassadors revealed at once the different interests of the Powers. England and Prussia, non-catholic states, worked conscientiously at reform. Austria, opposed on principle to any fundamental changes, because of their reaction in Lombardy-Venetia, concentrated on assuring the 'independence' of the Papacy which meant freedom to repudiate the suggestions embodied in the Memorandum. The main object of France was to get the Austrian troops out of Italy. The Memorandum was drawn up, presented, and then quietly shelved, the Pope announcing the imminent promulgation of reforms of his own. The troops of Austria were then withdrawn. But when the promised reforms appeared, they were so inadequate that they were at once rejected, Bologna rebelled, and once again Austria occupied the city. The reply of France was to despatch an expeditionary force and occupy Ancona.

Both from the diplomatic and the military point of view France mismanaged the Ancona expedition. She announced Cardinal Bernetti's consent, when, in fact, he opposed it. While the general in command broke his journey to take instructions from the ambassador at Rome, the second-in-command exceeded his orders, seized Ancona by force, and printed an inflammatory proclamation all about liberty. It was suppressed, but not before the Papal authorities had obtained a copy and circularized it to the Powers. Austria was furious and ordered Radetzky to block all the roads to Rome if the French troops moved from the city. War looked very near, but before going further Metternich consulted the Powers. Russia supported him, Prussia declared for neutrality, but England stood behind France. This saved the situation. So the Austrians at Bologna and the French at Ancona sat facing each other for six years until by mutual consent both forces were withdrawn. For the next ten years we hear little of the affairs of the Papal States; not that they were any happier or more peaceful. Blood feuds between Liberals and Papalini were endemic and the formation of the Centurioni, a body intended as a semi-military police, only made matters worse. Whether or not the first recruits were of the good material they were supposed to be, it is certain they rapidly degenerated into half-organized bands of Papal brigands whose ferocity knew no bounds. When, after the revolt at Rimini in 1845, the veil was lifted upon the true state of things by the brochure of Massimo d'Azeglio, *Gli ultimi casi di Romagna*, Europe was shocked at the results of Papal misgovernment.

The last echoes of 1831 had hardly died away when fresh trouble broke out, this time in Piedmont. This was the first and most elaborate attempt of Mazzini at insurrection. After organizing his new society of Young Italy in 1831 and the secret printing and distribution of his paper of the same name, Mazzini had opened his direct political campaign with an appeal to Charles Albert, on his accession to the throne of Sardinia, to put himself at the head of a nation wide revolutionary movement against Austria, in the name of Italian independence. When the only answer was an order to the police to arrest the author if he entered Piedmont (he was born at Genoa) Mazzini concentrated all his forces on seducing the loyalty of the army, overturning the throne, and rousing Italy against her oppressor Austria. It was an ambitious enough programme for a group of young men, without money or influence, whose only asset was their patriotic enthusiasm and the literary and organizing genius of their chief. In a surprisingly short time Mazzini had a network of propaganda spread between Genoa, Turin and Alessandria, with numerous groups of adherents both in civil life and in the army. But the police were very much awake. Copies of Young Italy and other documents found in a trunk opened by the customs enlightened them as to what was on foot. A year later a tavern brawl amongst some soldiers revealed the infection in the army, and a little later still the arrest of a young lieutenant, who broke down under examination and turned King's evidence, revealed the whole plot in detail. The King, thoroughly frightened, appointed a special commission to try the culprits. Altogether fourteen soldiers and civilians were executed, and the activities of Young Italy stamped out beyond recovery. For the rest of the King's reign there were no subversive efforts of the kind in Piedmont. In the meantime Mazzini had been collecting troops and money for the invasion of Savoy, convinced, as he always was, that the least spark would set all Italy aflame. Charles Albert knew all about it, writing an accurate forecast regarding it to the Duke of Modena some months before it materialized. The attempt was a miserable failure, largely due to the unfortunate choice of the Polish general Ramorino as the commander, and was not even a threat to the safety of the King or any part of his country. It was a bitter disappointment to Mazzini for it sadly discredited Young Italy, which for a time ceased to be regarded as an active force and dropped into the background.

The remorseless persistency with which the sects were hunted down by all the rulers of Italy, except in Tuscany, is evidence of the terrible fear they inspired. As every form of religious and social *bouleverse-ment* was believed to be their aim, so every form of bestial cruelty and outrage was accepted as their normal procedure. In a state such as Naples, where moral restraint on either side was almost unknown, it was a warfare without pity or quarter. 'I found in the archives of the 3rd Division', Pepe wrote in his memoirs, 'a document proving that upwards of two thousand ducats had been expended on poison and on the remuneration of those who poisoned bandits.' Immunity was granted to those who undertook to murder their companions; in some cases, as in that of the famous Vardarelli band, the government took them into its pay and having established confidence, had them killed by treachery. The ferocious struggle in the Papal states between the Liberals and the Centurioni was on the same level. During the investigation of Mazzini's plot in Piedmont Metternich forwarded to Charles Albert a horrible document issued in the name of Young Italy advocating every barbarous form of warfare. It would be an outrage on Mazzini to suppose he ever even heard of it, but it was issued in his name. It made an indelible impression on the King, who printed extracts from it in the official gazette. It was the belief that Mazzini sanctioned such methods that determined Charles Albert to stamp out Young Italy as one would some noxious reptile.[8]

The almost unintelligent obstinacy with which Metternich clung to this conception of the liberal movement, persistently identifying the ideals of the later leaders of its thought with the crude barbarism of Neapolitan or Romagnuol ferocity, is to be observed in his correspondence. As late as 1847 in a letter to the Grand-duke of Tuscany he writes, 'Between a Balbo, a Gioberti, a D'Azeglio, a Petitti, these champions of Italian liberalism, and a Mazzini and his acolytes, there is no other difference than that between poisoners and assassins, and if their wills are different, the difference disappears when it comes to methods of action'. The explanation of this attitude lay in Austria itself. The Empire was a congeries of states, differing in race, language and culture, whose delicate adjustment, a blend of expediency and experience, was held together by a common loyalty to the Crown. To touch it was to risk collapse, to reform it was more than Metternich could undertake; but he saw clearly enough, that any liberal or constitutional reform in Italy would at once be demanded in Lombardy-Venetia and if there, why not elsewhere in the Empire? So Metternich set his face as a flint against reform, however reasonable, lest the whole imperial structure should disintegrate.

The first phase of the Risorgimento was now over. There would be sporadic revolts, inspired by Mazzini, which served to keep Europe alive to the fact that Italy had not submitted to Austria nor been lulled into inaction, but as a whole, for the next ten years, Italy was quiet. It was a period of thought and education, in which in her own way she reflected for the first time the three great movements, nationalism, romanticism and industrialism, which were transforming European life and thought. Italy now entered upon a period of literary activity which had one peculiar feature, that everything was coloured by the one absorbing problem, her political future.

Her fiction, her poetry, her drama, even her dull trade journals, all alike revealed the underlying obsession. It was conspiracy on paper. The pioneer of the movement was the poet Alessandro Manzoni who in June 1827 produced his romance *I promessi sposi* (The Betrothed) which remained in solitary glory as Italy's great prose masterpiece. Here at once we see the subtle political influence, for though the story is set back in the days of Spanish oppression it might equally well be that of Austria, as his readers quickly understood; by so doing Manzoni set a fashion in the writing of historical fiction, which was later followed by many less gifted authors whose works are little read to-day. The romantic movement has been called 'the discovery of the middle ages' and there grew up in Italy a school of writers who turned to the past to arouse the present. Choosing episodes or periods of Italian greatness they sought to stimulate the patriotic pride of their readers by the heroic deeds of Italy in the past. Massimo d'Azeglio's *Ettore Fieramosca* and *Niccolò de' Lapi*, Grossi's *Marco Visconti* and the romances of Cantù and Guerrazzi, were all of this type, and there were many others. They were read by the cultured upper and middle classes, untouched by the propaganda of Mazzini, and were not without their effect in arousing patriotic ardour; but their intrinsic merit was not great, and few, if any, survived the passing of the active phase of the Risorgimento.

Another aspect of the literary movement, which stands by itself, was the work of Joseph Mazzini. His influence was European. From his asylum in Switzerland he founded Le Jeune Suisse and Young Europe, and indefatigible in his labour, spread his social and political ideas wherever possible. He was the apostle of Italian nationalism. He was the first to give the Risorgimento an ethical content. The first to realize the need for social and political education; the need to make Italians in order to make Italy. Italy, one and indivisible, under a Republican form of government, was his political creed, with Liberty, Independence and Unity as its triune banner. He gave the national movement a purpose and an ideal, and the youth of Italy a vision of greatness; teaching duty, self-sacrifice and patriotic self-dedication as the necessary preliminary to the grim business of action. His teaching reached the middle classes, he never touched the peasantry who took their politics from the parish priest, nor did he influence the upper classes. The poverty of his resources and the secrecy imposed on his methods by the unceasing activity of the police, limited his success, but all over Italy were groups of men who adopted his creed and followed him as the apostle of liberty.

The appeal to the past to stimulate the present, was by no means restricted to the historical novel, but is evident in all literary forms at this period. The wide interest in the drama, for instance, obviously offered a fruitful field for patriotic declamation. The classical dramas of Alfieri with their lurid denunciations of tyranny were already familiar, but something more in touch with reality than Orestes and Agamemnon seemed called for. The Francesca da Rimini of Silvio Pellico, though hardly a great work, contained patriotic passages which roused frantic applause, and his Eufemia da Messina was prohibited by the police for its outspoken sentiments. It was Niccolini who voiced public feeling most clearly. His Arnaldo da Brescia and Giovanni da Procida received rapturous applause, especially the latter with its setting in the Sicilian Vespers, the rising in the thirteenth century which expelled the Angevins from the island. A story is told that when performed at Milan the French Minister expressed himself most strongly to his Austrian colleague beside him, at the anti-French sentiments, only to receive the reply, 'Don't be upset: the envelope is addressed to you but the contents are for me'. It was of course inevitable that poetry should catch the patriotic note. Here again Manzoni was among the first in his poem on the Piedmontese rebellion of 1821, *Marzo 1821*, in which the single line, 'O day of our redemption!' expressed at once the longing in the hearts of the Italian people. The lyrics of Berchet, written however in exile, the patriotic odes of Mameli and many others struck the same note. Some, in a single poem like Mercantini's *Ode to Garibaldi* which became the Marseillaise of the Risorgimento, or Mameli's *Fratelli d'Italia*, achieved instant success. There was truth, however, in Cavour's remark that there were too many songs about freeing Italy, though this did not prevent him from adding his own untuneful voice to that of the other journalists, when in 1847 they marched past Charles Albert in the great procession in honour of the reforms, and adding *sotto voce* to his neighbour, 'We sing like dogs!' His one public appearance as a singer.

It would be natural to expect that the most obvious evidence of this patriotic feeling would be found in the Press. But in the first half of the nineteenth century the Press in Italy was almost non-existent, and the profession of journalist might well have been scheduled as a dangerous occupation. In the whole seven states of Italy there may have been some ninety publications altogether, including papers, magazines, trade journals and similar matter. It was not until 1847 that a genuine literary magazine, Predari's *Antologia*, was permitted in Piedmont, and the fate of the Lombard *Conciliatore* and the Florentine *Antologia*, both suppressed by the Austrian police, was plain evidence of the severity of the censorship. A single official gazette, containing government announcements and such other matter as it thought fit to publish, a few 'family' papers, and some trade journals, made up the bulk of periodical literature in each state. In spite of this a determined and not unsuccessful effort was made to produce a patriotic journal. In 1827 the editorship of an existing journal with the safe but forbidding title of *Annali universali di statistica, economia pubblica, storia e commercio*, passed into the hands of G. D. Romagnosi, one of the finest intellects in Italy. His policy was aimed at drawing Italy from her condition of backwardness and isolation into the main stream of European progress, not by means of rebellion like Mazzini, nor by historical comparisons like the romantics, but by political economy, trade statistics, and industrial information and encouragement. He gathered round him a group of able assistants, Carlo Cattaneo, Cesare

Correnti and others, and set to work to create a well informed and interested public opinion bent on the economic and industrial revival of Italy. The *Annali* was definitely patriotic; but Romagnosi had his eyes not on the present like Mazzini nor on the past like the romantics, but on the future. He did not abuse Austria but simply ignored her, turning all his attention to the industrial progress of France and England. By a stream of information about new inventions and developments, by statistics of production and distribution drawn from all over Europe, he pointed the moral of Italian backwardness. Italian industries such as wines and silk received special attention. Advice and information regarding markets and prices, reforms and new methods, were given, and wherever possible, the contrast between Austrian methods and those of the progressive states were stressed. His outlook was always national. A railway scheme for the whole peninsula, a universal standard of weights and measures, a plea for a common programme of technical and university education, reveal the width of his views. After ten years as editor Romagnosi died, but the movement went on and widened, and later reviews such as the *Rivista Europea* and the *Politecnico* developed and improved the original idea. Thus did the influence of Industrialism, Romanticism and Nationalism make their separate contributions towards the redemption of Italy, and as we approach the critical years of the early forties, their combined force, aided by external events, gave Italy, at last, a consciousness of her destiny as a nation.

The event in Europe which most directly affected Italy, was the death in 1835 of the Emperor Francis II. It removed a narrow bigoted bureaucrat, who, impervious to new ideas, preferred obedience to education and a police barracks to a university, yet lit by rare and unsuspected flashes of an underlying humanity which won for him the sobriquet of 'vater Franz'. The personality of an Austrian Emperor was of greater importance than that of any other ruler in Europe, and the fact that the son and heir of Francis II, Ferdinand, was mentally deficient and a mere figurehead, was a tragedy for the Empire. A brave face, however, was put upon a bad situation and for thirteen years the Empire was governed by a triumvirate, Metternich, Count Kolowrat and the Archduke Louis. Metternich dealt with all foreign relations and policy and Kolowrat with internal affairs; the Archduke was a nonentity. The effect of this new state of things was to impose on Metternich a policy of peace. The difficulties between himself and Kolowrat, the agitations of Kossuth in Hungary, the uselessness of the Emperor and the ominous creaking of the entire imperial fabric, made the thought of war a nightmare.

While Italy lay quiet, scarcely recovered from the terrible epidemic of cholera which swept both north and south in 1835 and the following years, most severely in Sicily, where suffering and superstition led to a fanatical outbreak of rebellion in 1837, crushed with unsparing severity by Naples, the Eastern Question darkened the European horizon and threatened a general war. France, under the bellicose Thiers, stood facing England and Austria, and in 1840 war seemed inevitable. Once again Louis Philippe prevented it, dismissing Thiers and replacing him with the pacific Guizot. Though Italy as a whole was unaffected, the crisis inevitably involved Sardinia which from now onwards becomes the centre of significance in Italian politics.

It was essential if the states of Italy were ever to act in unison, that there should be one, free and independent of Austrian influence, to take the lead and form a rallying point around which the forces of the peninsula could gather. The choice lay between Naples and Sardinia, for they alone had armies. The young King Ferdinand II of Naples, nephew of the French Queen and married to the pious Christina of Savoy, was one of whom the Sardinian Minister wrote, not inaptly, 'he is dominated by a laziness and heedless indifference which nothing can rouse: it is the fatalism of the *lazzarone*'. Nevertheless he began his reign with some symptoms of energy and liberalism. He issued a political amnesty: resisted Austrian pressure to sign an offensive and defensive treaty, as his grandfather had done: took an active if superficial interest in the army, and flirted with the idea of a French alliance. All this brought him into bad odour at Vienna. He was said to have his eyes on the crown of Italy for which purpose he was enlarging the army and seeking French support. In January 1836, however, his wife, whom he treated abominably, died, after giving birth to the last of the line to ascend the throne, the feeble Francis II. In May, Ferdinand, with indecent haste, paid a round of royal visits, to Florence, Modena, Vienna and Paris, in search of a new Queen. Finding wives for royalties was a speciality with Austria—'tu felix Austria nube' was still true, and she did not miss her opportunity, for the numerous brood of Archdukes (Francis II had seven brothers) had always—

'. . . daughters sly and tall
And comely and compliant. . . .'

and Ferdinand was duly provided for. Even before the Queen's death, in his passion for inside information, Metternich had however assured a knowledge of all that went on in the Royal circle at Naples by providing the widowed Queen Mother with an Austrian paramour, the Baron Smücker. After his second marriage Ferdinand returned to the fold and all thought of leading Italy died away.

There remained Charles Albert of Sardinia. He was an unknown quantity when he ascended the throne, for he had lived in semi-retirement since his return from the Spanish war. His reputation, however, both with the liberals and the royalists, was still deeply tainted with the memories of 1821, both regarding him as a traitor to their cause. He found the Kingdom in a lamentable condition. Charles Felix in his later years thought of little except amusing himself. The Ministers went their own way: the army was neglected: the finances were in disorder: the real directors of the national policy were the Austrian and Russian Ministers at Turin and the Papal Nuncio, who treated the country as an Austrian satellite state. There were spies and informers everywhere and everything was passed on to Vienna. All this was deeply resented by Charles Albert, but he lacked the moral courage to make a general clearance of all the lay and clerical 'austriacanti' who surrounded the throne and occupied all the important posts in the government. An absolutist, a religious ascetic, above all a legitimist, the King was severely handicapped in taking a firm line by the fact that while he hated Austria, he hated Louis Philippe still more. Warmly attached to the elder branch of the Bourbons, who had been his strong supporters in 1821 and after, he regarded Louis Philippe as an irreligious bourgeois usurper. In 1832 he had done his best to drive Austria into war with France, signing a military convention with Vienna, and writing in his diary, 'I have written a letter to Metternich in which I have put forward every possible reason to increase his indignation (against France), telling him that if Austria wished to make war on France, I was quite ready to begin it'. But Metternich was not to be stampeded.

Charles Albert's first task was to become master in his own house. Fortunately he found in his Foreign Secretary, Count Solaro della Margherita, the very man that was required. A pure-blooded Piedmontese of the provincial nobility, a diplomat by profession, Minister at Naples and then Madrid, Della Margherita was as jealous of his country's independence as the King, and determined to assert it. In a few years he procured the recall of four Foreign Ministers, including two Austrians, for undue interference, and retired two old and tried servants of the crown, the Ministers in London and Paris, for too much servility to the Courts to which they were accredited. This broke the back of the old system and Charles Albert was at last his own master. Metternich was naturally disgusted at the treatment of his representatives and informed the Sardinian Minister that the third should have orders to 'keep quiet and never to push himself forward but always to wait until they came to fetch him'. A new role for Austrian Ministers at Turin.

Having reorganized the army and the finances Charles Albert was now free to carry out his own policy. Abroad, he warmly supported the Duchess de Berry, providing her with nearly a million francs from his private purse with which she bought the 'Carlo Alberto', the ship in which she made her descent on France.[9] He espoused the cause of Don Carlos in Spain and of Dom Miguel in Portugal. In so doing he irritated France and England and lost the foreign trade of both Spain and Portugal. In fact for some years he had not a friend in Europe. His attitude towards Austria was enigmatic. His behaviour was correct but cold. He was neither friendly nor unfriendly, and Metternich, whilst affecting to approve highly of his attitude, grew increasingly puzzled and suspicious. When the crisis of 1840 came, the results of this policy of complete independence became painfully clear. Sardinia proclaimed a strict neutrality, but no one would agree to respect it. England told the King that his only policy was to fight with Austria: France said bluntly that whether neutral or not a French army would occupy Piedmont, and Prince Schwarzenberg, the Austrian Minister at Turin, toured the defences in the Alps and spoke of immediate steps, such as the Austrian occupation of Alessandria. It was well for Italy that war never came, for, had it done so, Sardinia could never have played the part she did a few years later.

Of greater ultimate importance to Italy was the King's internal policy. Charles Albert ruled as an absolutist. Every Minister reported to him weekly and nothing was done without him. The police, the double censorship, were as severe as in any other state. Education was in the hands of the Jesuits. The Press was negligible. Every day he received the Vicario, the head of the urban police, and listened to his report of all the rumours, gossip and crime in the capital. Spies and informers were ubiquitous. His personal life was admirable. He had neither vices nor passions. He worked long hours, lived in the simplest way, and tried to do what he believed to be his duty. He was devout even to asceticism. His policy was summed up in the phrase, 'tout améliorer et tout conserver', which in practice meant political stagnation and economic betterment. He was interested in economics, and writes about 'his little library on social and economic questions', and he felt it safe to allow freedom of discussion and the publication of books and pamphlets on current problems. More than a hundred were issued on the silk industry alone. He turned the Council of State into an economic Council to whom the recommendations of the Chambers of Commerce were sent and from which he himself was the final court of appeal. The previous government had had only one idea of raising money, to increase tariffs, and stop all exportation of raw materials in profitable industries, such as cocoons in the silk industry. The consequence was that smuggling had reached gigantic proportions. Charles Albert's new policy was not impressive. Tariffs were slowly reduced by about fifty per cent, but many industries only existed by state subsidies and remained small. As Cavour said later, 'they never grew up'. There was a gradual improvement, the revenue increased and the government was frugal, and in 1848 there was a good balance in hand. But the real value was not in the increase of wealth, but in economic knowledge. The country became educated on economic matters, the problems were understood even if the solutions were not known, and ten years later, when Cavour brought in his wide economic reforms, the country grasped their significance with a quick intelligence which was due in no small degree to the preparatory work of Charles Albert.

The great mistake which Charles Albert made was in thinking that he could keep apart his two opposite programmes, political silence and economic loquacity. Piedmont was as politically minded in these years as any other part of Italy, and when in 1842 the King was induced to permit the foundation of the Società Agraria or Agricultural Society, with a central committee at Turin, and provincial and local committees all over the country, the inevitable happened. For centuries public meetings had been forbidden, now they were permitted—to talk agriculture. No doubt they did, but it was a time to talk of many things, and if they began with talking of cabbages it was not long before they were talking of Kings. The whole organization became political and it was largely responsible for the creation of that public pressure which ended in the reforms and finally in the Constitution.

All this literary activity throughout Italy, as was to be expected, produced before long a series of political programmes. The first, by far the most logical and consistent as it was the most radical, was that of Mazzini, which postulated the expulsion of Austria, the abolition of the Temporal Power, and the union of all Italy under a republican form of government. This was to be brought about by a national rising *en masse*, provoked and heralded by sudden explosions wherever possible. Mazzini's programme was strenuously opposed by the Moderates or Reformers, a party of intellectuals whose base was in Lombardy. They regarded the Mazzinian policy of sporadic rebellion as futile and unnecessary, leading only to exasperation on both sides and the loss of valuable lives. Nor were they as a whole enamoured of a republic, though it had its partisans in their ranks. Their central idea was reform by co-operation between Princes and people within each state, leading up to the federal union of all Italy. Education, railways, banks, the modernizing of industry, must come first and then federation by consent. This programme received strong support with the publication in 1843 of the Abbé Gioberti's *Il Primato*, 'The civil and moral primacy of the Italians', in which the political solution advocated was federation under the Papacy with a College of Princes as an executive. The work, in spite of its seven hundred pages, was widely read and received with great applause, for Gioberti was determined that it should be read and not put on the Index, and he toned down his asperities and flattered every one, finding even a word of praise for the Jesuits and the egregious Ferdinand of Naples. *Il Primato* was perhaps the most elaborate piece of propaganda ever written. Its effect was to accentuate still further an existing rift in thought amongst the Reformers, between, that is to say, the Neo-Guelfs, who like Gioberti looked to the Papacy to lead, and the Albertisti, who were already speculating on the possibility of a lead from the House of Savoy. But the real weakness of the work was that it shirked the two vital questions which formed the crux of the whole problem, the Temporal Power and the Austrian possession of Lombardy-Venetia. The idea of leaving the States of the Church to be permanently misgoverned by Cardinals and Bishops revolted every one, and how to persuade Austria to quit Italian soil, was a problem Gioberti thought it well to leave unanswered.

The *Primato* was followed by Balbo's *Hopes of Italy* which abandoned the idea of Italy under the Pope and veered towards the leadership of the House of Savoy; but his solution of the Austrian problem, that with the break up of Turkey Austria would turn east and abandon Lombardy-Venetia, was fantastic. Other books of less importance making further suggestions appeared about this time, but the only one to reach public opinion outside Italy was D'Azeglio's brochure *On the recent events in the Romagna*. Prompted by the manifesto *To the Princes and Peoples of Europe* issued after the revolt at Rimini, it was a scathing indictment of Papal rule and shattered all thoughts of a regenerated Papacy so long as the present rule by priests was allowed to exist. D'Azeglio, already well known through his historical romances, was one of the few realists amongst the many idealists in Italy at this time, who looked the ugly fact in the face that, if his country demanded independence and freedom from Austria, she must be prepared to fight for it. Looked at from this angle the one hope for Italy lay in Charles Albert. Would he fight Austria? That was the single vital question. Determined to put this to the test D'Azeglio in 1845 made a pilgrimage from Rome through central and northern Italy to gauge public opinion and estimate what prospect there was of practical support for Piedmont if she threw down the glove to Austria. He reached two conclusions, first that the desire to fight Austria was a reality, and secondly, that there was little trust put in the Sardinian King. His journey over, D'Azeglio went to Turin and asked for a private audience of the King to whom he was well known. It was granted, and one autumn morning at 6 a.m. whilst the city still slept and the palace alone was ablaze with lights, for the King rose before dawn, D'Azeglio was ushered into the King's presence.

Charles Albert gave D'Azeglio an opening by inquiring where he had been lately. Then D'Azeglio spoke of his journey: of the generally expressed condemnation of the Mazzinian policy; the useless sacrifices and the futile risings. All sensible people, he told the King, deprecated conspiracy, but they knew force was necessary, they realized that Italy would have to fight, and all eyes were turned upon Piedmont and her King. Here he stopped and awaited the King's reply. He expected, he tells us, the usual colourless words of sympathy, instead, looking D'Azeglio in the eyes he said, 'Tell those gentlemen to keep quiet and not move, for at present there is nothing to be done: but they may be certain that, if the opportunity comes, my life, the life of my sons, my resources, my wealth, my army, all shall be given for the cause of Italy'. Such was Charles Albert's deliberate pledge to Italy and nobly did he redeem it.

The motto of Mazzini, 'Thought and action', both inflammable, was finding wide expression throughout Italy in the years after 1840. The chronic unrest in Sicily, the abortive rising of the Muratori at Bologna, the troubles at Rimini, followed by the quixotic attempt of the Bandiera brothers in 1844, with its tragic close before a firing squad at Cosenza, were all clear evidence of the quickened tempo of the national aspirations. There were new opportunities for interchange of ideas in the Scientific Congresses (whose members were drawn from all the states of the peninsula) which met annually in some city of northern Italy. Literature was becoming increasingly outspoken and there was a hitherto unknown freedom in the expression of public opinion, while Giusti's bitter epigrams gave a jagged edge to Italy's resentment at the conduct of Austria and her petty tyrants. The old and the new were at grips, and demands for social reform were meeting obstruction from reactionary ministers. When Cavour in 1846 proposed a bank for Turin it was at once turned down by the minister concerned as too great a novelty. Plans for railways were meeting with curious objections. The first line built, that from Naples to Portici, had to be constructed without tunnels on the ground of their moral danger. The Pope employed the same arguments, adding the reason, potent in the States of the Church, that they would bring malcontents into Rome. But the mere proposals revealed a new spirit.

Politically there appeared to be no change, but in Lombardy and in Piedmont there was a slowly increasing tension. The Lombards were bitter over the continual increase of Austrian officials, the slowness in an administration where everything had to be referred to Vienna, and the steady tendency to 'germanize' the country. In Piedmont, Charles Albert was pursuing a policy of contenting the liberals with small concessions without exciting the suspicions of Austria, but he was beginning to show clear symptoms of *italianità*. In a variety of small contentious matters with Austria, a contraband convention, the building of a bridge, the salt question, he consistently refused to meet Austria half way and showed himself difficult and unaccommodating. In his letters to Della Margherita we find him speaking of the 'necessity of showing ourselves completely independent of Austria' and again of 'bending all our thoughts to Italian independence', phrases which reveal an attitude of mind very different from the pro-Austrian leanings usually attributed to him. But nothing of this appeared in public and his enigmatic silence still caused distrust in his sincerity; as D'Azeglio wrote after his interview 'that is what he said, but God alone knows his heart'.

Thought in Italy, as elsewhere in Europe, was reaching a climax. It was no longer a vague hope but a deepening conviction that great changes were imminent. Things could not go on as they were. There was no certainty of leadership, there was no plans. There was not even a fighting spirit. It is upon moral grounds that Italy rests her cause. Monarchists, federalists and republicans each have their panacea, but all agree that change there must be. Clear-sighted as ever, Metternich saw the storm rising round him, but a sense of helplessness possesses him—*aprés moi le déluge* is his mental outlook, and the storm when it broke left him more helpless than ever, with the one thing he thought impossible, a liberal Pope.

On June 1, 1846, Gregory XVI died and after a short conclave Cardinal Mastai-Ferretti was elected as his successor, taking the title of Pius IX. A kindly, gentle priest, with a handsome presence and a fine voice, the new Pope had never made himself prominent and was generally unknown, and his selection was regarded as without much political significance. It was known, however, that he had shown humanity to the liberals in his diocese of Imola, that he was a friend of the liberal-minded Count Giuseppe Pasolini, at whose suggestion he had read both Gioberti and D'Azeglio. It was customary for a new Pope to issue an amnesty, but political criminals were habitually barred from this. A month after his elevation to the Papacy Pius issued a wide political amnesty which, though restricted by an oath of future loyalty and good conduct, was an unheard of concession, giving evidence of a liberal spirit hitherto unknown at the Vatican. The effect was electric. To the accompaniment of a chorus of praise from Europe (even the Sultan of Turkey sent a congratulatory embassy to Rome), the Pope entered boldly upon the path of reform. A series of commissions were appointed and plans made for railways and gas lighting, prison reform and education, communal and provincial administration. The States of the Church were to be modernized.

Amongst all these excellent administrative proposals, however, there were three political measures of fundamental importance. In March 1847, a law on the Press, permitted the publication of newspapers and journals under the supervision of a body of lay censors; in June a Consulta was granted, an advisory body of laymen under the presidency of a Cardinal; and finally, after a long struggle, came permission to form a Civic Guard. The method by which these results were obtained is of great interest and peculiar to the Papacy, though they were soon imitated at Florence and Turin. It might be called the process of 'pressure by acclamation'. The spontaneous display of devotion to Pio Nono in the kneeling crowds and the vivas, was before long cleverly organized into a form of political pressure. A body of progressives, amongst whom the most prominent were the Marquis Massimo D'Azeglio (returned to Rome from Turin), the doctor Sterbini and the popular wine carrier Angelo

Brunetti, known to all as Ciceruacchio, were behind the movement. The bouquets and the banquets, at which the national passion for rhetoric received *carte blanche* to expand itself, were soon supplemented by organized demonstrations of applause or silent disapproval, according as a wanted measure was passed or rejected by the Pope. Pio Nono was sensitive and vain: the incense of popularity was dear to him and its opposite abhorrent; and this subtle war on the Papal nerves, alternating between rapturous applause when he acquiesced, and a grim silence broken only by groans or threats (revealing the ugly temper of the Romans that lay beneath the surface) when popular measures were rejected, pushed the good Pope much further than he meant to go, without resort to the usual methods of force.

The repercussions of Papal liberalism were felt at once all over Italy. In May, by not dissimilar methods, Tuscany obtained a Press, and the *Alba* in Florence and at Pisa *L'Italia* at once began demands for further concessions. At Lucca a Civic Guard was granted in September, but the death of Marie Louise, which removed the princeling at Lucca to Parma, and caused the transference of Lucca to Tuscany, brought the full benefits won at Florence to the small state as well. Modena, where the new Duke, Francis V (his father died in 1846) was entirely under Austria, promptly asked for a garrison of his protector's troops. At Milan the appointment of a new Archbishop, this time an Italian, led to demonstrations whose nationalist character was unmistakable, as was the impressive funeral of Count Confalonieri, the martyr of the Spielberg, in the following January. Naples did not move, but there were disturbances at Reggio and Messina followed by executions and imprisonments as usual.

At Vienna the reaction to these events was a feeling of dismay. The prompt use of force, to which Metternich was averse, would only make matters worse and raise a storm of protest. But Metternich took precautions. The garrisons in Lombardy were strengthened and the timely appeal for troops from Modena gave him a valuable opening to exert influence in Tuscany if necessary. The tone of his letters to Lützow, his ambassador at the Vatican, is almost one of distress. He encloses notes, 'aperçus' to be read to the Pope: hints on forms of government: on the true significance of an amnesty and the real meaning of concessions. Realizing that Austrian action means trouble, he turns to France, trying to induce Guizot to take a firm line at the Vatican; but Guizot will not interfere with internal reforms and does nothing. But the patience of Metternich had limits. Commissions on prison reform and railways he does not mind, but when it comes to putting arms in the hands of the people by the formation of a Civic Guard, it is necessary to take steps. So, on the anniversary of the amnesty, when all Italy was en fête, cavalry, infantry and artillery, with fuses lighted all ready for action, occupied the Papal city of Ferrara, where Austria already had garrison rights. At once the storm broke; the Cardinal Legate protested, the Pope circularized the Powers, there was a shriek from the new Press, and Charles Albert offered to put all his forces at the disposal of the Holy Father for the defence of his states. The occupation of Ferrara was a bad mistake and involved Metternich in six months of worry and diplomatic warfare, until in December he felt beaten and withdrew the troops.

Metternich was no more successful elsewhere. The condition of Lombardy was causing grave misgivings. The administration seemed paralysed and the old Viceroy, the Archduke Rainer, was useless. Metternich sent Count Ficquelmont to try and vitalize the government. But nothing could be done, Milan laid the blame on Vienna and Vienna on Milan, and finding it hopeless, Ficquelmont resigned his commission and withdrew. The one live force in Lombardy was the army. Radetzky kept his sword sharp and ready for action and was eager to settle the Italian problem by force but Metternich would not permit it. The crux of the whole Italian situation lay with Charles Albert, for though the extremists everywhere were trying to drive the governments into war with Austria, the contributions they could make towards victory, apart from the Sardinian army, were negligible, and the state of things at Turin was as obscure as ever. The King's first care was to maintain law and order and prevent the country from falling into the condition of Rome and Florence. He had always hated crowds and demonstrations. The mob round the palace in 1821 had left upon him an unforgettable memory. All these vivas and rosettes and hymns to Pio Nono, from which Turin was by no means exempt, were thoroughly distasteful and everything was done to discourage them. As to war with Austria the position was complicated in the extreme. Charles Albert had not the least intention of provoking it. He knew very well the danger of flinging his small army against Radetzky and he had no illusions as to the fighting value of untrained revolutionary levies. Yet deep down in his nature there was a mystical crusader's vision of leading a victorious army under the banner of the Cross against the hated Austria, and of dying, like Wolfe, in the moment of victory. From time to time we see a flash of it in his correspondence, as in the message he sent to be read to the Scientific Congress at Casale. 'If ever', he wrote, 'God grants us the favour of being able to undertake a war of independence, it is I alone who will command the army, and then, I am resolved to do for the Guelf cause what Schamil has done against the great Russian empire. Oh the brave day that we shall be able to raise the cry of national independence!' 'He had one sole passion', wrote Della Margherita who watched him closely for thirteen years, 'Italian independence as his personal work.' But this quixotic dream was neutralized by a native caution. At his elbow was Della Margherita bent on preventing Italian adventures. The liberals worked hard to bring about his dismissal but could not. Nothing would induce him to resign and at every turn he opposed and obstructed the King's liberal tendencies. Nor did the King get any encouragement against Austria from abroad. No one wanted war. England urged reform but not war, neither France nor Austria wanted it, only the extremists in Italy favoured it.

The temper of resistance was rising in Piedmont. They hated Austria. They were sick of the King's policy of secrecy and silence and the plague of spies and informers. They wanted a free Press and a constitution, and freedom and liberty of expression. Its centre was Genoa rather than Turin, where under the inspiration of Goffredo Mameli, poet and soldier, destined to die in defence of Rome, and of Nino Bixio, Garibaldi's volcanic lieutenant and a future general of united Italy, processions and demonstrations culminated in an influential deputation to the King. But the first change came from events in the capital, where an assembly of citizens preparing to give a birthday ovation to the King, was rudely dispersed by the police and carabinieri with unnecessary violence. Strong protests followed which resulted in the dismissal of the Marquis Villamarina, the Minister for War, and, at last, of Della Margherita from the Foreign Office. A week later Charles Albert published his long expected reforms (October 1847). These included a free Press under a lay censorship, a court of Cassation, the transfer of the police from the Minister of War to that of the Interior, and a communal law by which members of the provincial and communal councils were eligible for election to the Council of State, together with the abolition of the exceptional Courts of Justice. For a brief space the King was raised to the pinnacle of popularity but the country was not satisfied. The new Press began to concentrate on the need for a constitution, Genoa was demanding a Civic Guard and the expulsion of the Jesuits, and the year closed in a struggle of will power between King and people as to whether parliamentary government or the old absolutism were to direct the future destinies of the country.

The same problem was troubling the Ministers at Florence, Rome and Naples, and the solution came from the south. The new year opened with the Tobacco Riots at Milan which revealed the rapidly increasing tension in Lombardy, involving clashes with the police and some fatalities, which roused ostentatious echoes of sympathy in Piedmont and Rome and impressive funeral services for the victims. It was a first indication of the national quality of the movement. Then on January 12th Palermo rose in revolt, expelled the garrison and put Ruggero Settimo at the head of the municipality. The bombardment of the city which followed was stopped by the protests of the foreign consuls. The example of Palermo spread quickly across the island. The constitution of 1812 was re-established and Sicily declared its independence. Afraid of losing his throne, Ferdinand hastily began reforms which culminated on January 29th in the proclamation of a constitution. Quickly drawn up on the French model of 1830, it comprised two chambers, one elective, the other nominated by the King, with a free Press and individual liberty. Ignoring Article 87 specially inserted to bring Sicily within its scope, the Parliament on the island declared boldly on April 13th, 'The throne of Sicily is vacant. Sicily will be ruled by its own constitution and will elect an Italian prince to the throne when it has revised its statutes. Ferdinand of Bourbon and his dynasty are for ever excluded.'

The example of Naples decided the other states. In Piedmont the pressure was irresistible and on February 8th Charles Albert promised a constitution and appointed a commission to draw it up. Three days later a constitution was likewise proclaimed in Tuscany. Like the rest of Italy, the Earthly Paradise had had its political troubles. These reached their climax in the revolt of the seaport of Leghorn, which, like Genoa in Piedmont, was the most radical city in the duchy. This decided the Grand-duke to submit and follow the craze for parliamentary government. Finally came Rome. On March 10th a ministry of laymen was nominated and five days later, the day on which Prince Metternich fled from Vienna to England, a constitution was proclaimed in Rome.[10] Of all these constitutional efforts one only was to last, that of Piedmont, which after twelve years of successful life in Turin was in 1860 extended to all Italy then united, and finally, ten years later, to Italy with Rome as its capital.

Whilst these events were transforming the peninsula, Europe was in revolution. On February 22nd France overthrew the Orleans throne and Louis Philippe fled to England. On March 3rd Baden obtained a constitution. From Germany revolution spread to Austria and on March 15th Metternich left Vienna. When this news reached Milan the city rose and in the famous 'Five Days' of street fighting reduced the Austrian garrison of thirteen thousand men to such a plight that on the 23rd Radetzky withdrew his troops from the city. The next day Charles Albert declared war on Austria, on the 26th his troops crossed the frontier and the first war of Italian independence began. The news of the 'Five Days' of Milan spread like wildfire over Italy. At Venice, Daniele Manin, rescued from prison by the people, at once took command of the situation and by a combination of audacity and determination seized the arsenal and compelled the Austrians to evacuate the city, and the Lion of S. Mark floated once again over the Republic of Venice. The princelings at Parma and Modena fled for safety, and Piedmontese troops arrived at Modena. It was the same at Florence though the Grand-duke remained. Like Manin at Venice, Leonetto Cipriani forced the weak hands of the government, volunteers were enrolled, the University of Pisa, both students and staff, volunteering almost to a man. Everywhere the Austrian arms were torn down. In Rome and Naples the organization of volunteers began and it seemed as if all Italy was rising at the call of national independence to a new greatness. In these first days it almost resembled a holy war, with the Pope's 'God bless Italy' ringing in every one's ears and the belief that his liberalism extended to the declaration of war on Austria. But volunteers are not like trained troops and enthusiasm is a poor substitute in war for organization and discipline; Italy had many bitter lessons yet to learn before she won her independence.

CHAPTER FOUR

THE MILITARY OPERATIONS IN 1848

WHEN Charles Albert crossed the frontier at Pavia, he had with him by his own account just over twenty-three thousand men. This small number was due to the despatch of part of the regular army to watch French movements on the western border and to the fact that mobilization was not complete. At Lodi he learnt that Radetzky had taken up a strong position at Montichiari behind the river Chiese. This position he decided to outflank by advancing to Cremona and ascending the Oglio, but Radetzky divined his intention and retired behind the Mincio within the famous Quadrilateral. The Sardinians met no opposition until they reached this new position. A brilliant little action gave them a bridgehead at Goito and a second at Monzambano and Charles Albert took up his position on both banks of the Mincio with the Austrians on the high ground beyond.

The ensuing campaign was fought out in an area represented by a right-angled triangle. The point of the angle was the Austrian fortress of Peschiera at the extreme southern point of Lake Garda. From here the river Mincio flows south past the villages of Salionze, Valeggio and Goito to Mantua, a distance of about thirty miles. This was the Austrian front. Eastwards from Peschiera ran the main road to Verona twenty miles away, which was Radetzky's headquarters. The hyposenuse of the triangle was the road running south-west from Verona to Mantua. The Austrian position was exceedingly strong. Holding the high ground rising from the river they overlooked the Sardinian lines and at the same time could reinforce any point of their front unseen by the enemy, while the two fortresses of Peschiera and Mantua protected them from any turning movement. Radetzky's strategy was quite simple: to remain strictly on the defensive until such time as he had received enough reinforcements to take the offensive. The position of Charles Albert was correspondingly difficult. To make a successful frontal attack he needed enough men to mask both Peschiera and Mantua to prevent an attack on his flanks. For he could not advance and leave the strong garrisons of the two fortresses to close in behind him. The same weakness made a wide turning movement round Mantua impossible. He could not stand still, nor could he mass his men at one point without the risk of uncovering Milan and Lombardy.

His first move was a reconnaissance in force towards Mantua which only revealed that it was strongly held, that the Austrians had flooded the marshes, and that the place was practically impregnable, except by a long siege. A week later on April 19th a similar move was made against Peschiera with the same discouraging result. It was then decided to reduce Peschiera by siege. The siege train at Alessandria was therefore sent for and in the meantime it became necessary to drive off the Austrians covering Peschiera. This led to the first battle. Charles Albert had by now received considerable reinforcements. The regiments had been brought up to full strength by the arrival of the reservists, and a force of some five thousand Tuscans and Modenese had also reached him. Another body of about the same strength, Lombard volunteers, was operating in the Tyrol and Roman levies were on their way, but under orders to remain south of the Po. The Tuscans were sent to the southern end of the front where they entrenched themselves at Montanara and Curtatone opposite Mantua. The Roman contingent, after long delay, passed through Venetia and joined the local levies blocking the road for Austrian reinforcements by the valley of the Brenta.

On April 30th Charles Albert attacked General D'Aspre at Pastrengo. This position not only covered Peschiera but kept open the valley of the Adige through which reinforcements could reach Radetzky from Trent and Rovereto. The battle started late, as it was a Sunday and the troops had to hear Mass. By four o'clock in the afternoon D'Aspre was dislodged from the heights and his troops were retiring in some disorder upon Verona. A vigorous pursuit might have dislocated the whole Austrian front but the King showed his lack of generalship by recalling his victorious army. In so doing he missed the one real opportunity offered him. It was a victory but fruitless, and brought the solution of driving out the Austrians no nearer. The moral effect of the victory was, moreover, completely neutralized by the Papal Allocution of April 29th in which the Pope declared the impossibility of his making war on any Christian nation. It was a great blow, for Italy had hoped to reincarnate in Pio Nono the warrior spirit of old Julius II, and it was true, that however little he meant to do it, his words and actions had greatly encouraged the people to beat their ploughshares into swords. The Pope's attitude was right and proper, for though he knew that he could not stop his people from joining in the struggle, his position made it impossible

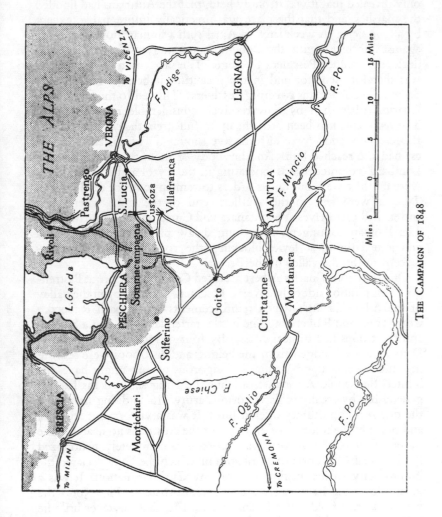

THE CAMPAIGN OF 1848

for him to sanction it. The next day Charles Albert again attacked the Austrians at Santa Lucia, but this time things went wrong. The staff work was defective. Orders did not arrive and the terrain proved unexpectedly difficult, and although by the end of the day the main objective was attained, the position could not be held and the Sardinian troops withdrew.

The battle of Santa Lucia was forced on the King by political pressure. The Ministers at Turin, now on the eve of the first general election, wrote insistently on the need of a victory, and the letters from the provisional government at Milan were in the same strain. The truth was that the situation was completely misconceived in both capitals. They were convinced that the Austrian army was utterly disorganized and that all Charles Albert had to do was to round up Radetzky's scattered forces and drive the remnants back into Austria. The exaggerated accounts of the setback at Santa Lucia produced a feeling of dismay, and a virulent campaign broke out in the democratic press against the army commanders and staff, which had the worst effect upon the morale of the army. During the month of May there was a lull in the fighting which was concentrated on the siege of Peschiera. During this interval the strength of the Sardinians was further weakened by the defection of the Neapolitan contingent. Ferdinand had promised forty thousand men, reduced finally to twelve thousand, but on May 15th there were fresh troubles at Naples, the army sided with the King, the Constitution was swept aside, and the troops sent to Lombardy were recalled. The general in command, Pepe, resigned, half of the regiments either disbanded or returned, but the rest, at the urgent prayer of the Milanese, rallied round Pepe who eventually led them to Venice where they were of great value later during the siege.

Towards the end of May the fall of Peschiera, which was not provisioned for a siege, was imminent, and Radetzky made an effort to save it. With some thirteen thousand men he slipped out of Verona, marched right across the Sardinian front undetected, and reached Mantua. The next day he threw his whole force against the Tuscans at Montanara and Curtatone. His aim was to roll up the Sardinian right, draw the King's main forces south, then to provision Peschiera and catch the King's army between two fires. The splendid defence of the Tuscans saved the situation. They fought like veterans, the students' battalion from the University of Pisa in particular showing splendid skill and courage. Though their losses were severe, and eventually they were compelled to retire upon Marcaria, they had given Charles Albert time to collect a force at Goito and forestall an attack. The next day Radetzky marched on Goito. The battle lasted all day until finally the Austrians were compelled to fall back on Mantua without achieving their purpose, for Peschiera surrendered the same day. The fall of Peschiera and the battle of Goito proved the high-water mark of Sardinian success. After two months of fighting no decision had been reached by either side. Charles Albert had failed to dislodge Radetzky, he had lost the Neapolitans and the Tuscans who had to be withdrawn, his only gain was Peschiera, and the Austrians had failed to crush Charles Albert at Goito. The war seemed to be approaching a stalemate.

Ever since the opening of the struggle the conduct of the war had been complicated by the political situation. The King left behind him a completely inexperienced cabinet, in which only two ministers, those of Finance and Public Works, had any political experience. The Premier, Count Cesare Balbo, was best known as an historical writer; the Foreign Secretary, the Marquis Pareto, was a democratic *exalté* from Genoa, and Count Ricci, Minister for Internal Affairs, was of the same colour. The electoral law was in course of preparation, and the tone of the Chamber of Deputies, when elected, was, of course, an unknown quantity. In the country generally, the complete defeat of Austria was regarded as certain, and the absorbing topic was the new 'Kingdom of Upper Italy' to be founded when the last Austrian was safely across the border. Moreover, France was now a republic and so was Venice, and there was a noisy republican party in Milan which from jealousy of Piedmont clamoured for Milanese self-government as an autonomous state. Mazzini was there in April urging republicanism, Gioberti followed him urging federalism, while the Albertisti pressed for union with Piedmont. During May and June the question of fusion with Piedmont was put to the vote. The duchies voted solidly in the affirmative, and to the general surprise, Lombardy did the same. Finally, in the first week in July Venice surrendered her republic and voted for union. Thus when the Piedmontese Chamber of Deputies met, all upper Italy was solid for union under the House of Savoy. The one reservation, proposed by Milan and accepted at Turin, was a Constituent Assembly to be summoned after the victory to consider the revision of the Piedmontese statute. This included the vexed question whether Turin or Milan was to be the capital of the new state. All appeared happily settled, when the one contingency overlooked, defeat in the field, materialized, and the new kingdom suddenly vanished in the smoke and flame of Custoza.

In spite of all their troubles at Vienna, the Austrian Government had found reinforcements for Radetzky. Twenty thousand men under Count Thurn were advancing through the valley of the Adige, and another fifteen thousand under General Welden by the Brenta. This information reached both sides, and Charles Albert planned to seize Rivoli and block Count Thurn's advance, while Radetzky decided to clear the road for Welden by attacking the Papal and Lombard troops under General Durando at Vicenza. The Sardinians seized Rivoli without much difficulty, and almost at the same time, Radetzky, with a greatly superior force, fell upon Durando. His success was complete. After a three days' battle Durando surrendered and Radetzky without wasting a moment hurried back to Verona, leaving the road clear for Welden. He was just in time, for Charles Albert had got word of his departure for Vicenza, and too late, advanced upon Verona. These two actions seriously altered the balance of forces. Charles Albert was weakened by the loss of ten thousand men and Radetzky strengthened by the addition of fifteen thousand, with another twenty thousand approaching from Rovereto; a force strong enough to drive back the Sardinian left and render it liable to a flank attack from Verona. The position of the King was getting critical.

Charles Albert made war much as he governed. He used his generals as his subordinates to carry out his plans, though no doubt he consulted them when he thought it desirable. The danger inherent in this mode of conducting war, was that if political matters distracted the King, military operations came more or less to a standstill. This happened now, just when Radetzky wanted a quiet time to plan his offensive, now that his reinforcements had reached him and he had superiority in numbers. For a month quiet reigned on the front, while the King, absorbed with political business, waited for reinforcements which never came, and the Austrians completed their preparations for a real offensive. The basic trouble was that both in Piedmont and Lombardy every one was so utterly convinced of the approaching defeat of the Austrians that instead of concentrating upon strengthening the army in the field, they gave themselves up to an orgy of political planning in the construction and constitution of the new Kingdom of Upper Italy. This was accentuated by what was happening in the higher ranks of the Powers, where England was working with France for peace, chiefly on the basis of the surrender of Lombardy, whereas at Turin they refused to consider it without the acquisition of Venetia as well.

'At Headquarters', wrote Della Rocca, 'ambassadors, diplomats and intermediaries, bringing advice or proposals for peace or mediation, were perpetually coming and going. A deputation arrived from Sicily to offer the crown to the Duke of Genoa, which was, however, rejected. Ministers came from Turin to take orders and entreat that the war should be pushed on rapidly. Parma, Piacenza and Modena sent deputations asking for help, while the Lombard representatives insisted on immediate action.'

After compelling Radetzky's withdrawal from Milan in the 'Five Days', the Lombards did nothing. In the middle of June the King wrote that there was not a Lombard soldier on the Mincio. The two divisions they undertook to send to the front never materialized, all they did was to urge the King to go on and win the final victory. Political pressure of the same kind came incessantly from Turin. At length, after planning a great advance into Venetia, promptly discarded for lack of troops to hold the Mincio in his rear, Charles Albert fell back on the hopeless task of besieging Mantua. By the middle of July he had thirty thousand men round the city. This was almost half his army. He had fifteen thousand at the northern end, stretching south from Rivoli to Sommacampagna, and ten thousand in the centre between Peschiera and Goito. Opposed to these twenty-five thousand, Radetzky, with Welden's fifteen thousand, had at least double the number of troops within a few miles of the front, without counting the twenty thousand under Count Thurn coming south down the Adige. Such was the disposition of the King's army when Radetzky struck on July 22nd.

The five days of fighting which constituted the battle of Custoza opened with an attack by Count Thurn on the Sardinian position at Rivoli. This was successful. De Sonnaz was forced back across the main road from Peschiera to Verona and took up his position at nightfall on the high ground of Sommacampagna between the Mincio on his left and the road from Verona to Mantua on his right. His new position brought him within reach of a flank attack from Verona, and the next day, heavily engaged both in front by Thurn and in flank by Radetzky, he was driven first westwards from the high ground to the shelter of Peschiera, and then southward beyond Valeggio, on the Mincio north of Goito. The noise of battle as it came south reached the King's headquarters at Marmirola, and realizing the seriousness of the position, he broke up the siege of Mantua and leaving a containing force, to prevent a sortie from the garrison in his rear, prepared to march north. His most obvious course was to follow the river road to Goito, but unexpectedly he gave orders to take the north-east road and to concentrate at Villafranca, half way to Verona. The weather was unbearably hot (98 degrees in the shade) and hundreds of men fell out on the long road north but by evening the army was concentrated at Villafranca. The soundness of Charles Albert's strategy is open to question. To have joined De Sonnaz at Goito would have concentrated the full strength of the army and kept it in touch with any available reserves and with supplies. It was what was expected by Radetzky, for his troops were now formed up across the river facing south. On the other hand an attack from the east took the Austrians in the flank and had the element of surprise. The army rested the next day (24th) until 4 p.m. and then advanced to the attack. The battle of Staffalo, as it has been called from a village on the line of advance, was a complete success. The high ground was captured and the Austrians driven back to the Mincio, two thousand prisoners including fifty officers were taken and the army bivouacked for the night in high spirits. Radetzky was now compelled to change his front from south to east. It was a brilliant piece of staff work to do this in a single night with an army of sixty thousand men. But he had his share of luck. The Sardinian attack was timed for 4 a.m. but the failure of the commissariat saved the Austrians from being caught in the midst of a complicated manoeuvre and by the time the Sardinians were ready to advance Radetzky's new front was securely established.

The advance, however, never came; for the high hopes of victory held the night before were sadly dashed when they realized the strength of the enemy. In the absence of De Sonnaz and the covering force left at Mantua, Charles Albert had probably no more than twenty-five thousand men. Radetzky, with the addition of Thurn, must have had more than double that number. It was now the Austrians who attacked and the Sardinians who defended. The grim battle of Custoza, taking its name from another village in the vicinity, raged all day under the July sun. The diversion for which the King hoped, an attack by De Sonnaz on Valeggio, never came: his troops were too exhausted. Despite their great numerical superiority, which enabled Radetzky to withdraw his troops and rest them during the fighting, the Austrians failed to dislodge the Sardinians from their position. But as night fell their ammunition gave out and retreat was inevitable, and they slowly withdrew to Villafranca. The praise that Radetzky lavished on his troops is sufficient evidence of the splendid courage of the defence.

Custoza was a defeat, but it was not yet a disaster. The next day, taking his prisoners with him, the King took the cross road from Villafranca and joined De Sonnaz at Goito. The addition of two thousand prisoners, however, had exhausted the commissariat, and the army arrived weary and famished. Here, for the first time, discipline broke down. Ill news spreads apace and the rumours of defeat arrived before the King, and at once the Milanese contractors who supplied the army fled for safety, taking their stores with them, and the hungry troops pillaged Goito for food, unearthing, happily, large stores of pilfered supplies. To remain in Goito was impossible, for the military situation of the army grew more dangerous hour by hour. The neglect of De Sonnaz to garrison Volta and the failure of the desperate effort to retake it, compelled the King to ask for an armistice. But the terms included the handing over of the duchies, and Charles Albert would not surrender those who had chosen him as their King. The retreat continued. Two days later he was at Cremona; an attempt to defend the line of the Adda was foiled by the demoralization of some units who left their positions and retired on Piacenza. This, in truth, was the only defensible position, and the one which the staff expected to occupy, but the King thought otherwise. A quixotic sense of loyalty to those who had chosen him, and the hope of checking the full tide of Austrian vengeance, decided him to attempt the defence of Milan.

Early on the morning of August 3rd the remains of his army, twenty-five thousand out of what at one time was sixty thousand, reached Milan and were disposed in a wide arc round the city. The King himself would not enter Milan but took up his quarters at a poor *osteria*, the San Giorgio, outside the walls. The next day the Austrians attacked, concentrating on the Porta Romana near the King's quarters. That evening the King moved to the Greppi palace within the city. The grim events of these days came as a rude shock to the complacency of the Milanese. In great haste a Committee of Safety was appointed and vigorous steps taken, which should have been taken months before. But the spirit of the 'Five Days' was no longer in evidence. All who could had left the city and the call for defence was utterly inadequate. Charles Albert and his staff toured the city and were convinced of the hopelessness of defending it. That night at a Council of War it was decided to ask for terms and two generals were despatched to the Austrian headquarters. In the morning they returned. Twenty-four hours were to be allowed for the withdrawal of the army, forty-eight for all those who wished to leave the city, the Porta Romana to be handed over on August 6th. These terms were accepted. When news of the armistice reached the city, where at last the citizens had begun to construct defences, there was an angry cry of betrayal. A furious crowd rushed to the Palazzo Greppi shouting death to Charles Albert, but were kept outside by the national guard on duty. All day the King and his staff were besieged. Deputations interviewed the King and bitter charges were made on both sides, but at last reason prevailed and the Archbishop and the Podestà were sent to Radetzky's headquarters to try and get better terms, but returned without success. The city had to accept its fate. Late that night word reached the army of the King's plight and the crowd disappeared like magic when the quick step of a company of Bersaglieri was heard approaching. Two hours later the army left Milan and within two days was on Piedmontese soil. The first war of Italian independence was over.

Charles Albert's conduct of the campaign has been very adversely criticized. That he was not the equal of Radetzky as a general is evident: except in courage, he led, however, an army inferior in nearly every necessary quality. In staff work, in discipline and training, in cohesion and power of manoeuvre, the Austrians were far superior. Nor should we forget that while Radetzky had a free hand, and at the critical period received large trained reinforcements, Charles Albert was sorely hampered by political problems, additional troops never materialized, and he was forced into premature action by the pressure of political uncertainties. Ten years later Napoleon III, with an army four times the size, after two resounding victories, when faced with the same problem, made peace at Villafranca rather than attempt to force the Quadrilateral.

The rising of Italy in 1848 was no effort for unity, an aim which as yet had but few supporters beyond the more far-seeing Mazzinians. It was a purely anti-Austrian movement. Charles Albert could never have made Italy, for he would never have invaded the States of the Church. There is a passage in his diary where he writes, 'if once we could obtain the duchy of Parma it would be less difficult to get Modena. This is the constant aim of my policy for which I shall work with perseverance and warmth'. The events of 1848 made Lombardy a further possibility, and this, with the more remote prospect of Venetia, comprised his entire ambition. To form this Kingdom of Upper Italy, not to make Italy, was his one and only objective.

CHAPTER FIVE

THE AFTERMATH: 1849

THE blaze of enthusiasm which marked the opening of the first war of independence had its source not only in hatred of Austria but in the liberalism of Pio Nono. That a Pope should bless Italy and wish her independent, should grant an amnesty and initiate reforms, was so unexpected and untraditional that it lent an atmosphere almost of benediction to the whole national effort. But with the Papal Allocution of April 29th and the subsequent defeat of Charles Albert the spirit of the movement changed colour. We can now detect a steady growth of the more extreme opinions, as happened in the early phases of the French Revolution. Mazzini is behind it and summed it up in the words, 'the war of the Kings is over, the war of the people begins'. It is evident in Piedmont, Tuscany and the Papal States. Its central idea is a Constituent Assembly and a Republic, and it is accompanied by a rising tendency to violence, animosity against the rulers, and in some quarters a demand for the renewal of war with Austria.

The Allocution had revealed the hopeless contradiction involved in the dual personality of the Pope. As a temporal prince he could arm the people through the medium of a Civic Guard, he could enroll troops to keep order, who at need might shoot down his own subjects, but as the spiritual head of Catholicism he could not declare war against any Christian nation. Equally anomalous was the relation between the Pope and his government. All the government proposals had to pass through the sieve of the College of Cardinals before the final sanction of the Pope permitted their translation into laws. There were two foreign secretaries, one dealing with the spiritual and the other with the temporal aspects of the problems arising with other countries, and the Pope's insistence that he must have 'absolute freedom of action that there may be no obstacle to carrying out what he believed to be in the interest of religion and the state' hampered the ministry at every turn.[11] Under such peculiar conditions governments were unlikely to have a long existence. The first ministry under Count Mamiani, an exile of 1831, resigned in the middle of July, after ten weeks of perpetual friction with the Papal authorities. On August 3rd Count Odoardo Fabbri succeeded him—the day the Austrians occupied Ferrara. The people clamoured for war but the Pope merely protested, without result. A week later, General Welden tried to do the same at Bologna, again the Pope protested, but this time the people of Bologna took up arms, and after a sharp action drove the Austrians from the city. On August 26th Parliament was prorogued until November 15th and shortly afterwards Count Fabbri resigned to make way for Pellegrino Rossi.

Few men could have been chosen better equipped to bring order and decent government into the States of the Church than Count Rossi. An Italian by birth, a convinced liberal, a man of wide political knowledge and experience, an economist and financier, who had held chairs at Geneva and the Sorbonne, and a peer of France, he had been sent to Rome two years before as French ambassador and political and financial adviser to the Pope. He threw himself into his new task with all his power, preparing a whole series of measures on railways and telegraphs, army and police reform, to be submitted to Parliament when it reassembled. He was working too on a scheme of federation between Rome, Turin and Florence, a counter project to that of Gioberti at Turin, whose representative, the philosopher Rosmini, was already in Rome with proposals of a like kind. But Rossi was not popular. He was, perhaps, too much of a doctrinaire; too superior, too efficient, and too cold, to appeal to the Romans, and one suspects he lacked a sense of humour. That he somehow offended all classes and failed to win the support of any, is unfortunately true. Especially was this the case with the extreme democrats, the members of the Circolo Romano, to whom Rossi's attitude towards war with Austria, which he discouraged, regarding it as hopeless, was a bitter cause of offence. What Rossi might have done for Italy is, however, an idle conjecture, for on November 15th as he ascended the steps to open the first sitting of the new Chamber he was stabbed to death by an unknown hand. The indifference shown by the members of the Chamber of Deputies at this foul and foolish deed, and the open satisfaction, even rejoicing, displayed by the populace, is evidence enough of the moral condition and the political sagacity of the Roman people.

With the death of Rossi the extreme parties redoubled their efforts to get control of the government. On the 16th a crowd headed by the members of the Circolo Popolare assembled at the Quirinale demanding the promulgation of Italian nationality, convocation of a Constituent Assembly, war with Austria and a government including Galletti, Sterbini and Saliceti, all extremists and anathema to the Pope.

The day following a more threatening crowd assembled; attempts were made, the French Minister d'Harcourt wrote to Paris, to set fire to the palace, but it was frustrated by the Swiss Guard who arrested the ringleaders. Finally the Pope yielded, and a new Ministry of which Galletti and Sterbini were the dominant members came into power. A week later on November 24th Pius, in disguise as a simple priest, left Rome in the carriage of Count Spaur and sought peace and safety at Gaeta in the Kingdom of Naples. Thus the year 1848 in the States of the Church closed with the abandonment of Rome by the Pope, the collapse of the moderate or reformist party and the assumption of power by the extremists, in whose programme a Constituent Assembly, a Republican form of government, and war with Austria were the avowed objectives.

During this period a parallel movement was developing both in Tuscany and in Piedmont. At Florence the news of Custoza led to the fall of the weak Ridolfi Ministry, which was followed by that of Gino Capponi, who promised more energetic measures of defence and the upholding of national independence. But in Tuscany as in the Roman States it was the extremists who were the active force, and it was not Florence but the radical city of Leghorn which was shaping the policy of the state. Dominated by the turbulent poet-politician Domenico Guerrazzi, the city broke into revolt and the attempt of Cipriani to master it with a force of two thousand men only made matters worse. The arrival, however, of a popular hero in Montanelli, a second poet-politician, who had been wounded at Curtatone and taken prisoner by the Austrians, restored order. His advocacy of the need for a Constituent Assembly added a new demand from the Circolo politico del Popolo and threw fresh difficulties in the path of the Ministry, and in October Capponi resigned. There was at once a popular demand for a democratic government and after a fortnight of indecision the Grand-duke, like the Pope, yielded. At the end of October Montanelli was called to the Presidency of the Council with Guerrazzi beside him as Minister for Internal Affairs, and a programme embracing a Constituent Assembly and political union with the ideals of Rome. A general election followed Capponi's fall and the new Parliament was called for January 10, 1849.

The course of events in Piedmont followed the same general lines but the problems were more complicated. When the news of Custoza arrived, the new Ministry, which had been designed as representative of the 'Kingdom of Upper Italy' with Count Casati, President of the

Provisional Government at Milan as Premier, at once resigned. Before doing so, however, they appealed urgently to the Ministers of France and England at Turin for immediate mediation, and at the same time sent Count Ricci to Paris to approach the government for the loan of a general and twenty-five thousand troops, to take command of the Sardinian army and repair its losses. On the return of the army to Piedmont Count Casati and the Abbé Gioberti hastened to the King's headquarters at Vigevano and having informed him of the steps already taken, begged him not to prolong the armistice but to prepare for a renewal of the struggle, assuring him of the speedy arrival of a French army. To this the King, painfully aware of the real condition of his troops, returned a definite refusal, and sent his Chief of Staff, General Salasco, to make terms with Radetzky. These included the recall of the fleet from Venice and the withdrawal of all troops from the duchies. The prompt mediation of England and France, however, saved Piedmont from invasion and her soil remained free from Austrian occupation. These terms were certainly not unduly severe, but when they were known there was a furious outbreak in the press, which stigmatized them as unacceptable and dishonourable, for it was held that the vote of the duchies and of Lombardy-Venetia for union with Piedmont constituted a *de jure* right to the establishment of the Kingdom of Upper Italy, regardless of the fact that Austria was in possession. Their army had been beaten, not the spirit of the people, and they clung to their moral right to Italian independence with a tenacity which, in spite of defeat, in the end convinced Europe and led to victory. As to the French army which never arrived, it was England's determination to prevent French interference in Italy, backed by the general state of France herself, that accounted for its failure to appear.

Charles Albert had now to appoint a new Premier. Public opinion pointed strongly to Gioberti, but the King, who had no fancy for an ex-priest as his Prime Minister, turned to a tried servant of the State and invited Count Revel to form a government. He accepted on two conditions, that there must be a strict inquiry into the conduct of the campaign and that the King must submit to the appointment of another commander-in-chief. Charles Albert acquiesced, and what is known as the Revel-Pinelli Ministry took office. The new Minister for War, General Dabormida, however, refused to gratify the democratic thirst for a holocaust of generals. Changes were made, some were retired, but the morale of the army was maintained as far as possible, and there was no public inquiry. The attitude of the King, revealed in a letter to the Minister for War, was worthy of his position. After remarking that in his opinion such an inquiry would have been both impolitic and revolutionary, and productive only of discontent and indiscipline, he added—

besides this measure would have had no serious consequences for the officers attacked, for I beg you to believe, that I have enough courage to have assumed the entire responsibility and faced the inevitable unpopularity: for I should indubitably have covered them with my name and my orders: then, after such an insult, I should have abdicated the crown, which I only still wear from a sense of devotion to my country at this critical time.

As to the French general, those approached revealed a strange reluctance to assume the task of reorganizing the Piedmontese army and attacking the victorious Radetzky and the idea was given up.

In the first shock of defeat parties had disappeared and all classes had united to save the country. When that stage was passed and the expected invasion did not take place, the old divisions reappeared. Gioberti had not hitherto identified himself with any party, but now, wounded in his self-esteem by the King's selection of Revel instead of himself, he joined the extreme democratic section and in the Circolo Politico Nazionale at Turin, for Piedmont had its democratic 'circles' as well as Rome and Florence, he thundered against the new Ministry, demanding a general election at which he hoped to be borne to victory and the premiership. The country was rapidly splitting up into two parties, for and against a renewal of the war, but everything depended on the outcome of the Anglo-French mediation. England urged the complete withdrawal of Austria, but the creation of a strong northern Italian Kingdom was by no means desired by France, and the hope of any satisfactory solution gradually faded. The revolt of Hungary the first week of October followed by a fresh outbreak at Vienna and the flight of the Court to Olmütz, gave a fresh impetus to the war party in Piedmont, and when the Chambers met in the second week in October the Left demanded a full-dress debate on the policy of the government. Their motion for immediate war was, however, lost, and had not the Ministry foolishly demanded the appointment of a committee to report on its policy it might have weathered the storm. But the report when it came was virtually a vote of censure and its position was so shaken that before long resignation became inevitable.

In the meantime Austria recovered. Before the close of October Prince Windischgrätz crushed the revolt in Vienna and in Prince

Felix Schwarzenberg Austria found the strong man she needed. His announcement that not a foot of imperial soil would be surrendered nullified the Anglo-French mediation, and faced with the alternative of signing a humiliating peace or breaking the armistice, and possibly a second Custoza, the Ministry resigned. The King had no alternative but to summon Gioberti, and with him came the Circolo Nazionale, pledged to a renewal of the struggle; and thus, as in Rome and Florence, the close of 1848 saw power in the hands of the men of the Left, the democrats, whose creed was war with Austria with a Constituent Assembly and republicanism in the background.

Although there were now democratic governments alike in Rome, Turin and Florence, in none of them was there unanimity of opinion, nor was there any common policy between them. Rome was divided into constitutionalists such as Mamiani, who desired the return of the Pope and the maintenance of the existing constitution, and democrats such as Galletti and Sterbini, who looked first for a Constituent Assembly and then a republic. The scope of 'the Constituent' was in itself divided, for some wanted a 'Roman', limiting its action to the Papal States, and some wanted an 'Italian', which meant legislating for Italy. Moreover, the 'Italian' was differently interpreted, some meaning a federal pact which would leave the individual states free to adopt their own form of government, others that it meant imposing a republic on all members of the constituent body. On these points the circles met all over the Papal States, some supporting a Roman, others an Italian 'Constituent'. Finally on December 29th a decree was issued by the government for the convocation on February 5th of the assembly of Roman States with full powers, and the ambiguity as to its scope was cleared up a fortnight later when it was announced that it would be Italian, not merely Roman. To this the Pope replied on January 1st with an edict which stigmatized the 'so-called general national assembly of the Roman State' as a 'monstrous act of masked treason . . . abominable alike for the absurdity of its origin no less than the illegality of its form and the impiety of its aims' and forbade his subjects to vote at the elections. We gather some idea of the bitterness of the feeling at Rome when we read that on January 7th a demonstration organized by Ciceruacchio, carrying torches and chanting the *De profundis* and the *Miserere*, solemnly consigned the Papal protest to the public latrines.

A parallel movement was taking place in Florence. On January 10th the new democratic parliament led by Montanelli and Guerrazzi was opened. The former presented to the Grand-duke the decree for a Constituent Assembly and the inauguration of a federal pact, which while 'respecting the existence of the separate states and leaving their forms unaltered' would 'strengthen and assure the liberty, union and absolute independence of Italy'. The Prince consulted Guerrazzi who advised him to accept it as 'a guarantee to Piedmont in case of victory and as a useful instrument in case of defeat', adding, that it would be a safeguard against republican impetuosity. With some misgiving the Grand-duke signed it on January 21st. The next day it was presented to Parliament and was accepted and passed by both Chambers. Thirty-seven deputies were to be sent to represent Tuscany in the Roman Constituent Assembly, elected by universal suffrage. But on the 30th the Grand-duke committed the same mistake as the Pope and left Florence for Siena, from where, before leaving to join Pius at Gaeta, he wrote to the President of the Council that 'as it is now proposed to expose me and my state to the greatest dangers, that is, to force both myself and many good Tuscans to suffer the censures and denunciations of the Church, I must refuse to adhere to the law, which I do with a tranquil conscience'.

The withdrawal from their states of the Pope and Grand-duke was an error, for not only did it show a lack of courage but it put an effective weapon in the hands of the extremists. At Rome, the Constituent Assembly met on February 5th in the Palace of the Cancelleria, after hearing Mass at the Church of Aracoeli as was customary. On the 9th, after two days of debate, by a majority of 131 to 5, the motion of the deputy Filopanti was passed, which read:

The temporal Power of the Pope has fallen in fact and in law: all necessary guarantees for independence in the exercise of his spiritual power will be provided: the form of government is a pure democracy with the glorious title of the Roman Republic.

That evening the Republic was proclaimed in the city, followed the next day by a *Te Deum*. When the events in Rome were known, the Pope at once appealed to the Catholic Powers for armed intervention to restore him to Rome and free the States of the Church from 'the faction of *miserabili* that exercise there the most atrocious despotism and every sort of crime'. The union of Tuscany with Rome, however, did not materialize. The withdrawal of the grand-ducal assent complicated matters, and Guerrazzi was anxious to postpone it. Mazzini came and harangued the crowd, urging the formal declaration of the republic and immediate union with Rome, but it still hung fire. The government was meeting much opposition. Many supporters of Leopold had followed him into exile. The country districts dreaded war and favoured their Prince. The troops were unreliable. The whole country was in a state of utter confusion and rapidly getting out of hand, and when in March came the news of Charles Albert's defeat at Novara, all idea of union with Rome vanished.

In Piedmont the democratic movement was neither so violent nor so subversive as in Rome and Tuscany, for the country was content with its constitution and loyal to the House of Savoy. Gioberti, how-ever, made a mistake in identifying himself with the Circolo Nazionale. Had he stood aloof, he might have formed a coalition govern-ment from all parties; as it was, he had to form his Cabinet from among the extremists. He made another mistake in immediately dissolving the chamber which had brought him to power, for the new one, when it met on February 1st, proved more radical than its predecessor. Gioberti took the portfolio of Foreign Affairs. He had a definite policy of his own. Though he expected war with Austria he hoped that before it broke out he would have concluded a real alliance with Rome and Tuscany. That was his first aim; his second was to prevent the restoration of the Pope to Rome by a foreign power: he wanted to make it an Italian not a Catholic ques-tion, and he hoped that the *kudos* for bringing back the Pope would fall to Piedmont. A vain and self-centred person, with an immense confidence in his own ability, Gioberti consulted no one. Neither the King nor the Cabinet was aware of his diplomacy and this proved the cause of his fall.

In pursuance of this policy, realizing that the Powers would never allow a republic either at Florence or Rome, Gioberti first approached the Pope, offering him an asylum in Piedmont or sufficient troops to restore him to Rome. But Pius refused. He had lost all confidence in Italian governments and was resolved to appeal to the Catholic Powers, which he did. Then Gioberti approached the Romans, trying to find a common ground for reconciliation with the Pope, but they were bent on a republic. He then considered force, and thought of landing troops at Ancona, but the King forbade it. Finally, he asked Papal permission to send troops to Rome but Pius replied that if he gave his consent to such action to Piedmont he must also give it to Austria. Failing at Rome, Gioberti tried the same methods at Florence, but Ferdinand likewise refused, for Piedmontese policy was viewed with deep suspicion. She was generally regarded as a greedy, ambitious little country eager to dominate Italy, and not to be trusted. But when Leopold abandoned Tuscany and the situation grew more and more disturbed, Gioberti decided on armed intervention. He collected a force of some nine thousand men under General La Marmora at Sarzana on the Tuscan border, destined, when the moment came, to restore order, organize the Tuscan forces, and in case of war with Austria to be prepared to attack Lombardy from the south. Such was the state of things when the Chambers met on the first of February.

The previous day, news had reached Turin that the Constituent Assembly at Rome was to be 'Italian' and not 'Roman', and the Circolo Nazionale had at once sent a deputation to Gioberti to nominate delegates to represent Piedmont. To their utter surprise Gioberti absolutely refused, on the ground that a federative system should leave each of its components full liberty as to their own form of government, whereas Rome intended to impose republicanism on all the Italian States. The next day in the Chamber, the Left taxed the Premier with splitting Italian unity, but the Right supported him, and he retained the confidence of the Chamber. When his attitude was known at Rome he was at once deprived of his Presidency of the Circolo Popolare, the erasure of his name by the committee being accompanied by the typical rhetorical imprecation, 'May the curse of infamy rest upon this wicked man who armed his country for fratricidal war', a sentiment uttered 'with groaning heart'. But it was the resignation of General La Marmora from his post as Minister for War, to take command of the troops at Sarzana, which proved Gioberti's undoing. Questions were asked in the Chamber and the whole design to occupy Tuscany by force was revealed. Neither the King nor the Cabinet were in the secret and Gioberti found his most intimate colleagues in furious opposition to his policy. Charged with sending Italians to fight Italians, his position became untenable and he offered his resignation, though firmly convinced that the King would not accept it, so indispensable did he believe himself to be. Charles Albert, however, was of another opinion, and his resignation was, to his surprise and annoyance, accepted. The new Premier, General Chiodo, was a mere figurehead, the real power being in the hands of Urbano Rattazzi and his colleagues of the Circolo Nazionale, whose policy was the repudiation of the armistice and war.

Whilst Gioberti in the secrecy of the Foreign Office had been carrying out his personal policy, the rest of the Cabinet had been steadily engaged on 'democratizing' the fabric of government and the army. Each Minister arrived with a queue of 'aspiranti' behind him, for whom places had to be found, and the civil service was thrown into disorder. Their most thorough work, however, was the new army. As a new commander-in-chief had to be found also, the King, on the recommendation of a Polish officer attached to the army, invited General Chrzanowsky, known as a military writer rather than a commander in the field, to take over the post of chief of staff, General Bava in the meanwhile being appointed commander-in-chief. This arrangement did not last long for General Bava was foolish enough to publish an account of the recent campaign in which his criticisms of the other commanding officers was so severe and in such bad taste that he was removed and replaced by Chrzanowsky. According to the Minister Tecchio, speaking in the Chamber for the Minister for War, the army was doubled in numbers and flourishing, burning with thirst for revenge and destined 'not to stand still but to go forward; not to sicken in the marshes of Mantua but to pluck the laurels warmed by the Italian sun'. A very different picture of the reality, from the military point of view, came from the Duke of Savoy, in command of his division at Casale, in which the lack of discipline, the want of training of the new officers, and the general tone of the troops was bitterly criticized. Confidence between the men and their officers had been weakened, politics had been introduced among the rank and file, and too often indiscipline was condoned. The democratic principles did not work well for the cohesion and fighting value of the new army.[12]

The situation of the country was in truth becoming desperate. The failure of mediation brought the government face to face with a peace dictated by Austria. The cost of the army was exhausting the resources of the Treasury. Piedmont too was full of refugees from Milan and elsewhere, and the stories reaching them of the treatment of the Lombards by the Austrians was rousing a feeling of such exasperation that the desperate chances of war seemed the less of two evils. At the end of February the Ministry decided to denounce the armistice, which ended on March 12th. The King presided at the final Cabinet meeting and the next day left Turin for army headquarters, while Rattazzi informed Parliament of the government's decision. A state of war was to begin on March 21st. Charles Albert nominally took the supreme command, while Chrzanowsky, for whom the rank of 'General-Major' was devised, was the commander in the field.

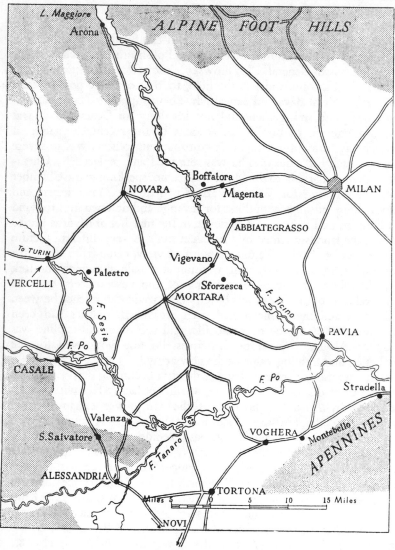

THE CAMPAIGN OF NOVARA

The campaign of Novara was one of the shortest and most decisive in history, for it occupied only six days. War was declared on March 20th and on the 26th Charles Albert was beaten and surrendered. The Austrian army was in high fettle. Cheers and massed bands greeted the announcement of war. Everything was ready. During the last days of peace Radetzky concentrated his whole force at Pavia on the southern extremity of Piedmontese territory where the Ticino joined the river Po. From here it was possible to invade Piedmont by two roads; the main road, which ran north-west from Pavia to Mortara, or by crossing below the junction, on Lombard territory, to take that which ran west on the southern bank by Tortona to Alessandria. The Austrian dispositions were completely unknown to Chrzanowsky. Opposite Radetzky he placed the weakest division of the army under the worst of his commanders, his compatriot Ramorino, the hero of Mazzini's attempt on Savoy in 1834, lauded by the democrats as a great general. His orders were to hold the strong position of La Cava in the angle of the two rivers, and if attacked, to send word at once to headquarters for support. His force numbered only six thousand men. But on the night of the 19th Ramorino withdrew his main force to the southern bank of the Po by the bridge at Mezzanacorte, leaving only a feeble detachment under Colonel Manara at La Cava.[13]   The intention of Chrzanowsky was apparently to march directly on Milan by the main road from Novara, which crossed the Ticino by the only permanent bridge north of Pavia, at Boffalora, expecting no doubt to find his path barred by the main Austrian army. When the armistice ended, Radetzky crossed the Ticino at Pavia, brushed aside the small force at La Cava, isolated Ramorino by destroying the bridge crossing the Po at Mezzanacorte, and marched on Mortara, held by the reserve division under the Duke of Savoy. Chrzanowsky crossed at Boffalora, marched east as far as Magenta, unopposed, and then marched back again to await news of the Austrians. Uncertain as to the Piedmontese positions, Radetzky detached a force under Strassoldo to explore the area on his right flank. Strassoldo made contact with the Piedmontese at Sforzesca and held them all day whilst Radetzky marched on Mortara behind him. In the evening the Austrian main force fell on the Duke and drove him back in the gathering darkness into Mortara, where a desperate action was fought through the night, until at dawn the Duke disentangled his division and regrouped it behind the town. When information arrived of the disaster at Mortara a council of war was held. The King and Chrzanowsky advocated a dawn attack on Mortara by all available forces, but it was overruled by the generals who were insistent that the morale of the troops was unequal to such a desperate attempt, and it was decided to fall back on Novara for a final struggle. The next day the army retired on Novara and took up position. The following morning the Austrians attacked. The battle raged all day, but Radetzky had the last reserves; the Piedmontese left gave way, dragging the centre with it, and the battle was lost. There was now no alternative to surrender and General Cossato and the Minister Cadorna, attached to the army, were sent to ask terms from Radetzky. These included the occupation of Alessandria and Novara and the surrender of the person of the Duke of Savoy as a hostage for the fulfilment of the Austrian terms. To such humiliation Charles Albert would not yield. The council of war was adjourned: two hours later it again assembled and the King for the last time addressed his generals.

'To the cause of Italy,' he said, 'my life has been dedicated. For that I have risked my throne, my life and that of my sons. I have not succeeded. I recognize that my person is the one obstacle to peace. Since to-day I have failed to find death on the battlefield, I make my last sacrifice for my country, I lay down my crown and abdicate in favour of my son, the Duke of Savoy.'

That same night Charles Albert, accompanied by only two attendants, left Novara. He was stopped by an Austrian picket on the Vercelli road and conducted to Count Thurn's headquarters, the one Austrian commander who had never seen him. He was not recognized and as the Count de Barge he was permitted to pass through the Austrian lines. Without returning to Turin he traversed Piedmont and southern France, crossed into Spain and travelled on to Oporto. Here he lived four months in complete seclusion and died on July 28th.[14]

The victory of Novara removed the only real obstacle to an Austrian re-conquest of Italy. Venice was under blockade and the recall of the Piedmontese fleet rendered it at last effective. There remained Tuscany and Rome. The condition of Tuscany was one of utter political and social confusion. There were three parties, and Guerrazzi. The Republicans, who even after Novara clung to union with Rome and a republic; they were, however, the least important party. The Legitimists, who wanted the return of the Grand-duke, preferably without, but even with, the Austrians; finally the Constitutionalists, who wanted the Grand-duke to return but dreaded an Austrian occupation above anything, and who hoped that Leopold would trust his subjects and return without them. As to Guerrazzi, he would have liked an autonomous state without the Grand-duke, who, better informed than others, he knew to have been intriguing with Vienna. But Guerrazzi would not commit himself. He detested the Austrians and knew what his fate would be at their hands, but he could not rouse the people to self defence nor stop their demands for the return of Leopold, and his attitude was without decision. The conduct of the Grand-duke was typical as an Archduke of Austria, but despicable as an Italian sovereign. Dreading the loss of his little throne, he wrote humbly to the Emperor, the young Franz Joseph, begging for Austrian troops to replace him safely in the Palazzo Pitti. The Emperor's reply was cold, and certain reputed remarks of Prince Schwarzenberg about the necessity of removing him, added to his fears. He was, however, forgiven and put in touch with Marshal Radetzky, with whom he arranged for the occupation of his states by Austrian troops. All this he concealed from his subjects.

On April 11th matters came to a head. The presence in Florence of a body of undisciplined troops from Leghorn resulted in a riot. The next day the Municipality at last took action. Co-opting five leaders of the Constitutional party including Gino Capponi, Bettino Ricasoli and Luigi Serristori, they suppressed the assembly, nullified its acts, dismissed the extraordinary tribunals and declared the Grand-duke re-established in power. Guerrazzi was arrested and imprisoned, and a deputation sent to Gaeta to ask Leopold to return. After keeping the deputation waiting for a week, Leopold accepted, and on May 1st nominated Count Luigi Serristori as his commissary with absolute powers, to restore order and to prepare for the restoration of the constitutional régime as previously established. On the 5th of May the Austrians occupied Lucca, after garrisoning Parma, Modena and Pontremoli. On the 10th they reached Leghorn. In a blaze of fury the populace, without leaders or organization, fought to stop their entry, and it was not until the next day that they forced their way into the city. It was the last protest of Tuscany. On the 25th they occupied Florence without resistance. Leopold returned on July 28th. His return under Austrian protection was never forgotten. He regained his throne but he lost the respect of his people; and ten years later it was one of those same constitutionalists, Bettino Ricasoli, whose support in 1849 restored him who declared his deposition.

The restoration of the Pope was a question of European interest but primarily to the Catholic Powers. The first to move in the matter was Spain, who as early as December 1848 in a circular note to the Powers from the Foreign Secretary, the Marquis Pidal, had proposed a congress. The proposal met with general acceptance except at Turin, where Gioberti at once replied that it was an Italian not a Catholic question and should be dealt with by the Italian people. Gioberti's views found support both in London and Paris where both governments were anxious for a peaceful solution and held that if force was necessary it should be provided by Italy. France then proposed a conference of the Catholic Powers at Gaeta, whose representatives should determine not only the means by which the Pope should be restored to his capital, but also the basis of a stable form of government which would prevent the renewal of the old abuses. Austria, though with obvious reluctance, accepted the French proposal, and on March 30th the conference met under the Presidency of Cardinal Antonelli, France, Austria, Spain and Naples each sending a delegate. It at once became clear that no support was forthcoming for the French point of view. Neither the Pope nor any other Catholic Power would hear of anything else except unconditional restoration. All alike regarded a peaceful solution as impossible and narrowed down the question to what number of troops would be required and who should supply them. Austria alone was prepared to provide the thirty thousand which Antonelli suggested would be necessary. The restoration of the Pope without conditions, by Austrian arms, France would not permit, and while the delegates continued their discussions at Gaeta, the government at Paris decided on action. The position was very delicate, for while French Catholic sentiment demanded the Papal restoration, republican sentiment was opposed to the suppression by French arms of the sister-republic at Rome. The solution devised in this difficult state of feeling was the immediate despatch of ten thousand men under General Oudinot to occupy Civitavecchia. From there he was to occupy Rome, if possible without conflict, and to restore the Papal authority without suppressing the republican government. In the presence of a 'friendly' French army it was hoped that a *via media* between Papal reaction and republican government would be found without recourse to violence. It was believed that the French would be received with open arms, that the republican forces would at once disintegrate, and that the Pope, grateful for restoration, would return to the ingenuous liberalism of 1846; all of which were illusions. On April 25th General Oudinot disembarked at Civitavecchia, advancing on Rome during the following days. Serious opposition was not expected and Rome, it was anticipated, would be in French hands by May 4th.

The lights of liberty in Italy were going out one by one. Piedmont was crushed, Venice blockaded. Ferdinand II had wreaked his vengeance on Sicily and she too lay under the triumphant bayonets of reaction. Austria ruled in Parma, Modena and Tuscany. Only Rome was left. But the fate of the Eternal City was no longer in the hands of men of the calibre of Carlo Bonaparte and Sterbini, but of two men whose love of liberty and Italy was dearer than life, Mazzini and Garibaldi, and under their inspiration Rome rose to greatness. The military position was wellnigh hopeless. Four armies were converging on the city, for Spain had landed five thousand men under Fernandez de Cordova at Gaeta who, blessed by the Pope, were marching on Albano. Naples, with sixteen thousand under the King, crossed the border towards Velletri; Austria after a hard fight had subdued Bologna and was moving on Ancona, and Oudinot approached from Civitavecchia. Yet Rome decided to resist. The last of the Roman Republics would go down, but at least it would go down fighting.

On the last day of April Oudinot attempted to force his way into Rome, only to be soundly beaten by Garibaldi and forced to retire to Civitavecchia, from where he urgently demanded from the government large reinforcements. This required time, and while the French representative at Gaeta, the Duke d'Harcourt, pressed Cardinal Antonelli for a Papal proclamation of the terms of his future government, which might bridge over the chasm that divided republicans from papalists, a new agent, De Lesseps, was sent to Rome, professedly to try once more to make a friendly settlement for the entry of the French army into the city. But De Lesseps was being used as a catspaw, for the real object was to gain time. The military honour of France had been compromised, and defeat must be wiped out in victory. De Lesseps was well received in Rome and after two proposals had been rejected he was at last successful, but the terms agreed upon exceeded his instructions and would never have been ratified in Paris, and he was at once recalled, and the army now being heavily reinforced, Oudinot ignored De Lesseps and again marched on Rome.

With his army raised to thirty thousand men and a full complement of sappers, scaling ladders and siege guns, Oudinot opened his attack on Rome on June 3rd. From the first the city was doomed, but the Romans put a desperate defence, full of heroic exploits which have passed into history, and a month was required before the position of the defenders became hopeless. Early on July 1st, while Mazzini in the Assembly still urged with all his eloquence resistance at any cost, Garibaldi, haggard and battle-stained from the desperate struggle of the previous night, arrived and bluntly told the deputies that defence was no longer possible. The next day Garibaldi left Rome with some five thousand of the remaining troops on his great retreat across Italy to Ravenna. Pursued by four armies, his little force, defying capture, melted away amongst the Apennines and he himself, after hairbreadth escapes, at last found safety in Tuscany, guided in the final stage of his journey by a patriotic priest, Don Giovanni Verità. The next day Oudinot marched through the silent streets of Rome, dissolved the Assembly, and sent the keys of the city to be laid at the feet of the Pope. A Junta of Cardinals arrived in due course to rule the city under the bayonets of France until such time as His Holiness thought fit to return. Alone amid her lagoons Venice still held out some weeks longer, but in August she too was forced to surrender, and all Italy lay prostrate under Austria and triumphant reaction.

Despite the wave of unjustified optimism, not only in Italy but in England, and the corresponding pessimism in Austria, which alike had anticipated an Italian victory and the expulsion of the Austrians from Lombardy-Venetia, the defeat of Italy in 1848 was to be expected. When we discount the extravagant hopes, the flood of patriotic rhetoric, the ignorance of war and the complete failure to grasp the military realities of the position, and look at the actual situation, no other outcome was likely; unless Radetzky committed a bad blunder or Charles Albert revealed military genius, neither of which took place. For what the Sardinian army was so hopefully expected to do, was to force one of the strongest defensive positions in Europe, in the face of an army as numerous and far better trained than their own, perfectly familiar with the terrain, and commanded by an experienced general, who, as a divisional commander at Wagram and chief of staff at Leipsic, had probably forgotten more about war than Charles Albert ever knew. Outnumbered and outgeneraled, Charles Albert was defeated, and after Custoza the war was won. But the Sardinian troops fought splendidly and upheld their reputation, as did the Tuscan levies at Curtatone, and Garibaldi's little army in the defence of Rome, and the Venetians in the defence of their city. Those who did fight, fought well, but they were not enough.

The significance of Italy's effort in 1848-1849 is not, however, to be judged only by the adverse military decision, for it revealed both the strength and the weakness of the whole national movement. Its strength lay in the nation-wide expression of its hatred of Austrian domination. From now onwards it was clear that Italy was simply held down by force, and at the first opportunity would repeat her frantic struggle for freedom. Moreover, the national aim was clarified. Republicanism as a solution died with the Roman republic and Gioberti's federalism disappeared with Pio Nono's reversion to absolutism, but the idea of monarchy was strengthened. Charles Albert's last desperate attempt at Novara had won the heart of Italy, and the young Victor Emanuel's loyalty to the Constitution, in spite of all the cajoling of Radetzky, had between them lifted the House of Savoy to the first claim on Italy's hope and gratitude. It was not yet 'Italy and Victor Emanuel' but it soon would be. Its weakness lay primarily in the impossibility of creating a national army when all the material was in the hands of the rulers, adverse to the national movement and ready to call in Austria. But besides this, there were two deep-seated weaknesses which were certain to complicate any forward movement. The first was political inexperience; the second, the now ingrained habit of conspiracy. These two failings were the legacy left by Metternich. In his determination to suppress every manifestation of self-government, throughout a period of over thirty years, he had not only robbed Italy of all political experience but had forced her into a mentality of chronic conspiracy. The quick Italian mind was full of political ideas but with no practical experience of the difficulties of realizing them. Carried away by their inveterate love of rhetoric, conceiving the ends without considering the means, they made the 'business of government' a vocal panorama of unattainable ideals. The effect of the spirit of conspiracy, on the other hand, was to create the belief that in order to get things done, it was necessary to work against the government rather than with it. This feeling, that the hand of the government must be forced, that it would always accept the *fait accompli*, was to retard the national political development and to create endless embarrassments for successive governments for many years to come.

The rising of 1848 was a spontaneous expression of national feeling but completely unco-ordinated and therefore defeated in detail. After it, once more patrolled by Austria, Italy sank back into inaction. But the movement had now a rallying point in Piedmont and a statesman in Cavour: conspiracy became national and radiated discreetly from a centre at Turin: the policy of isolated effort was abandoned, and the traditional policy of the House of Savoy of playing France against Austria, rejected alike by Charles Albert and Mazzini, was once more brought into action in the extremely capable hands of Cavour. The age of conspiracy has passed into that of diplomacy.

CHAPTER SIX

FROM CONSPIRACY TO DIPLOMACY
CAVOUR, 1849-1859

THE history of Italy during the ten years that followed the collapse of the national effort in 1848-1849 and which ended with the war of 1859, is centred in the political life of Piedmont and in the work of one man, Count Cavour. Elsewhere in Italy the old system is at work again as if the agitation of the previous two years was a bad dream. Those most deeply compromised have fled abroad. Garibaldi is in America, Mazzini in London and Manin in Paris, and around each of them are grouped bands of refugees. Austrian garrisons now keep order at Florence, Modena and Parma, and control the Legations with troops at Bologna, whilst the Pope is kept secure on his throne by the presence of French bayonets. This is not to say that the spirit of revolt is dead, but that, as in 1831, its centre was now outside Italy. Mazzini was as busy as ever weaving new plots and combinations which before long produced disastrous results in Lombardy and Piedmont. In Naples, the policy of Ferdinand was to imprison every one against whom the least suspicion of possible subversive activities was directed, and to keep them there indefinitely. There is a story related of a prominent English resident, one of whose Italian friends was thrown into prison in this way. Knowing the Chief of Police he at once endeavoured to procure his release. The official expressed his regrets, adding that he was most anxious to oblige him, and that if at any time he wanted anybody put *into* prison it should be done at once, but that the one thing he could not do was to get any one out again. It was this iniquitous system which Gladstone, after watching the whole procedure of Neapolitan justice, condemned with such vigour in his letters to Lord Aberdeen.

Lombardy was held down by force, with Radetzky in command as civil and military governor, but even this did not stop the Lombards from conspiring. In London, Mazzini had formed a National Italian Committee, one of whose activities was the issue of a loan to be subscribed both in Italy and in England. Another was an anti-Austrian printing press, established at Capolago on the Swiss border of Lombardy, which introduced leaflets and pamphlets into Austrian territory. The activities of the police in arresting agents of this latter led to several executions, and the discovery of a share certificate in the loan had even more disastrous results. The trial which followed the investigations of the police, was known as the Process of Mantua or 'The Martyrs of Belfiore'. Priests, professional men and landowners, were found to be implicated, nine persons were executed in 1852 and thirty-two others condemned to years of imprisonment in irons. This severity led to an outbreak at Milan the year following, which though hopelessly ineffective, produced the first breach between Austria and Piedmont over the sequestrations of the property of Lombard *émigrés* now in possession of Piedmontese nationality. In the States of the Church the old order was restored by Papal decrees, enforced in the Legations by Austrian bayonets: the Romans, however, were more gratified by the return of the Pope than grieved over the loss of the Republic, and soon settled down under the accustomed system without complaint. There was no further internal trouble in Rome, even when Cadorna occupied the city in 1870.

It would be a mistake, however, to regard this general inaction as an acceptance of the *status quo*. The masses in Italy, it is true, never took a real part in the movement. Outside Piedmont, the peasantry never moved. Naples was sunk in apathy and corruption, and even in 1860 Cavour's attempt to promote a rising against the Bourbons was a complete failure. The whole strength of the Risorgimento was in the liberal element in the cities and after 1848 there was a marked change in their attitude. There is no longer any agitation for reform: in fact, a reform movement is what they are afraid of, because it might lead to apathy. The whole political system is now under condemnation. Austria, the princelings, the temporal power of the Pope, all must go and unity and independence must be established. Some years later Daniele Manin in reply to a speech on Austro-Italian reconciliation by Lord John Russell, voiced the conviction of Italy when he said, 'We don't want Austria to reform, we want her to go'. How this was to be brought about no one could tell, but before many years were passed a new hope was born which this time was to achieve unity.

From the wreck of the Italian political institutions in 1849 there was only one survival, the constitution granted by Charles Albert in Piedmont. It provided for a Premier or President of the Council, who, like the Senate, was nominated by the King, and a Chamber of Deputies numbering two hundred and four, elected on a narrow franchise. The Chamber met in the Palazzo Carignano, the Senate in the Palazzo Madama. The Deputies quickly grouped themselves into the Conservative Right, the Democratic Left, and a wavering section of Moderates in between. The Chamber had a President or Speaker, to which position Gioberti on his first return to Italy had been unanimously elected. At first members spoke from a rostrum, a great stimulus to democratic oratory, until Cavour abolished it and made members speak from their places. The hall in which they met was arranged in tiers facing the President and the bench of Ministers. After Novara, the young King Victor Emanuel induced his friend the Marquis Massimo D'Azeglio to accept the Premiership, though he had scarcely recovered from a wound in the thigh received at Vicenza which sometimes necessitated Cabinet meetings at his bedside. A painter by profession, a soldier and a writer, D'Azeglio's qualification as first Minister lay in his sterling character, rather than in political gifts, of which he had few, for he had neither administrative nor political experience. Almost his first task was the suppression of a revolt at Genoa, where the extremists had seized two of the forts and raised the old republican cry of independence. It was easily suppressed by General La Marmora, happily without bloodshed. Then came the peace treaty, the terms of which the Left opposed with such determination that D'Azeglio at length dissolved the Chamber and strained the constitution by inducing the King to issue a personal appeal, known as the Proclamation of Moncalieri, for loyalty and support. The new Chamber accepted the peace treaty. After this the members settled down to work. Amongst those who had lost their seats in the wave of democratic victories which had led to Novara, and now regained them, was Count Camillo Cavour, editor of *Il Risorgimento*, elected as one of the members for Turin, which seat he held for the rest of his life. A convinced liberal, whose opinions had caused his resignation from the army, Cavour had taken up farming and made a fortune by the application of machinery and modern methods to the family estates. Interested from his youth in politics, he had travelled much in Switzerland, France and England, studying agriculture, parliamentary government and modern industry. He knew most of the leading political figures in France and some in England. He was recognized as a financial expert, interested in all kinds of business ventures, banks and mills and railways, and all the progressive forms of modern industry. A man of great ability and wide knowledge, gifted with courage and determination, he stood politically between the two extreme parties, opposed equally to the reactionary tendencies of the Right and the democratic excesses of the Left, and, in consequence, was condemned by both. Amongst his many gifts there were two of peculiar value for the future of his country: he was a born parliamentarian, with a genuine knowledge and practical understanding of constitutional government, a true appreciation of liberty, and what we should call a House of Commons temperament—and he was a modernist. He took small interest in Italy's historic past, her art and literature were beyond his ken, his whole outlook was to the future and his interest was centred on modern progress, scientific advance, industry and finance. He was the one great statesman Italy produced in the nineteenth century and the architect of Italian unity.

The presence of D'Azeglio as first Minister, was a guarantee to the Powers that Piedmont would follow a policy of reason and moderation. His policy was aimed at keeping the ship of state on an even keel and avoiding those contentious political measures which were calculated to arouse violent opposition and party bitterness. Although D'Azeglio prided himself that he understood Italy and the Italians, Cavour, nevertheless, had a truer appreciation of what Piedmont expected than the Premier. He realized that the new Constitution, if it was to satisfy expectations and justify its existence, must deal promptly with those very reforms which D'Azeglio was anxious to postpone, amongst which stood out prominently the relations with the Church. Even from 1848 the government had been working at Rome to induce the Pope to agree to a new Concordat; to regulate the relations of Church and State under the new form of government; in particular, to permit the abolition of the Foro Ecclesiastico or Ecclesiastical Courts, which duplicated the whole legal system of the country and doubled the expense of litigation in all cases which came within the orbit of the Canon Law. The most recent representations had been made at Gaeta by Count Cesare Balbo, and after his failure, by Count Siccardi. To all alike the Pope returned an uncompromising refusal and at last the government decided on legislation. The Siccardi Laws, abolishing the Foro Ecclesiastico, were passed in March 1850 and the speech made by Cavour on that occasion laid the foundation of his parliamentary reputation. After this Cavour's advance was rapid. In October he accepted the post of Minister of Agriculture, Commerce and Marine. His great ability and masterful energy converted what was regarded as the least important position in the government into the most vital. In a series of commercial treaties with Belgium, France and England, Cavour practically committed the country to a policy of free trade, cutting down the tariffs on imports to a minimum but at the same time opening fresh markets to Piedmontese exports. This involved a considerable immediate loss to the Treasury, and Cavour took over the Ministry of Finance, floated an internal loan for immediate requirements, while he negotiated another of three and a half millions in England. With this he paid off the balance of the Austrian war indemnity, freed the finances from the hold of the Rothschilds, and used what was left for the railways under construction.

It was a maxim of Cavour that in politics there is nothing so absurd as rancour, and he gave an example in dealing with the English loan, for he at once asked Count Revel, a political opponent and one of his severest critics, to go to England to negotiate it, which he did. This spirit of putting the country first was one of the secrets of Piedmontese strength. It was now becoming obvious to every one that D'Azeglio's retirement and the accession to power of Cavour was merely a matter of time. To Cavour the problem was how to secure a stable majority which would enable him to carry out his programme. There were two centre parties in the Chamber, of which he himself led the one and Rattazzi the other. Neither was strong enough by itself to assure power, but together they would dominate the Chamber. To this union of forces Cavour had for some time been urged by his friend Castelli, but he had hitherto ignored it; however, a circumstance now arose which rendered it imperative.[15] This was the *coup d'état* of Louis Napoleon, with the return to absolutism and empire which it foreshadowed. Pressure was almost at once brought to bear at Turin to control her press, by both France and Austria, supported by the more extreme Right in the Chamber. The result of this was the Deforesta Press Law, which transferred actions against the Press from juries to special magistrates, in cases where foreign countries or rulers were concerned. Cavour viewed this support of the reactionary parties with great misgiving, and to strengthen the liberal element in the Chamber, joined Rattazzi and formed the centre party which was to give him a steady majority for the eight years of his Premiership. His action brought about D'Azeglio's resignation, but the King refused to accept it and ordered him to reconstruct the Ministry, leaving out Cavour. Had Cavour been vindictive he could have made the position of the new Cabinet impossible, but instead, he made it as easy as he could by resigning his portfolios and going abroad. The inevitable change could not, however, be long delayed and in November 1852 D'Azeglio again resigned, advising the King to call Cavour. This he did, and the Great Ministry came into being.

The man to whom the destinies of his country were now entrusted came to his task not only with a clear idea of what was to be done, but with a definite plan as to the steps to be taken to achieve it. Cavour's ultimate aim was the deliverance of Italy from Austria and the formation of an Italian Kingdom. But the events of 1848 had convinced him that Charles Albert's motto, 'L'Italia farà da sé' (that Italy would win her own salvation), was not practical, and that she must revert to her traditional policy of a French alliance. To lessen the danger of French dictation, he hoped to enlist the sympathy and support of England, whose liberal policy might be used as a counterpoise to Napoleonic absolutism. Thus Cavour's primary object was to win the joint support of the two Western Powers, and he rightly foresaw that nothing would be more effective to this end, than law, order and prosperity, in Piedmont herself. Sound constitutional government, firm, moderate and progressive, resulting in material prosperity, would not only raise Piedmontese prestige abroad, but would focus the eyes of Italy on Piedmont and enhance the contrast between the Austrian methods of force and political stagnation and the freedom and progress of the little Subalpine Kingdom. Cavour had already given a considerable fillip to trade, and many schemes were afoot for further advance. Nor had his holiday abroad been wasted. He had been to Paris and London, interviewed Palmerston and dined and had an audience with Louis Napoleon, he had calmed French fears of a reversion to radicalism, had introduced Rattazzi, who made a good impression, and returned with a knowledge of the leading political figures in the West and their views, which was of great value.

In November 1852 the new government took office. Cavour immediately avoided a clash with Rome by withdrawing the Civil Marriage Bill which in his absence D'Azeglio had mismanaged and which had been, moreover, the direct cause of his fall. After that came the budget, with the usual deficit and plans for additional taxation, economies, and further loans. For the next two years Cavour was plunged in reform, roads and docks and railways, and all the expensive but essential foundations for commercial advance. The country was already showing signs of increased prosperity. Parliamentary life had taken firm hold, and business was now conducted in the Chamber of Deputies in a manner which won warm praise from for all observers, especially the English Minister, Sir James Hudson, whose reports to Lord Palmerston paid tribute to the steady progress of the country and its sound political life. Cavour broke his first lance with Austria over the sequestration of the property of the Lombard *émigrés* in Piedmont, which followed the Mazzinian rising at Milan in 1853. It was handled with ability and firmness, and when it became obvious that no satisfaction was to be obtained from Vienna, despite the illegality of Austrian action, a full statement of Piedmont's case was drawn up and circulated amongst the Powers, and the Piedmontese Minister was then recalled in protest. The moderation and dignity of Piedmont's attitude was in striking contrast with the angry bullying tone of the Austrian Foreign Secretary, and Cavour came through his first diplomatic battle with increased prestige. It was an essential part of Cavour's diplomacy to reverse the opinion generally held in Europe regarding Italy: to show that she was not a hot-bed of conspiracy against law and order, but a people driven to exasperation by oppression of a foreign Power, and thus to shift the moral support of Europe from Austria to herself. The sequestration question gave him his first opportunity, for Austria was in the wrong, and he made full use of it. There were other forces working in the same direction. The sustained indictment of Austria in the writings of Mazzini, the translation into English by Gladstone of Farini's *Lo Stato Romano*, the publication of such works as the *Rinnovamento* of Gioberti, with its revised programme in favour of unity under Victor Emanuel and the abolition of the temporal Power, and the histories of Ranalli and Gualterio, were all alike helping to change European opinion as to the treatment of Italy by Austria.

Not the least interesting aspect of Cavour's political life was his handling of the Chamber of Deputies. Although, in fact, he exercised a parliamentary dictatorship, it was accompanied by such tact, ability and humour, that it never occasioned irritation or revolt. Cavour was perfectly at home in the Chamber. Debate stimulated and clarified his thought, and he was never at his ease when the Chamber was not sitting. He loved the stress and storm of debate and was always ready to cross swords with a vigorous opponent. Normally he interfered very little. He would sit throughout a long session, playing with a paper-knife and apparently inattentive, but he missed nothing. He had a mathematical brain, which in his early years as a young engineer in the army, he had trained by forming the habit of working out his calculations mentally, without having recourse to paper and pencil. This faculty he used in his speeches and in debate, and he could carry a long series of facts, deductions and inferences in his mind, and reproduce them in logical order, without making a note. At the close of the sitting he would rise and sum up with admirable lucidity the arguments of both sides, explaining or refuting as he thought necessary, and marshalling his own case with such skill that there was seldom any other conclusion to be drawn but his own. If the sitting was stormy and he was heckled, he had at his command a pungent irony, the gift of the quick retort and a keen sense of humour, all of which weapons he was an adept at using. The democratic orator, Angelo Brofferio, who in the early days of a rostrum and galleries crowded with the rhetoric-loving populace, aroused tumultuous applause with his resounding periods, quickly learnt to be very cautious in provoking the caustic wit of the President of the Council, who so persistently deflated him, that a duel between them became one of the relaxations of the Chamber. 'I will try and arrange a little *boutade* with Brofferio for your amusement', Cavour once wrote to a friend coming on a visit to Turin. He prepared his speeches without committing a word to paper, except figures, testing the effect of special passages on his private secretary from whom he would invite criticism. He was never a real orator. His delivery was somewhat hesitating and his command of Italian limited, but his speeches, closely reasoned and filled with facts, covering every aspect of the question, produced a sense of inevitability which as a rule carried through his measures without difficulty.

With the dawn of the year 1854 the political horizon was darkened by the shadow of the Crimean War. It was the 'European complication' which Cavour had anticipated, and upon the probability of which his desire for friendship with the Western Powers was based. 'It is above all upon France that our destiny depends,' he wrote in 1852, 'for good or ill we must be her partner in the great game that sooner or later must be played out in Europe.' Cavour had now to turn his attention from domestic problems to the wider sphere of European politics, and exploit if he could, to the advantage of his country, the new international situation created by the Crimean War. He had done a great work in his three years of office. In 1850 the deficit was no less than seventy-seven millions with a revenue of ninety millions. In 1853 the revenue was increased by thirty-two millions and the expenses reduced by twenty millions, leaving a deficit of twenty-five millions, and he spoke of establishing an equilibrium in the next budget. But a sound budget was for Italian Finance Ministers a will-o'-the-wisp for many years to come. They are still pursuing it.

It seldom happens that a small power is in a position to put a great power under an obligation, but this was precisely the opportunity offered to Sardinia by the war with Russia. England with her small army was in need of troops, and a contingent from Sardinia would be very welcome. Cavour saw his opportunity and decided to offer fifteen thousand men. In January 1854, previous to bringing the matter before the Cabinet, he sounded the King, who at once agreed. He then approached the British Minister, to whom he made a definite offer, which Sir James Hudson embodied in a despatch; but before sending it he read it to the Foreign Secretary, General Dabormida, who to his surprise told him that the matter had never been discussed by the Cabinet, that personally he did not agree with the proposal which must be regarded as the President's private opinion. So Sir James tore it up and wrote a private letter to Lord Palmerston describing the position. Cavour's treatment of his Cabinet was certainly not complimentary, but he well knew that nearly all would oppose him and to strengthen his position he wanted to have a definite request to put before them. When the question was discussed by the Cabinet, only one member supported him, and so, for the time being, Cavour appeared to drop it. His proposal was soon common property and met with general condemnation. No request for troops came from the Western Powers and Cavour could only wait. In the meantime opinion in Parliament and Press began to appreciate better the advantages of the alliance. Time was on the side of Cavour, and the King spoke out in favour of the treaty. The cause of the delay, which lasted throughout 1854, was Austria. Both sides were pressing Austria for an alliance. Her position was very difficult, for she would not fight against Russia, whose help in 1848 had saved the monarchy, nor would she fight against the Allies, for fear of an attack by France and Sardinia when she was committed in the East. Her assistance, however, was so much more valuable than that of Sardinia, that as long as there was the least hope of her joining the Western Powers, the offer of Turin was kept in abeyance. At last in December Austria signed a non-committal treaty with the Allies. She did not promise troops, but merely stipulated that if peace was not in sight by the end of the year, the three Powers should deliberate upon further steps. At the same time Sardinia's offer was accepted and in January, eighteen thousand Sardinian troops were embarked in English transports for the Crimea. It had been a hard struggle for Cavour. He had had to convince the Cabinet, the Chamber and the nation, and had had to dismiss his Foreign Secretary and take over his portfolio, before the treaty was signed.

Cavour defended the alliance before the Chamber a month later. The debate showed very clearly the difference between the European outlook of Cavour and the *municipalismo* of the majority, summed up in the phrase of Brofferio that the treaty was neither 'just, rational, useful nor necessary'. In his reply to criticisms of the smallness of the English army and its lack of any striking success, Cavour revealed his understanding of English character and his trust in her policy in a passage deserving quotation:

'As to the disasters of the English army, which it would be useless to deny', he said, 'I do not consider that this should be any reason for us to doubt the final result of the campaign, nor to induce us to believe that England is not in a position, and has not the determination, to make equal, if not greater, efforts than her allies. The history of all wars in which England has taken part shows us that at first she always suffers reverses, starting with forces out of proportion to her powers; but that the disasters and failures which she suffers, instead of discouraging her, have the effect of stimulating her to greater efforts and sacrifices, and that while her adversaries, after some successes, begin to lose courage and exhaust their resources, she, as the war progresses, gains in strength and attacking power.

'This, gentlemen, happened in the great wars of the French Revolution. In 1792 and 1793 the English experienced nothing but reverses, their means, in comparison with their allies, being very small: the others grew weary: but the longer the English fought the greater grew their army to such a point that in 1814 I believe they had four hundred thousand men in their pay. What has happened in Europe has happened several times to them in India. Nearly all their early efforts turned out badly, and it was not until after a real disaster that the English used means adequate to their task. All remember the expedition to Cabul in 1839, which resulted in the complete destruction of the English army. Well, after this immense disaster, which has scarcely a parallel, many people prophesied the ruin of the English power in the East. But this prophecy, very far from being realized, was shown to be completely false, when the next year the English returned to Cabul with an army more than twice the size. What took place in the French revolutionary wars, and has now happened in Cabul, I believe will repeat itself in the Crimea. I am, then, convinced that we can put full trust in our allies, assured that we shall find them as the war progresses not weaker but stronger than ever before.'

Though Cavour did not put it in epigrammatic form, this passage may well be the origin of the phrase that England 'loses all the battles but the last'.

During the most critical period of the negotiations for the Crimean alliance and throughout the months that followed up to May 1855, the Chamber was engaged in one of the most violent political struggles it had experienced in its short life. The cause of this was a government Bill known as the Law on the Convents. It was the necessary corollary to the Siccardi Laws. The Bill was sponsored by Urbano Rattazzi, and Cavour, engaged in the alliance negotiations, did not speak until late in the debates. The Law had been preceded by an investigation into the wealth of the Church, which afforded ample justification for the terms of the measure. It provided for the suppression of 334 convents with an average of 16 inmates apiece, leaving 274 containing 4,050 inmates. Religious Orders engaged in teaching, preaching, or care of the sick, were excluded. It also provided for the removal from the annual budget of the sum of nearly one million lire a year in support of the poor clergy: for a drastic reduction in the salaries of the Episcopate: and the establishment of an Ecclesiastical Bank for the repartition and distribution of clerical incomes. The Bill was bitterly opposed by the clericals and unhappily was accompanied by three deaths in the royal family, the Queen, the Queen Mother and the Duke of Genoa, the King's younger brother. The struggle roused such intense feeling outside Parliament, in the press and the public, that Cavour feared for the morale of the country. The real crisis arose when the Bill, having passed the Chamber of Deputies, came before the Senate, which was the clerical stronghold. Cavour had made a tactical error in persisting in regarding it as a financial measure rather than, what it really was, a matter of principle. At the critical moment the Bishops offered to provide the million of lire and thus render the Bill unnecessary. The King accepted the offer gladly and insisted on its being brought forward. It was now a question of submission to Rome. The government resigned. The King, distracted with grief, determined to end the struggle and sought a new Prime Minister. No one would accept, and at last Cavour had to be recalled. The crisis was over. The Senate passed the measure after some slight amendments and the King signed it with a good grace. The Bill on the Convents was the coping-stone to the new political system. The old mediaeval system was broken, and Sardinia was now a modern state fully equipped to go forward unhampered by the restrictions of the past.

In the Crimea on the 16th of August the alliance was sealed at the Chernaia, when as comrades-in-arms with the French, the Italian troops repulsed the Russian attack, winning warm praise from General Pélissier, the French commander-in-chief. The victory was fully exploited by Cavour and a wave of pride swept over Italy, and the bold policy of the King and Cavour was recognized as fully justified, for the stain of Novara was wiped out. The war continued throughout the year but in January 1856 the Czar accepted the mediation of Austria and peace became assured. The preliminaries of the Peace Conference was a time of great anxiety at Turin, the point at issue being whether or not the Sardinian representative would be admitted on an equal footing with the Great Powers. Austria naturally opposed it, pointing out with some justification that it might impose responsibilities which a small country might find beyond its powers. The question was not finally settled until Cavour, nominated as Sardinia's representative, actually arrived in Paris, where he was at once accepted as an equal. Sardinia had joined the alliance without any conditions, and so far all she had gained was prestige, at the cost of two thousand men (mostly from cholera) and a heavy financial burden. Cavour aimed at some increase of territory, at Austria's expense; he would have liked the duchy of Parma. His other objective was to put the condition of Italy on the agenda, provoke a discussion and, if possible, obtain a condemnation of Austria's policy and position in Italy. As this had nothing to do with the purpose of the Congress, it would require great skill and pertinacity to carry it through. Cavour worked very hard, but all hope of territorial compensation had soon to be abandoned. 'Austria', Napoleon told him, 'would go to war sooner than let you have Parma.' So Cavour concentrated on bringing up the Italian question. He induced Lord Clarendon, the English representative, to promise to speak first and he primed him well with information. He kept the Emperor fully informed of everything. It was impossible to drag in Italy until the Peace with Russia was signed, but at the close of the Congress, on April 8th, Count Walewsky, the President, was instructed by the Emperor to introduce, as a supplementary subject upon which the Emperor thought it desirable to have the opinion of the Conference, the questions of the occupation of Greece, the excesses of the Belgian press, and the condition of Italy. Walewsky, who throughout was pro-Austrian rather than Italian, did his best to minimize the importance of these questions, and the Conference got a shock when Lord Clarendon rose, and passing over Greece and Belgium in a few sentences, proceeded to denounce the occupation of the Romagna by Austria, the misgovernment of the Papal States and the appalling condition of the Kingdom of Naples, with a warmth and vigour of language which Cavour himself would not have dared to use. 'He charged', as one of the

secretaries present wrote, 'like Lucan at Balaclava'. To the onslaught
of Lord Clarendon the rest of the delegates replied with pained
surprise, and with the Austrian delegate, Count Buol, at their
head, pleaded that they had no instructions to deal with a question
so far outside the purpose of the Congress. The speech of Cavour
was very moderate, but he drove home Lord Clarendon's points and
made it clear that the existing state of things in Italy put Sardinia in a
most difficult and dangerous position. Lord Clarendon had more than
fulfilled Cavour's most sanguine expectations. He had made Italy a
European question, and awakened the conscience of her statesmen to
a state of things which, unless remedied, meant another European war. After this the Congress broke up. Cavour went to London
and saw Palmerston, who toned down considerably the hopes of
English support aroused by the enthusiasm of Lord Clarendon, and
after a final audience with the Emperor in Paris he returned to Turin.
He had won a European reputation at the Congress: Italy had found
her spokesman and produced the ablest statesman in Europe.

The Congress of Paris forms a definite turning point in the history
of the Risorgimento. From Italy's point of view its importance does
not lie in the terms of the treaty, which had nothing to do with her,
nor in the few anaemic sentences with which the sitting of April 8th
was recorded by Benedetti in the Protocol. It lies in the fact that for
the first time the Italian Question had been placed before Europe by
her responsible statesmen, and could no longer be ignored. It brought
to an end the first phase of Cavour's policy, based on the hope rather
than the belief, that the problem of Italy could be solved by diplomacy
alone, for the attitude of Austria had made it abundantly clear that
nothing but force would induce her to surrender her Italian provinces.
Cavour saw no other issue now except war, and he bent all his energies on winning the help of his two allies. Napoleon had already
given him a lead. 'Austria will give way on nothing', he said to
Cavour; 'at the moment I cannot present her with a *casus belli*: but
make your mind easy, I have a presentiment that the actual peace will
not last long'. In his final interview with Clarendon, and in the Note
directed to his allies on April 16th, he stressed the critical situation
of Piedmont with uncompromising directness. Inaction, he declared,
would redouble revolutionary activity in Italy and throw her into the
arms of Mazzini: only with the active help of her allies could the
conditions in the peninsula be rectified. Some incautious words of
Clarendon had led Cavour to anticipate armed intervention from
England if Sardinia was driven to war, but his interview with Pal-

merston had quickly shown him his mistake and his hopes were now centred on the Emperor.

The policy pursued by Cavour between the Congress of Paris and the outbreak of war three years later, was based upon a twofold conviction. The first was reliance on the help of Napoleon. Though he had nothing to rely on but the verbal assurances of the Emperor and his own intuitive appreciation of Napoleon's policy and character, it is clear that Cavour felt assured that France would make war on Austria, and before very long. His second conviction was that Sardinia was safe from attack by Austria unless she was prepared to face both her allies as well, for that they would both come to her help, in the event of an unprovoked attack by Austria, he felt certain. It was this sense of relative safety which made Cavour so audacious both in words and actions at this time. He adopted a policy of complete disregard for Austrian susceptibilities, which, if the tempo was quickened, would speedily become a policy of exasperation, as in the later stages it did, and finally drove Austria into delivering her famous ultimatum and thereby provided Napoleon with an admirable reason to come to the help of Sardinia. The first indication of this attitude was the Appropriation Bill for the rebuilding of the fortifications of Alessandria, which Austria, with cynical disregard for other people's property, had dismantled before evacuating the city after its occupation in 1815. The Bill was opposed in the Chamber on the grounds that it was a deliberate provocation of Austria, to which Cavour replied that if Austria was allowed to fortify Piacenza, which did not belong to her, and in which she had only garrison rights, Sardinia was more than justified in fortifying an important military centre on her own soil. Austria was annoyed, and more so when the Lombards, not only subscribed to a fund opened by Manin to present a hundred cannon to the refortified city, but sent a further sum to pay for a memorial to the Piedmontese army to be erected in Turin. Cavour's next step was to print and circularize abroad his Memorandum of April 16th, to find out the opinion of the Powers on his new policy, and he also made use of a visit abroad of General Dabormida, to gather unofficially the impression made on foreign Cabinets. The result was not unsatisfactory, 'be cautious' was the general verdict. Though personally friendly to General Dabormida when he visited Vienna, Count Buol, so the British Ambassador wrote to Lord Palmerston, was very irritated at the general behaviour of Sardinia, though he did not show it officially as yet.

In words as well as actions Cavour went to the verge of provocation. Addressing the Chamber on his return from Paris regarding the results of the Congress, he spoke as follows:

It is certain that the negotiations in Paris have not bettered our relations with Austria. We are bound to confess that the plenipotentiaries of Sardinia and Austria, after having sat beside each other for two months, and after having co-operated in the greatest political work of the last forty years, have separated without personal animosity, indeed I ought to bear witness to the courteous behaviour of the chief of the Austrian Government, but they have separated with the intimate conviction that the policies of their two countries were further than ever from reaching agreement, that the principles to which they adhered were irreconcilable. [*Bene! Applausi.*] This fact is grave, we cannot deny it: it may cause difficulties, it may provoke dangers, but it is the inevitable, fatal, consequence of that loyal and liberal system which King Victor Emanuel inaugurated on his accession to the throne, of which his government has always sought to make itself the interpreter and to which you have always leant firm and valid support. [*Bravo! Bravo!*] I do not believe, gentlemen, that the thought of these difficulties will make you counsel the King's Government to change its policy.

These were bold words. Candour could scarcely go further and the applause which greeted them revealed the spirit of the country. Twice Piedmont had faced Austria and been defeated, and she was ready to do it again. 'Those Piedmontese devils', old Radetzky once said, 'are always the same.' Cavour then brought his speech to a close with a passage still more irritating to Austria, emphasizing as it did the general condemnation in Europe of her Italian policy:

Our policy during these last years has taken a great step forward: for the first time in our history the Italian question has been discussed in a European Congress, not as at Laibach and Verona, with a view to intensify the sufferings of Italy and to reforge her chains, but with the openly manifested intention of bringing some remedy to the evils which oppress her, with the open expression of the sympathy which the great nations feel towards her. The struggle may be long, the fluctuations of fortune many, but trusting in the justice of our cause we await the final issue with confidence.

In preparation for the struggle which he saw ahead, Cavour next drew around him all the live forces in Italy. He had already seen and won over Daniele Manin, the old Venetian republican leader, while at the Congress; he now got in touch with Garibaldi, who had returned from America and bought his rocky home at Caprera. He told him his hopes, and encouraged him to prepare the ground for the future. More important was his new friendship with La Farina, the indefatigable secretary of the National Society. They met almost daily at dawn and to the slogan of 'Italy and Victor Emanuel' the National Society began to rouse the people for unity and independence. Alone amongst the active elements in the country, the republicans, with Mazzini at their head, were impervious to the value of any other method of national redemption than futile risings and the old ideal of conspiracy. The previous autumn there had been one more such effort in Sicily under Count Bentivegna, which, according to Brofferio, should have been supported by the government. It met with no encouragement from the Ministry. Such movements, Cavour had replied, would receive neither sanction nor assistance, for they were convinced that they did far more harm than good to the national cause, and only created fresh difficulties for the Ministry in their relations with foreign courts.

When Cavour returned to Turin from Paris he wrote to his friend Castelli that he left Count Buol 'frightened at the general marks of sympathy which the Italian cause aroused throughout Europe'. It led to a change of policy at Vienna. The Emperor of Austria, advised of the general feeling, decided on a policy of leniency. It will be remembered that the two Ministers at Turin and Vienna, had been recalled to their respective capitals following the decree of sequestration imposed by Austria on the Lombard *émigrés* after the Milan rising of 1853. The sequestration order was now removed, and it only required the nomination of the Ministers to resume normal relations. Before this took place the Emperor paid a visit to Milan, and Victor Emanuel, as an act of courtesy, proposed to send a delegate to meet him. But at the critical moment the Austrian police committed a blunder, arresting and expelling as an undesirable a Sardinian Senator, M. Plezza, visiting friends. Victor Emanuel was furious, refused to nominate a delegate, and ignored the visit of the Emperor. This so irritated Count Buol that he sent an angry note to Turin demanding explanations and denouncing as provocations the fortifying of Alessandria, the hundred cannon, and the conduct of Sardinia in general. Cavour sent a cold and dignified reply, and shortly afterwards Austria withdrew Count Paar from Turin and Sardinia then recalled her chargé d'affaires, and all diplomatic relations between the two countries were thus severed. The policy of leniency towards Lombardy was not, however, changed. Following the Emperor's visit, which was accompanied by various acts of grace, the release of prisoners, an amnesty for some classes of exiles, and the cancelling of various communal debts to the state, the Archduke Maximilian was appointed Viceroy.

He was young and attractive, cultured, and filled with zeal to do his best to win over the Lombards. But it was too late. The upper classes stood aloof. His actions were adversely criticized, his invitations refused, his motives misinterpreted, and in spite of his best efforts the policy of conciliation proved a failure. This new attitude of Austria caused Cavour considerable uneasiness, nevertheless. It was warmly supported both at Vienna and Turin by England, who persisted in believing that a little goodwill on both sides would even now reconcile Italy to the *status quo*—as if the desire for unity and the existence of Lombardy-Venetia in the hands of Austria, were just small matters that could be easily forgotten and forgiven. The blindness of English politicians to the real desires of Italy and the depth of her craving for freedom and independence, when they conflicted with her own love of peace and quiet, reduced Cavour at times almost to despair.

Cavour's programme of frigid correctness towards Austria and quiet preparation for the future in Italy, was rudely broken in June of this year (1857) by a new Mazzinian effort. It came at a moment when Cavour had great schemes on hand. He was not only busy pushing forward the strategic railway extensions and occupied with the negotiations connected with the piercing of the Mont Cenis tunnel, but he had appropriated large sums for the transfer of the naval base at Genoa to Spezia, and the conversion of Genoa into a first-class commercial port by the extension of docks and loading facilities, to enable her to deal with the largest mercantile vessels and become the rival of Marseilles as the first commercial port in the Mediterranean. At the end of June Mazzini's new plan matured. There was to be a descent on the coast of Naples and a simultaneous rising at Genoa, aimed at seizing the forts and procuring weapons to be despatched to arm the Neapolitans. Both attempts were a dismal failure. Pisacane and his three hundred patriots landing at Sapri, were either killed or captured, and the attempt at Genoa fizzled out in a few scuffles. It brought, however, the usual crop of recriminations from Paris and London. Cavour was equal to the occasion. Writing to his ambassador in London, he deliberately magnified Mazzini's effort, but pointed out that 'the great European revolutionary party' had its headquarters in London, which harboured all the most dangerous conspirators who hatched their plots under cover of English liberty, adding that he regretted that one Englishwoman (Jessie White Mario) was amongst those arrested. He took the opposite line in dealing with French reproaches, minimizing the outbreak, and stressing the fact that if this was all the revolutionary party could do, they might be disregarded. The storm soon blew over and before long Napoleon was once more quite friendly.

In November this year there was a general election in Piedmont. It was fought with unusual vigour. There was a strong feeling against Rattazzi, to whose want of energy and sympathy with the Mazzinians the events of June were attributed. Cavour supported his colleague and this led to co-operation between the Right and the Clericals, in a determined attempt to upset the government. The result was an opposition so strong that Cavour was doubtful as to his ability to carry through his programme. However, the by-elections went in his favour and the Chamber carried a Bill excluding clerics, and this restored his majority. A scapegoat was, nevertheless, required, and Rattazzi left the Ministry.

The role which Sardinia had played in European affairs since the Congress of Paris imposed a difficult and delicate task upon Cavour, which a statesman of smaller calibre could never have sustained, for her prestige far exceeded her power. The status of equality which Sardinia had then obtained put her on level terms with her allies in those problems which remained unsettled when the Congress closed. Cavour had since acted as arbitrator in the intricate boundary question of Bolgrad and had settled it to the satisfaction of both sides, but his real difficulty lay in trying to keep in with two allies whose policies and interests, once the binding force of the military alliance was removed, tended steadily to diverge. On the question, for instance, of the union of the Principalities (Moldavia and Wallachia, afterwards Roumania) Cavour sided with France, both believing that a single strong state was far better than two weak ones, while England wished to keep them separate, holding that united they would fall at once under the sway of Russia. Cavour's support of union irritated Lord Clarendon and was at once interpreted as subservience to France. The rigid attitude of Sardinia towards Austria, was likewise a source of complaint, because English friendship with Austria was a matter of principle, as a check, when needed, on either France or Russia, and the irritation of Vienna at Sardinia's attitude and her friendship with France, disturbed English relations with Austria. To Cavour, good relations with England were essential but friendship with France was vital, and throughout 1857 he had a hard task to keep in with both. But he knew that Cabinets change and he relied for support on English public opinion, which at bottom was with Sardinia, and he was right to do so, and though at the close of the year his relations with France were closer than with England, the latter's fundamental sympathy was not lost. The new year, however, was to imperil his friendship with both.

The Parliament which met at Turin in the closing days of December 1857 was destined to be the last, the next would be that of the Kingdom of Italy. The new year was only a fortnight old when the news came of Orsini's attempt on the life of the Emperor and Empress as they went to the opera. In due course came violent recriminations from Paris accompanied by demands and threats. Almost equally strong were the protests made in London, which culminated in the defeat of Palmerston's Conspiracy Bill and the resignation of the government. Mazzini, though this time innocent of connivance in the outrage, had to bear the responsibility, and at Turin the hand of the government fell heavily on his partisans. Many were exiled, and his paper, *L'Italia del Popolo*, was hounded to death by confiscation and prosecution. Another Press Law was passed to limit still further criticism of foreign governments and articles directed against their rulers. When the French Minister, La Tour d'Auvergne, read M. Walewsky's despatch to him, Cavour strongly resented the tone of it. He was prepared, he said, to apply the full rigour of the existing law, but nothing would induce the government to alter the constitution at the dictation of a foreign power. Strongly as Cavour spoke, it was, however, the proud bluntness of the King which had the most unexpected results. Victor Emanuel had sent General Della Rocca to congratulate the Emperor on his escape and his report as to what Napoleon had said to him was so menacing that the King's pride and anger were roused. 'If what you write are the actual words of the Emperor', he wrote to the General in reply, 'tell him in your own words that one does not treat a faithful ally in such a way: that I have never tolerated compulsion from any one: that my path is that of untarnished honour and that to this I hold myself responsible to none but God and my people: for eight hundred and fifty years my race has held its head high and no one shall make me lower it: yet, for all that, I have no other wish than to be his friend.' Forwarding the King's letter to Della Rocca, Cavour added that it would do no harm if he committed the indiscretion of reading it to Napoleon, but not to let it out of his hands, as it contained a phrase about 'perfidious Albion' which he regretted. The enigmatic *parvenu* on the throne of France had never before been addressed in such a tone and his reaction to it was not what was anticipated. 'Now that is what I call courage', he exclaimed, 'your King is a brave man. I love his answer.

Write to him at once and put his mind at ease and express my regret
at having caused him pain'. In short, far from producing a breach
with France as Cavour feared, the King's letter clinched the wavering
determination of Napoleon to go to the aid of Italy and face war with
Austria. Orsini's bomb had had strange repercussions.

From now onwards Napoleon worked steadily in his own peculiar
way towards war with Austria. His methods were devious and his
purpose sometimes obscure. He published, for instance, Orsini's
last letter with its fervid appeal to the Emperor to free Italy. Cavour
was dumbfounded. 'How can we fight successfully the doctrine of
regicide', he wrote, 'when France transforms the assassin into a
martyr?' But the object of the Emperor was to popularize the future
Italian adventure in France and win public opinion to support it.
In the same way he instigated the publication of Orsini's final repudiation of regicide, in the official Piedmontese Gazette, a document which
Cavour described as a direct provocation of Austria. It was not long
before further steps were taken. The first week in May came a communication from Paris proposing the marriage of Prince Napoleon,
the Emperor's cousin, to the King's daughter the Princess Clothilde,
coupled with the offer of an alliance for war with Austria and the
formation of a Kingdom of Upper Italy. Thus began, hidden in the
deepest secrecy, the conspiracy between Cavour and Napoleon against
Austria, which a year later led to the war of 1859. In June, the
Emperor's intermediary, Dr. Conneau, came to Turin, and in July,
when the parliamentary session ended, Cavour went to Switzerland
for a holiday and on the 24th, at the Emperor's invitation, he joined
him at Plombières where the two arch-conspirators planned the future
of Italy. At this famous meeting the purpose of Cavour was to probe
the Emperor's mind, to let him talk and reveal his ideas, while he himself reserved his own opinions. There was to be a Kingdom of Upper
Italy, stretching from the Alps to the Adriatic, to include the Romagna: a Kingdom of Central Italy to be offered to the Duchess of Parma:
the remaining Papal States under the Pope, and Naples. Italy was to
be a confederation of these four states under the presidency of the
Pope. To achieve this there must be an army of three hundred
thousand men, of which France would supply two-thirds. The price
to be paid to France was Savoy and possibly Nice, to be sealed by
the marriage of Prince Napoleon to the King's daughter.

In reply to this elaborate settlement of Italy, devised without any
regard for Italian wishes, still less on the principle of a plebiscite, to
which Napoleon owed his own throne, Cavour said very little,

though his mental reservations must have been considerable. There was little likelihood of Italy acquiescing in the exploded ideals of Gioberti or being content with a reshuffling of her territorial divisions, but it would have been impolitic to suggest it. The vital matter was the French army in Italy and the expulsion of Austria, the settlement would come later. The next day Cavour, having written a full account to Victor Emanuel, crossed the border into Germany where at Baden he sounded German and Russian opinion before returning to Turin. His first task was to reconcile the King and his fifteen-year-old daughter to the marriage with the Prince, then aged thirty-seven, for on this hinged the success of the whole plan. That accomplished, he took into his confidence the leaders of the army and the National Society—La Marmora, La Farina and Garibaldi—to prepare the country for war. To Paris he sent his confidential secretary Count Nigra, whose tact and judgement throughout the long and difficult preparations proved of inestimable value. The war was to begin in the late spring of 1859 and to Cavour it was left to find the *casus belli*, which must be non-revolutionary and one in which Austria was clearly the aggressor. In consultation with the Emperor at Plombières, Massa and Carrara had been pitched upon as a likely source from which to make trouble, but it faded out quickly and Cavour relied on the policy of exasperation to goad Austria into a declaration of war. So far nothing had been put upon paper and the entire plans were dependent on the good faith of the Emperor. To translate these verbal arrangements into a formal treaty of alliance now became Cavour's primary object. Fortunately, Napoleon's keen anxiety to see the Prince's marriage successfully concluded put a trump card in Cavour's hand, for he made the treaty the pre-condition of the marriage. There were plenty of difficulties over the treaty, for France wanted all the glory and none of the expense, proposing that the Sardinian army should be relegated to the south bank of the Po and employed in 'mopping up' operations following the French victories, and that Sardinia should feed and pay both armies as well as handing over Nice and Savoy. All this had to be modified. However, by the end of the year a satisfactory compromise was effected and the treaty was ready for signature.

No less difficult was the time factor, for both armies must be ready together, lest Austria should, by a 'preventive' attack, overwhelm the Sardinians before France could come to her assistance. To synchronize their preparation was difficult, for Napoleon wanted money and to float a loan took time, whereas Cavour could not face a postponement. Italian enthusiasm might evaporate and the expense of keeping the army on a war footing once it was mobilized might mean bankruptcy. Yet another difficulty arose from diplomatic suspicion. Complete secrecy soon became impossible. Though the Emperor kept his Foreign Secretary in the dark, the mission of Prince Napoleon to the Czar at Warsaw leaked out, and before the end of the year the Chancelleries of Europe were alive to the approaching struggle. The position was not too reassuring. If Russia could be relied on for a friendly neutrality, the attitude of Prussia was disturbing, and though England was unlikely to interfere actively, all her diplomatic weight would be against war. These were days when the lightest words of Kings and Emperor vibrated through the diplomatic web to the boundaries of Europe, and on the opening day of the new year (1859) the words addressed to Baron Hübner, at Napoleon's reception of the Diplomatic Corps, reverberated throughout the Chancelleries. 'I regret', he remarked to the Austrian Ambassador, 'that my relations with Austria are not as good as I could wish, but I beg that you will write to Vienna that my personal sentiments towards the Emperor remain the same.' These words were generally interpreted as meaning war. 'The Emperor', wrote Cavour, 'has opened the year with an outburst (*algarade*) that recalls the style of his uncle on the eve of declaring war.'

The Sardinian Parliament met ten days later and the address from the throne was a matter of anxious deliberation. Victor Emanuel, however, was determined not to be outdone by Napoleon and he spoke boldly of completing 'the great mission entrusted to us by Divine Providence'. The address was then sent to Paris for the Emperor's approval, and it was Napoleon who, changing the final paragraph, added the famous sentence, 'though we respect treaties, we cannot remain insensible to the cry of grief (*grido di dolore*) that reaches us from so many parts of Italy'. The speech created a tremendous sensation and opened the floodgates of European diplomacy in protest against the approaching war. A week later Prince Napoleon arrived in Turin with the signed treaty of alliance and on January 30th his marriage to the Princess Clothilde took place in the Royal Chapel.

In the diplomatic struggle which now commenced, in an endeavour to prevent the war, the lead was taken by Lord Malmesbury, who had followed Palmerston at the Foreign Office. Perhaps the most general feeling perceptible in Europe during these months was the underlying distrust of Napoleon. Europe had not forgotten his uncle, and if the French army routed Austria and dictated peace at Vienna, as Napoleon said might be necessary, the old danger of French domination would become a live issue and the former coalition would have to be revived. This is seen in the cautious attitude of Prussia, determined not to be taken unawares, and in the silent and watchful attitude of Russia. Malmesbury took his stand on the sanctity of the treaties of 1815, that there must be no territorial changes in Italy: in so doing he had the hearty support of Austria whose possessions and policy in Italy was based on that settlement. As it was the fixed purpose of Napoleon and Cavour to change the map of Italy, the one to re-divide it, the other to unite it, there was small chance of a common denominator being found with English policy. Besides, England would not fight in support of her policy, for the sympathy of the nation was with Italy not Austria. The complicating factor was the difficult situation of Napoleon. Unlike Cavour, who had the nation with him, the Emperor was almost alone in his determination to make war. His Ministers, especially his Foreign Secretary, Walewsky, were against him, and his only support came from a small inner circle of intimates headed by Prince Napoleon. The bankers could find no money: stock fell on the Bourse: trade and business were all for peace. In this awkward situation Napoleon adopted a tortuous policy, what might be termed an elastic defence, alternately retreating and advancing, confusing the issues, putting forward suggestions which he knew were futile, and all the time hastening preparations for war.

Cavour, on the other hand, had a relatively straightforward if difficult policy, namely, to goad Austria into sending Sardinia an ultimatum. This would put her wrong in the eyes of Europe, fulfil the conditions demanded by Napoleon and bring France, in pursuance of the terms of the alliance, to his help immediately. His chief cause of anxiety was the possible success of English pressure on Napoleon, leading to a joint note from the Powers, and the search for a solution not by war but by diplomacy through such medium as a congress, which would never sanction the unity of Italy nor even the formation of a strong state in the north with Piedmont as its centre.

Austria's reply to Napoleon's speech to Hübner had been the despatch of the 3rd Army Corps into Lombardy, for she put more trust in soldiers than in diplomacy and this clearly aggressive action strengthened Cavour's diplomatic hand. He replied with an Appropriation Bill for fifty million lire. This was opposed by the extreme Right in both Chambers on the ground of provocation; but Cavour was able to make out a good case for his action, as purely defensive, and pointed to the increased Austrian army. Both sides were insistent on the defensive nature of their military moves. 'We shall not declare war', Buol announced and Cavour was equally emphatic. The first article of the Alliance stated, 'In the event of war breaking out between H.M. the King of Sardinia and H.M. the Emperor of Austria, as the result of an aggressive action on the part of Austria, an offensive and defensive alliance will be signed between the Emperor of France and the King of Sardinia'. This imposed on Cavour the necessity of provoking Austria and to do so he adopted the policy of 'defensive provocation'. The loan, which was raised entirely in Italy, much to Cavour's satisfaction, was followed by a Bill for the reorganization of the National Guard. This was the method chosen to defeat the clause in the treaty which stated that 'no free corps were to be raised'. Hundreds of volunteers were flocking into Piedmont to join the army, from Lombardy and the Duchies. They were incorporated nominally in the National Guard, but in reality were trained as a special force of volunteers destined to be commanded by Garibaldi. At the outbreak of hostilities they totalled twelve thousand. This was the contribution of Italy to the war, outside Piedmont. They were a further source of irritation to Austria for most of them were her subjects.

In France the troubles of the Emperor increased. England was exerting every kind of pressure, from the Queen's personal letters to the activities of her ambassador, Lord Cowley. Further, there was disconcerting news of Prussian preparations. Napoleon took a step back. In a long article in the *Moniteur* he avowed his guarantee of help to Italy but only in case of aggressive action by Austria. Having obtained some satisfaction from Paris, England sent Lord Cowley to preach peace at Vienna: he got many assurances but the steady increase of troops sent into Lombardy belied the words of the Ministers. Cavour then, with the consent of Napoleon, 'called up the contingents', bringing up all the regiments to war strength. It was practically mobilization. The next step was taken ostensibly by Russia but inspired by Napoleon. Through Kisseleff, the Russian ambassador to France, a congress was proposed. Cavour fought it with all his strength, for no help for Italy had ever come by this means. The first suggestion was to limit it to the five great Powers, Sardinia to be excluded. Then Austria proposed to include all the Italian States, except Piedmont. While this was being debated England summoned Sardinia to disarm but Cavour agreed only if Austria disarmed first. Austria of course refused. No amount of pressure would make Cavour give way so long as France maintained her refusal to coerce Sardinia. Then came Lord Malmesbury's final proposal, simultaneous disarmament by all three states, France, Austria and Sardinia. Napoleon gave way and, provided that Sardinia was admitted to the congress, agreed. The joint note, from France and England, drove Cavour to the verge of suicide, but the timely advent of his friend Castelli saved him.[16] He was forced to yield, and telegraphed his willingness to disarm on equal terms with France and Austria. No answer had yet come from Vienna upon whom the entire responsibility for peace or war now rested. If she agreed to disarm, attend the congress and sit beside Sardinia, it would be peace. Unknown to Europe Austria had, however, decided to take the law into her own hands. She refused to disarm, sabotaged the congress, and sent an ultimatum to Turin giving her three days' grace. It was war. Cavour's policy of defensive provocation had triumphed. Austria was the aggressor and the terms of the treaty came into force.

CHAPTER SEVEN

THE MILITARY OPERATIONS IN 1859

THE Austrian ultimatum was presented at Turin on April 23rd and was formally rejected by the government on the 26th. The general military situation on that date was as follows: Austria had by then some 230,000 troops in Lombardy-Venetia, of which 70,000 were required to keep order and perform garrison duty, leaving 160,000 available for immediate action. This force was distributed along the eastward curve of the river Ticino to its junction with the river Po at Pavia. The chief centres of concentration being Abbiate-grasso, lying almost due west of Milan, Bereguardo, further south, and Pavia, with Milan, Lodi and Piacenza, as bases behind them. Opposed to them was the Sardinian army of 60,000, upon whom fell the double task of covering the capital and safeguarding the vital railway from Genoa to Alessandria and Turin, by which the French troops coming by sea from Algeria and Marseilles would arrive. To cover the capital La Marmora had constructed defence works on the river Dora Baltea twenty miles east of Turin, but after consultation with the French experts sent beforehand, they were only lightly held and the army was concentrated between Casale and Alessandria, with the King's headquarters midway at San Salvatore, and strong forces guarding the passage of the river Po at Valenza and Bassignana. In this position they not only protected the railway but threatened the left flank of an Austrian force advancing on Turin.

When Napoleon made his famous remark to Hübner at the opening of the new year the French army was ill prepared for war. Tremendous efforts had, however, been made since and by April the Army of Italy, numbering 200,000 men divided into four army corps, was equipped and ready. A fifth corps under Prince Napoleon was formed a little later, and with the Imperial Guard, 360 guns, and three cavalry divisions completed the entire force. The 1st and 2nd corps were to come by sea, and the 3rd and 4th by the Alpine Passes. No time was wasted. By April 29th French troops were reaching Susa and disembarking at Genoa, at the rate of no less than 10,000 a day. One hundred thousand men were, in fact, transported into Italy in twenty-five days.

Marshal Gyulai, the Austrian commander-in-chief, began his

advance on April 29th. The country between the Ticino and Turin is intersected by a series of rivers, roughly parallel, and all flowing south. By May 2nd the army had crossed the Terdoppio, the Agogna and the Sesia, and had occupied Mortara, Novara and Vercelli, whilst a brigade of Urban's reserve division had been sent north to seize Como. At the southern end of the line a bridge was thrown across the Po below Pavia and three brigades advanced on Castelnuovo, Voghera and Tortona (May 3rd). Unfortunately for the Austrian plans the weather broke, heavy rain swelled the rivers, carried away the pontoons and held up the advance. At the same time news came through of the rapid concentration of the French in the central sector around Alessandria, so on May 9th Gyulai ordered all troops to retire behind the Sesia. By that date the 3rd and 4th French corps were at Alessandria and the 1st and 2nd, arriving by sea from Algeria and Marseilles, were in force south of the Po between Novi and Tortona. In a despatch to Vienna, Gyulai explained that the enemy strength compelled him to abandon the idea of advancing on Turin or of forcing the Po at Valenza and Bassignana, and necessitated his covering Lombardy, which he proposed to do on a line between Mortara and Vercelli. Gyulai's analysis of the situation in the middle of May was that it was the Allies' intention to march on Piacenza, crossing the Po at Valenza and advancing on both sides of the river. To meet this threat he concentrated the bulk of his forces in the centre, and to clear up the situation south of the Po, and find out, if possible, the allied strength around Tortona and Voghera, he directed Stadion to make a reconnaissance in force from Pavia on the southern bank of the Po. This led to the first clash at Montebello.

Stadion now took over the command from Urban, whose reserve division had been the single unit across the Po, and with a mixed force of twenty thousand men advanced along the Stradella-Tortona road towards Casteggio and Montebello. Having occupied these two places without opposition, he sent forward a detachment to seize Genestrello, a position of tactical importance a mile or two further on. Voghera was held by a French division under General Forey, who on getting word of Stadion's movements, collected what troops were ready and at once advanced. The two forces met at Genestrello. Forey, though outnumbered at first, attacked. The battle lasted two hours. The *élan* of the French troops carried the day, and Stadion promptly retired on Pavia. Forey lost in all some seven hundred men, while Stadion not only lost double that number but failed in the objective of the reconnaissance. This action convinced Gyulai of the accuracy of his forecast that Piacenza was the aim of the allied army and he still further strengthened his left and centre at the expense of his right.

The action at Montebello was hardly over when fighting flared up in the north. Garibaldi, who was now an Italian major-general in command of the volunteers, was at Biella on May 17th with three thousand men; from there he crossed the Sesia and a week later was at Varese. Urban with a brigade was sent north to stop him. On the 26th he attacked Garibaldi at Varese but was beaten and retired to Rebbio where a second brigade joined him; but Garibaldi, who had followed him closely, again attacked him and drove him as far as Monza. On the 29th, strengthened by yet another brigade, he advanced and reoccupied Varese, while Garibaldi tried unsuccessfully to capture the fort of Laveno on Lake Maggiore; before, however, he could exploit his advantage, for Garibaldi's position was now difficult with the Austrians at Varese and Lake Maggiore behind him, much greater events further south brought Urban a hasty recall and removed all danger for the volunteers.

Napoleon arrived at Genoa on May 12th, exactly two months before the signing of the Peace of Villafranca, and was met by Victor Emanuel and Cavour. The Emperor then joined his army at Alessandria and preparations for the advance began. The problem was where to attack, in the south, the centre or the north. An advance in the south, by the right bank of the Po, which Gyulai thought most probable, meant moving a large army by a single road, that from Tortona to Piacenza, between the mountains on their right and the river on their left, with the Austrians in possession of the crossing below Pavia and the difficult and strongly held fortress of Piacenza blocking further advance. To attack in the centre meant a frontal effort on entrenched positions over a terrain intersected with dykes and streams and often under water. There remained the northern sector. This was the most lightly held; it opened the road to Milan and turned the Austrian right flank, necessitating, in the event of an allied victory, a general withdrawal from Lombardy. On the other hand, it entailed the abandonment of Genoa as a base of supply, and in case of defeat would find the army in a most precarious position with a neutral country, Switzerland, in their rear; above all it entailed a hazardous flank march across the enemy's front from south to north. This was, however, the plan which was adopted.

Vercelli had been evacuated by the Austrians on the 17th and was now occupied by the Italians, but east of the Sesia the Austrians held the whole area from Novara southward to Mortara with detachments occupying the villages right up to the river. It was now decided that the flank advance northwards of the French army should be covered by an Italian attack from Vercelli across the Sesia on the villages of Palestro, Vinzaglio and Confienza, to divert the attention of the enemy from the movement of the French divisions and drive the Austrians back upon Robbio. Three bridges were thrown across the Sesia opposite Vercelli, and on May 29th four Italian divisions crossed. On the 30th, the anniversary of Charles Albert's victory at Goito, they attacked. Severe fighting took place at Palestro, which occupied a commanding position on the plateau overlooking the river. The Italians, supported here by the French Zouaves, stormed the village and held it, while two other divisions seized Vinzaglio and Confienza, the Austrians withdrawing to Robbio. Gyulai, it was evident, had not yet grasped the extent of the French move northwards, for the next day he sent forward two divisions to recover the lost ground, now held by more than double the number of allied troops. Besides, Canrobert's corps had now concentrated at Prarolo, some two miles west of the river opposite Palestro, and had crossed it with three further divisions. In the fighting on the 31st the Austrians lost over two thousand men against six hundred allied losses, and that evening Gyulai telegraphed to Vienna that he had cancelled the attack for the next day owing to the great superiority of the allied forces.

After the defeat at Palestro the indecision of Gyulai became most marked, for he could not make up his mind which side of the Ticino to fight. He is said to have proposed to withdraw behind the Mincio, as Radetzky did in 1848, but that this was strongly opposed by Kuhn, his chief-of-staff, and that finally a compromise was reached by deciding to withdraw behind the Ticino. This was effected during the first three days of June, the main forces being concentrated at Magenta, Abbiategrasso and Binasco. The only permanent crossing of the Ticino was by the stone bridge at Boffalora, strongly held and defended by earthworks, but six miles higher up the river could be crossed by a ferry at Turbigo. This was at once seized by the Allies, a bridge was thrown across and on the 3rd MacMahon's 1st division crossed, and driving the Austrians from the village of Robecchetto, assured the passage of the river for the army.

The battle of Magenta which was fought the next day (June 4th) a s the first of the two battles which decided the campaign. The main ench forces were around Novara, while MacMahon's 2nd corps a s now across the river at Turbigo and Robecchetto. On the

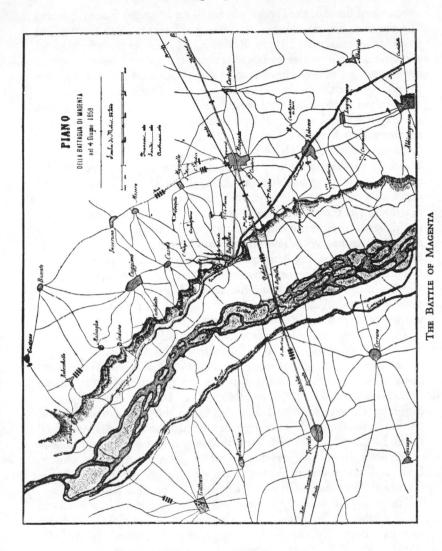

PIANO
DELLA BATTAGLIA DI MAGENTA
nel 4 Giugno 1859

THE BATTLE OF MAGENTA

morning of the 4th, the French advanced on Magenta from the north and the west. From Novara, the main road and railway went direct to Milan, crossing the river at Boffalora, and a mile further, crossing the Grand Canal, which ran below the rising ground beyond which lay the village of Magenta. It was along this road the main forces moved to seize the bridge, cross the river, and then the canal, whilst MacMahon's troops worked southward. The struggle began about midday and lasted until eight that evening. As the two French forces converged on Magenta, they formed a semicircle, steadily pressing in upon the village. The severest fighting was for the bridges, of which there were five across the canal, and for groups of houses and some farm buildings which lay beyond. These changed hands several times as fresh troops were drawn in to drive out the exhausted defenders. At the close of the fighting a desperate struggle took place in Magenta itself until the Austrians were finally expelled, their remaining troops withdrawing east to Corbetta. The losses of the French were 4,560, the Austrians, including prisoners, 10,000.

The battle of Magenta was on both sides a premature action. Neither army was fully concentrated and ready to fight. Only a portion of the Austrians had been engaged, for Gyulai was still uneasy as to an attack towards Piacenza and had considerable forces at the southern end of the front. Better generalship and superior fighting powers had given the Allies victory, but the night of June 4th must have been an anxious one for Napoleon. In fact, Gyulai gave orders that night for a renewal of the struggle the next day, to be concentrated on the recapture of Magenta. But the deplorable condition of the troops who had fought and the disorganization and confusion that reigned in the commands made an immediate renewal of the battle impossible. Melczer, in command at Milan, had at once ordered the immediate evacuation of the city, troops to be sent to Lodi and munitions to Verona, and this, with the report of the divisional commanders, decided Gyulai on a general withdrawal.

The plain of Lombardy is traversed by two main roads, a northern and a southern. The first crossing the frontier at Boffalora goes direct to Milan, Brescia, Verona and Venice. The other follows the river Po through Pavia, Piacenza, Cremona and Mantua. The whole plain is likewise transected by the series of rivers feeding the Po, the Adda, the Oglio, the Chiese and the Mincio, this last forming the eastern boundary of Lombardy. The victory of Magenta had opened the road to Milan, and while the Allies marched on the capital the Austrians withdrew to the Mincio by the southern road, thereby surrendering Lombardy to the victors. Napoleon and Victor Emanuel made their triumphant entry into Milan on June 8th, acclaimed with delirious joy by the populace, for the Italians have a genius for welcoming those who fight their battles for them; but the feelings of Victor Emanuel as he rode beside the Emperor must have been tinged with bitterness when he thought of the last time he saw the city, ten years before, after Custoza; with his father Charles Albert besieged in the Palazzo Greppi and the crowd hurling cries of treason and death, and the final exit from the city accompanied by unanswered gun shots from the roofs and windows. It was small wonder that the House of Savoy preferred the silent loyalty of their Turinese to the mercurial enthusiasm of the citizens of Milan. The next day the Emperor and the King left Milan for the front. More than one plan was made by Gyulai for a determined stand before reaching the safety of the Quadrilateral, but the steady pressure of the advancing French army quickly caused their collapse. On the night of the 6th he received stringent orders from the Emperor Franz Joseph to stand firm on the Adda, or if it was now too late, to take up a position between Piacenza and Lodi. Instructions were therefore issued to this effect, and to gain information of the movements of the French, Gyulai sent Roden to hold Melegnano, with orders to patrol everywhere and report on enemy activities. This was on the 6th. On the 8th a force six times as large attacked him; Roden put up a splendid resistance but the odds were too great and he was driven out with a loss of fifteen hundred men. This action determined a further retreat. Pavia was evacuated, the fortresses of Piacenza, Pizzighettone and Cremona were dismantled as far as possible, their heavy guns being sent to Mantua or destroyed, and the garrisons absorbed into the army and all the columns of the retiring troops were directed to the Mincio.

A new Austrian army was now appearing on the scene. As early as May 30th the 1st army was ordered to mobilize under the command of Count Wimpffen, with the Emperor in supreme command of both armies. On the 30th Franz Joseph proceeded to Verona. After the failure of the defence of the Adda, Gyulai had decided on defending the Mincio from behind the river Chiese, between Lonato, Montichiari and Castiglione, a line south and west of Lake Garda with the fortress of Peschiera upon which to retire. This was now given up and both armies were concentrated behind the Mincio, the second army between Peschiera and Goito, the first from Goito to Mantua. Nine bridges were thrown across the Mincio and by June 21st both armies were in their assigned positions. On the 18th Gyulai re-

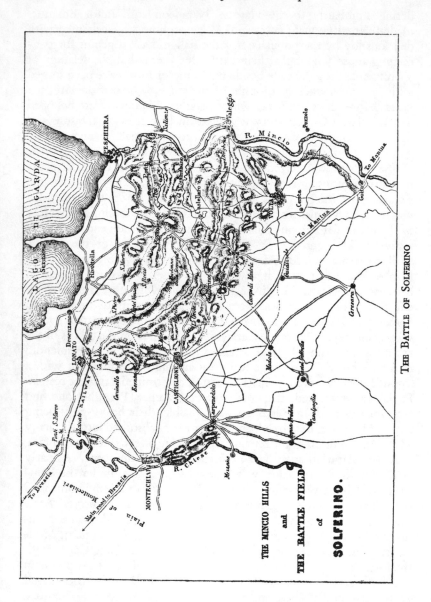

THE MINCIO HILLS
and
THE BATTLE FIELD
of
SOLFERINO.

THE BATTLE OF SOLFERINO

signed and was replaced by Count Schlick. The Emperor was now in command of an army numbering 190,000 men with 22,600 horses and 752 guns. While this concentration of the Austrian army was being carried through the Allies were steadily converging on the Mincio. Napoleon commanded a slightly smaller force, numbering 174,000 men with 14,500 horses and 522 guns. The only portion of the troops which had left France that was absent, was one half of the 5th corps under Prince Napoleon, of which one division had been detached and added to the 1st corps while the other had been sent to Tuscany, where, with the levies under General Ulloa and the volunteers of General Mezzacapo, it formed a body of nearly ten thousand. After the battle of Magenta, the flight of the Duchess of Parma and the Duke of Modena, together with the recall of the Austrian garrisons, left the Duchies unguarded, and on June 12th Prince Napoleon crossed the Apennines and before the end of the month occupied Parma.

The terrain over which the great final battle of the campaign, Solferino, was fought, was as unusual as it was difficult. The ground on the western bank of the river Mincio, as it flows south to Mantua, rises between Peschiera and Pozzolo to form a mountainous block extending six or seven miles from east to west and about the same distance from north to south. Roughly shaped like a triangle, it has its base on the Mincio and its apex the town of Castiglione, which lies in the plain beyond the last hills to the west. This block of hilly country is surrounded by the plain: within it lies the village of Solferino, midway along its southern side a mile or two from the edge. A circle of villages surrounds the block of hills. On the east side lies Pozzolengo towards the northern angle, in the centre lies Castellaro with Cavriano in the southern angle. From Castiglione a chain of villages, well out in the plain, runs eastward along the southern border of hills, Medole, Guidizzolo, Cereta and finally Pozzolo on the Mincio. Two miles north of Castiglione lies Esenta and due north again the larger village of Lonato.

Franz Joseph and his staff had no intention of remaining on the Mincio and awaiting the French attack. They calculated, from their information as to the position of the enemy, that by a sudden and unexpected advance they would intercept the French troops in the act of crossing the river Chiese. With this objective, orders were issued on the 22nd for the general advance of the army. On the 23rd they were to cross the Mincio and occupy the line Pozzolengo-Solferino-Guidizzolo and on the 24th to advance to that of Lonato-

Castiglione-Carpenedolo. On the same date the French staff issued orders for the advance on the 24th from the line Lonato-Castiglione-Carpenedolo to that of Pozzolengo-Solferino-Guidizzolo. Thus on the same day and on the same roads, each army would be advancing on the bases which the other was vacating. The only possible result must be a general action, in which the element of surprise would lie with the army which started first. This advantage lay with the French, whose movement was to start 'not later than 3 a.m.' whereas the Austrians were to move at stated times between 8 a.m. and 10 a.m. This advantage, however, might be held to be balanced by the fact that the French troops had had several hours of marching before the action began while the Austrians would be fresh. The Italian army was on the left of the allied line and their objective was thus Pozzolengo. The advance on Solferino in the centre was entrusted to the 1st and 2nd corps (mainly Algerian troops) and the Imperial Guard, while MacMahon with the 3rd and 4th corps on the right had the village of Guidizzolo as his objective.

The battle consisted of three separate actions, for the steep scarp of the mountains that fringed the southern edge of the block made it impossible for MacMahon to send help to the centre if needed, and the same was true of the Italians in the north, divided from the centre by almost the entire width of the hills; only the divisions held in reserve outside could be directed by the Emperor to one or other of the centres of conflict. The first contact was made on the southern sector with MacMahon's advance on Medole. The terrain here was partly cultivated, with farms and houses spread about round the villages but with stretches of open heathy land. It was some time before the Austrians realized the strength of the opposing forces but when they did a dour struggle began for every defensible point. The numbers engaged were about equal, and the battle lasted until the afternoon, when the general retirement of the Austrians to the Mincio became necessary, and their forces withdrew fighting obstinately to the last. Medole, Guidizzolo and finally Cavriana were stormed by the French but only after long hours of effort and repeated setbacks. In the northern sector, Benedek, in command at Pozzolengo, observed the advance of the Italians as early as 6 a.m. He at once sent forward two brigades to hold the high ground about San Martino, covering Pozzolengo, which he reinforced later. Here the battle raged all day until the general Austrian withdrawal across the river in the afternoon. No impression could be made by Victor Emanuel on the defence of San Martino, but, at least his pressure was so severe that Benedek had to refuse the request for help for the centre and concentrate all his strength on the safe withdrawal to the Mincio. But the crux of the whole battle lay in the epic struggle for the village of Solferino and its environs. The village itself lay high up, in a depression surrounded by higher ground. North-west of it rose a conical hill called the Bocca di Solferino, from which were flung out two spurs, the one on the left called the Monte di Cipressi from a ridge of cypresses on its summit, the other being occupied by the Church of St. Nicholas. This was surrounded by a high wall enclosing the school, a belfry and the priest's house as well as the church itself. Close by was another walled-in enclosure, the cemetery. Two narrow roads wound up between the hills to the church and village. From this group of buildings the ground sloped down towards the plain in a series of sharp ridges called the *Scale* (ladders) *di Solferino*, each one commanded by the ridge above it, forming a natural outwork of great strength. Such was the terrain, strongly occupied by the Austrians, which the troops of Marshal Baraguey d'Hilliers assaulted. The struggle was long and made at tremendous cost, but the French would not be denied. Ridge after ridge was carried at the point of the bayonet, but, as the French approached the summit, it was necessary to bring up the guns to breach the walls of the enclosures. After tremendous labour this was at length accomplished and in one great final assault, into which Napoleon threw all his last reserves, the whole position was carried. The capture of Solferino broke the back of the defence, for from this central position the remaining points of Austrian resistance could be taken in rear and Franz Joseph now issued orders for a general withdrawal to their original positions across the Mincio. This was carried out skilfully and in order, for the French were themselves too much exhausted for further efforts and no fresh troops were available. About 5 o'clock a violent thunderstorm, accompanied by torrents of rain and an intense darkness, broke over the battlefield, putting an end to the fighting and enabling the Austrians to disengage their forces. The losses of the Austrians at Solferino were nearly 22,000 officers and men and the total losses of the French were over 17,000.

No movement took place in either army until the 28th. On that day Franz Joseph, after consulting his generals, decided to retire to the line of the Adige. That night, leaving their watch fires burning, the army dropped quietly back and a week later were in their new positions. There was no suspicion in the French army or in Italy that the campaign was about to close. In fact all indications pointed to an advance. The troops of Garibaldi and the Italian division under Cialdini, had already secured the army's left flank by the occupation of Lavenone, Gavardo and Salò on Lake Garda. An allied fleet had now reached the Adriatic, and based on the island of Lossini, was in position to attack the forts of Venice. The siege of Peschiera was about to be undertaken and the siege guns were already in transit from France. On July 2nd the French crossed the Mincio, establishing their headquarters at Villafranca and Sommacampagna, names redolent of Charles Albert's campaign in 1848. But all these preparations for the due fulfilment of Napoleon's promise, to free Italy 'from the Alps to the Adriatic', came to nothing when suddenly, after giving a hint to Victor Emanuel, the Emperor on July 6th sent General Fleury to Franz Joseph's headquarters with a request for an armistice. This was signed on the 8th. On the 11th the two Emperors met at Villafranca, and the next day, two months from his landing in Italy, Napoleon signed the terms of peace and the war was over.

CHAPTER EIGHT

THE POLITICAL REACTIONS OF
THE WAR

WITH the outbreak of hostilities Cavour took over the War Office, vacated by La Marmora who was attached in an ambiguous capacity to the staff of the King as military adviser. Though he already held both the portfolios of Foreign and Internal Affairs, Cavour carried out his triple duties with amazing efficiency, for all three ministries were housed in the same building and he slept where he worked. At his meeting with Napoleon at Plombières Cavour had taken care not to contravene the Emperor's proposals for the re-division of Italy, but it is clear from the policy he adopted that he had every intention of thwarting them, for his objective was Italian unity. Of the four suggested divisions, he welcomed the formation of the Kingdom of Upper Italy, agreed with the retention of the Papal States, but on a reduced scale, for his interpretation of Napoleon's phrase 'from the Alps to the Adriatic' meant from 'the Alps to Ancona' because he wanted the Romagna. Naples he left aside for the time being, but he rejected the idea of a Kingdom of Central Italy. To prevent this his policy was now directed.

The events in the early part of the year, Napoleon's words to Hübner, the *grido di dolore* speech and the marriage of Prince Napoleon, had naturally created great excitement throughout Italy. On March 14th to clarify the attitude of the Grand-ducal government, Cavour had instructed his Minister at Florence, Boncompagni, to propose an alliance between the two states in view of the approaching war. It was an astute move, for if it was accepted, it put a spoke in the wheel of any Kingdom of Central Italy, and if it was refused, it at once separated the Grand-duke from the national movement. But Leopold, an Austrian Archduke, put upon his throne by Austrian troops after 1848, had small option in his choice and it was refused. The result was to consolidate the unitarian party and with Boncompagni at its head an agitation for the removal of the dynasty began. Cavour waited patiently until the crisis came, and on April 24th, the day after the presentation of the Austrian ultimatum, Boncompagni was instructed to demand from the Tuscan Foreign Minister a formal declaration in favour of Piedmont. The reply was evasive, but the

Grand-duke knew what it meant. He refused to abdicate, but three days later, undisturbed by any hostile demonstration, with all his family he took the road to exile.

After the withdrawal of the Grand-duke there was great confusion in Tuscany. Boncompagni, for the moment the most important figure, was lacking in decision. He made a wise choice, however, in selecting the Baron Bettino Ricasoli as the new head of the government. But opinion was far from unanimous about union with Piedmont. Some wanted the young Archduke Ferdinand with liberal guarantees, others desired an autonomous state under a new line, and amongst these, the Prince Napoleon, as son-in-law of Victor Emanuel, had his adherents. Ricasoli, however, supported by Cavour, was determined on union and Boncompagni received secret instructions to prepare it. The first proposal of the government was to offer the dictatorship of the duchy to Victor Emanuel. But this opened difficult questions and the delegates were referred to Napoleon to whom they exposed the confusion reigning at Florence. Napoleon then decided to send Prince Napoleon with his division to Tuscany to keep order and forestall any Austrian attempt at a *coup de main*. The King, in the meantime, refused the dictatorship but accepted a provisional 'protectorship', leaving open the final destiny of the duchy until after the war. It has often been said that the presence of the Prince and his division was the first step to the formation of the Central Italian Kingdom to which he was secretly destined. There is no evidence for this. The Emperor denied it, as did the Prince, and his well-known support of Tuscan union with Piedmont discounts all the rumours of his aspirations to the throne.

After the battle of Magenta and the Austrian evacuation of Lombardy, both the Duke of Modena and the Duchess of Parma sought safety in flight. Provisional governments were at once installed, both of which asked for union with Piedmont. This was accepted, and a Royal Commissioner was appointed for each, Count Pallieri at Parma and Luigi Zini, and later L. C. Farini at Modena. At the same time M. Vigliani, a prominent Piedmontese magistrate, was nominated Governor of Lombardy. As Lombardy and the duchies had been included in the 'Kingdom of Upper Italy' there was no difficulty with Napoleon over these appointments, though he was not too pleased at the promptitude with which Cavour gathered the fruits resulting from French efforts. It was a different matter when it came to the Romagna. On June 11th Austria withdrew her garrison from Bologna. The Cardinal Legate at once left the city for Rome, and Bologna, after an outbreak of rejoicing, nominated a provisional government whose first act was to telegraph to Victor Emanuel and offer him the dictatorship. Almost immediately the scattered garrisons throughout the Papal States were withdrawn and the example of Bologna was followed everywhere. Not only did the revolt spread throughout the Romagna, but it penetrated into the Marches, as far south as Perugia, all alike throwing off the Papal yoke and calling for absorption in Piedmont. The Allies were now face to face with the thorny problem of the Temporal Power.

Cavour had long ago made up his mind that the temporal power of the Pope must be abolished, and the personal opinion of Napoleon was very much the same, for he was disgusted at the Pope's refusal to reform and at the hopeless futility of his notions of government. But it was not a question to be solved on personal predilections. The Temporal Power was regarded by the whole Catholic world as the guarantee of Papal independence, and by none with greater intensity than the Catholic party in France, upon which the stability of the Napoleonic government rested. To occupy the territory of the Holy Father with French troops or to permit the Italians to do so, except for Papal safety, like the garrison of French troops in Rome, might lead not only to a general protest and outcry, but to clerical opposition in France. Victor Emanuel was advised on all sides, 'refuse the dictatorship, refuse the protectorate, but accept all help for the war'. While the outcome was still in suspense, the Pope ordered Colonel Schmidt with his two thousand Swiss troops to suppress the revolt in Perugia. This he did with such brutal thoroughness that Europe was shocked. This sample of Papal ideas of restoring order convinced Napoleon that action would have to be taken. He threw the responsibility on Victor Emanuel, refused to allow French troops to cross into Papal territory, and endeavoured to minimize the Italian occupation as merely a temporary expedient to ensure order. So Cavour sent Massimo D'Azeglio, the former Premier, to Bologna with sufficient troops to keep order and officers to train the new levies.

Napoleon had not the fibre of a successful general. He had never seen the realism of war until General Bourbaki took him over the field of Palestro, and the sight revolted him; and now came the slaughter of Solferino; after this his mind was set on peace. He had plenty of reasons for dissatisfaction with the military situation and for uneasiness in regard to the political. His losses were severe and reinforcements were not easy to find. The Italian response to the call for recruits was feeble in the extreme. From the letters of Cavour and the King, Napoleon had been led to expect a great national rising, but the reality was otherwise. The Italians were lavish with cheers and compliments but parsimonious when it came to fighting material. They much preferred that the battles should be fought by the French and the Piedmontese. All the efforts of the National Society produced only twelve thousand out of twenty millions. They have not altered much since. The task still before the allied army meant more severe fighting, for the resources of Austria were far from exhausted. No less disquieting was the political aspect. The guidance of the national movement was rapidly slipping from the Emperor's hands. He was consulted and treated with all respect, but it was to Cavour that every one turned for advice. The Kingdom of Central Italy was still in the clouds and that of Upper Italy incomplete. His relations, too, with Victor Emanuel had deteriorated and were not without a tincture of jealousy. The King's love of fighting had inspired unpleasant comparisons. Had not the Zouaves after Palestro made him the first corporal of the regiment, as another French regiment had done to his father before him, when he fought with the Grenadiers at the storming of the Trocadero at Cadiz? To all these reasons was now added the unpleasant but indubitable fact that Prussia had four hundred thousand men in arms on the Rhine. It was time he considered the safety of France. So Napoleon, after showing a pessimistic letter from the Empress to Victor Emanuel, had sent General Fleury to Franz Joseph to ask for an armistice, and without wasting a day, drew up peace terms and finished the war.

By the terms of Peace Lombardy was to be surrendered to Napoleon, who would give it to Victor Emanuel: Venetia with Peschiera and Mantua were to remain with Austria: the dispossessed Princes were to be restored, but without force being used: Italy was to be a Confederation under the Pope. On getting word in a telegram from La Marmora that the armistice was being signed, Cavour and Nigra hurried to headquarters. He was not consulted; the Peace was signed unknown to him, and he felt no responsibility for its execution. Late in the evening the King returned with the Peace terms signed. A terrible scene followed. When Cavour, distraught with impatience, heard the terms all his control gave way. The whole fabric he had raised crumbled before his eyes. Austria, ensconced in Venetia with Mantua and Peschiera in her hands was still master in Italy, and now admitted on an equal footing with the rest of Italy as a member of the Italian Confederation under Papal presidency. The Dukes of Tuscany and Modena to return : Lombardy won as a gift from Napoleon. After a furious outburst of denunciation, Cavour resigned, and the next day returned to Turin and shortly afterwards left Piedmont for Switzerland. As to Napoleon, dissatisfied and frightened, knowing that he had betrayed Italy and left his self-imposed task half done, nervous for the safety of his throne and country, he hurried back to Paris, leaving orders for the bulk of his forces to follow him with all speed. Prussia, thwarted in her aim, demobilized with angry mutterings to wait for another opportunity to rise against her hereditary enemy. This first tentative and immature effort at Pan-Germanism had failed, but it is well to remember that all the formative elements of the German creed were already in being. Bismarck was active, his eyes already on Schleswig-Holstein. Treitschke was lecturing on history at Leipsic. Aryanism and Racialism, Pan-Germanism with its correlative anti-semitism, were being discussed and formulated, ideas whose ripened fruit is poisoning the world to-day.

Before leaving Turin Cavour had given his last directions to the disputed provinces. Parma was to prepare the act of union with Piedmont at once. As to Tuscany, he had told her envoy Bianchi to prepare a Liberal government, to resist diplomatic pressure, and refuse the return of the Grand-duke. 'If Tuscany holds firm it may save everything', he added. The official recall of the Royal Commissioners had followed the conclusion of peace and D'Azeglio had returned from Bologna; but at Modena, Farini, after resigning his official post, was promptly elected dictator, first at Modena and then at Parma and Bologna, which, with the inclusive title of Emilia, he proceeded to govern with energy and firmness. No less decided was Ricasoli's conduct at Florence. These two men saved Italy. For the six months Cavour was out of office, despite the protests of La Marmora's new Ministry and pressure from the representatives of France, they held firm to union with Piedmont, rendering the return of the old order impossible except by armed force. Farini was anxious for the two states to join forces, but Ricasoli, with greater political perspicacity, realized that by so doing they would be creating just that Kingdom of Central Italy which was Napoleon's objective, and all he would have to do would be to name the individual for whom they had prepared a throne, so he insisted that their policy should be 'identical but distinct'. To make his policy quite clear Ricasoli called an Assembly which passed unanimously two resolutions. The first, that they would never receive back the House of Lorraine; the second, that it was Tuscany's firm intention 'to make part of a strong Italian Kingdom under the constitutional sceptre of King Victor Emanuel'. Similar resolutions were passed by the three states under Farini, and all alike were presented and received by the King, who promised to make their wishes known to Europe but made no mention of annexation. Both dictators then set to work to 'piedmontize' their states, unifying the currency, the customs and the postal arrangements, and while Farini numbered the new regiments in continuation of those of the Piedmontese army, Ricasoli put up the royal arms on all public places and headed public documents with the title, *Regnando S.M. Vittorio Emanuele*.

The destiny of Emilia and Tuscany was at the same time the subject of earnest deliberation at Zurich, where the Plenipotentiaries of Austria, France and Piedmont, were assembled to sign the Peace Treaty. Austria wanted the compulsory return of the dispossessed rulers, France a Central Kingdom, and Piedmont union. Outside the Conference England was all for union, Napoleon forbade annexation and likewise the use of force, which checkmated Austria. The government at Turin was too weak to take decided action and referred every suggestion to the Emperor. It was Cavour who divined the cause of Napoleon's obstructive attitude and was prepared to provide the remedy. On leaving Turin the Emperor had said to Victor Emanuel, 'You will pay me the cost of the war and we will say no more of Savoy and Nice'. When he got back to Paris, however, he was soon made aware of popular discontent with the outcome of the 'Italian adventure'. On the surface it had been a remarkable *tour de force*. In two months France had transported a quarter of a million men to Italy, won two resounding victories without a single check, rescued Lombardy for Italy, made peace, and was back in Paris almost before Europe had realized that the war had begun. Napoleon's prestige had risen sharply, France's military reputation was increased, and Piedmont was to pay the expenses. But France had got nothing but glory, and highly as she prized it, she liked it best when accompanied by increase of territory. The exchange of Savoy for Lombardy was an old suggestion in European diplomatic annals, Queen Elizabeth had once discussed it with the Venetian ambassador, and in well-informed French circles it had been an open secret that this was to be the *quid pro quo* France was to receive; it was enshrined, moreover, in the Treaty of Alliance, with Nice added. So Napoleon began to scheme to get the coveted provinces. A visit of General Dabormida, the Foreign Secretary in the new government, gave Napoleon an opening, and he suggested that Nice and Savoy might be accepted instead of cash for his expenses. But the general reminded him of the unfortunate phrase 'from the Alps to the Adriatic', and that not having been fulfilled, the Savoy and Nice clause did not apply. So the deadlock continued.

After two months' holiday Cavour returned to Piedmont, and his farmstead at Leri at once became a centre for envoys and diplomats. He offered to help the government but he was a poor consultant, for the delicate operations he suggested could only be successfully performed by himself. As in the parliamentary debates, so now, the varied opinions and information he received from correspondents and visitors, clarified his thought, and before long he was busy with new plans and a fresh policy. It was based on the conviction that the original terms of the alliance must be fulfilled. Savoy and Nice must go, but Italy must get Tuscany and the Romagna in exchange. Cavour now wanted to get back to power: he had not long to wait. The government, faced with the prospect of Cavour in opposition, for Parliament was to meet in the new year, resigned, and after a difficult interview with the King, who still smarted at Cavour's outburst at Monzambano, he found himself once more President of the Council.

His first act was to dissolve the Chamber and order a general election which was to include the nomination of deputies from Lombardy, Tuscany and Emilia. This he followed with a circular letter to his agents and diplomats abroad announcing that, as Europe had failed to agree on the settlement of Italy, she was now entitled to deal with her internal problems herself. He then let Napoleon know privately, as did Victor Emanuel, that they were prepared to surrender Savoy and Nice in exchange for Central Italy. His plan was to hold a plebiscite in both areas, for he was certain that Nice and Savoy would vote for incorporation in France, by means, if necessary, of judicious manipulation. He intended, however, to have parliamentary sanction and to regularize the exchange of territory by constitutional methods. Cavour's hands were at this point much strengthened by the work of Lord John Russell, who induced Napoleon to adhere to a four-point programme, non-interference by France and Austria in Italy, a plebiscite, the withdrawal of French troops and no interference in the internal affairs of Venetia. The winning of Central Italy now appeared assured and Cavour hurried on the plebiscite. But it was not to be all plain sailing. Cavour had hitherto kept Nice and Savoy in the background, but now Napoleon became suspicious that Italy having got her quota might repudiate the cession of Nice and Savoy, so he inspired strong articles in the Press demanding his share of the spoils. This infuriated England, who wrote about the shame of sacrificing the cradle of the race. Cavour denied and prevaricated, insisting that he would neither cede nor exchange Italian soil, but added to Sir James Hudson, that if Savoy of her own will voted for incorporation in France, Italy would accept the verdict, as it would accept that of Tuscany and Emilia. Napoleon regarded Cavour's constitutional methods as mere finesse, and impatient for his pound of flesh, under the pretext of withdrawing the French forces from Italy, marched troops into Nice and Savoy before the plebiscite. This made the outcome inevitable and in due course Tuscany and Emilia voted themselves into Italy and Nice and Savoy into France. The new state of things was then regulated by an open treaty accepted and sanctioned by Parliament.

Having been out-manoeuvred by Cavour over Central Italy, Napoleon had seen his original four-part division of the peninsula reduced to three. He now became uneasy lest by turning south it should be further reduced to two, by the absorption of Naples. In the heat of his anger after Villafranca Cavour had declared that the treaty should never be executed. He would turn to Naples, become a conspirator, anything to prevent the treaty from being carried out. This outburst merely brought to the surface ideas long latent in his mind, for, as he wrote in a calmer moment, he had foreseen that when the national aims were blocked from going east, they would inevitably turn south. But Cavour's policy did not include for the present an attack on Naples. Before that was feasible the Papal States had to be dealt with. He wanted to work from north to south and deal with the centre first. He had already an assurance that the French garrison would leave Rome during the summer. When that took place a condition similar to that of the Romagna after Magenta would soon be created. If Naples stepped in to keep order, that could at once be regarded as a breach of non-intervention, and dealt with by force if necessary. But until that situation materialized he would be content to bring order and organization to the new provinces and weld together the Italy already redeemed. In May 1859 King Ferdinand of Naples had died and his feeble son Francis succeeded him. Cavour, badly in need of more troops, had offered him an alliance which had been refused, and since then there had been little intercourse between the two states. In March 1860 the Piedmontese Minister at Naples wrote warning Cavour that a plot was on foot to recover the Romagna by Neapolitan arms. It was a strange combination of forces, consisting of Francis II, Cardinal Antonelli the Papal Foreign Secretary, the Archduchess Sophia at Vienna and the Queen Mother at Naples, supported by Mons. Ginelli, the Papal Nuncio, and the Spanish ambassador, Bermudez di Castro, who talked openly of the 'great Catholic league'. Cavour instructed his Minister to act with great reserve, but with vigour if the Neapolitan troops occupied any Papal territory. It was not, however, to be Neapolitan aggression but Piedmontese which opened the southern problem.

Sicily was the conspirator's paradise. The hatred of the Sicilians for the Neapolitans, the long tale of ill-treatment meted out to them, the poverty and misery of the peasantry had made incipient rebellion a chronic condition amongst the mass of the people. Since the failure of Pisacane's expedition in 1857, Mazzini had turned his attention to Sicily, so too had La Farina, himself a Sicilian, with the resources of the National Society. Their principal agents were Nicola Fabrizi, whose headquarters were in Malta, Francesco Crispi, the future Italian Premier, and Rosalino Pilo. Unrest had naturally been increased by recent events, and the results of their efforts was a rising at the Gancia Convent at Palermo on April 6th. In itself it was a small affair and was quickly stamped out by the police, but it was symptomatic of a larger movement. News of what was taking place in Sicily quickly reached Cavour. It was an inopportune moment, for four days before, the King had opened the first Italian Parliament amid great popular pride and interest. Turin was full of deputies and the city was given over to festivity. Cavour found time, nevertheless, to consult his Minister for War, General Fanti, as to a suitable officer who might be sent to guide and stimulate the movement; for Cavour, though anxious for peace with Naples, had no compunction in helping to create trouble for her in Sicily. One never knew what opportunities might emerge. Fanti suggested Colonel Ribotti, who had taken part in Bentivegna's rising in 1857. Ribotti, however, was never sent. While Cavour was thus engaged, the news had reached Genoa, and Nino Bixio and Crispi at once hurried to Turin to endeavour to induce Garibaldi, who was now a deputy, to take command of an expedition to the island. After much persuasion he consented. But Garibaldi hesitated. There were twenty thousand troops on the island. The value of the local support he would get was small and unreliable. The strength of Sicilian resistance lay in street fighting, where every one could join in and defend barricades or hurl coping stones from the roof tops and leave off fighting when they chose. The local levies, the *squadre*, without leaders or discipline, were of small fighting value. For a month there was indecision. In the meantime preparations went on. Garibaldi's request to the King to take with him a brigade of his old Hunters of the Alps who had fought under him in 1859 and were now part of the regular army, was refused, and he had to rely on volunteers. Before long they were flocking to Genoa. Arms and stores were being collected. The expedition was becoming a national conspiracy. The King was supporting it with money, Cavour knew all about it, and so did diplomacy. Talleyrand, the French ambassador, went to Genoa to see for himself and kindly kept Cavour informed of all that was taking place. It was nothing less than a filibustering expedition organized with the knowledge of the government, and a breach of international law. Then a second expedition organized by the National Society under the leadership of Colonel La Masa amalgamated with Garibaldi, and thereby made it impossible for Cavour to stop it, for the political party supporting the National Society was the backbone of Cavour's parliamentary majority, needed to pass the Bill on the cession of Nice and Savoy. At length, the first week in May, the expedition, numbering eleven hundred men, steamed out from Quarto near Genoa in two old merchant ships commandeered from the Rubattino company, and, as Cavour put it, the fate of Italy was 'once more on the high seas in the midst of storms and dangers'. 'But what can we do?' he added, 'as long as Italy is not made we cannot think of reposing in the calm of the past years'.

The expedition of the Thousand is an oft told tale. It thrilled Italy as no other episode in the whole Risorgimento ever did. A week after Garibaldi sailed *The Times* correspondent wrote, 'Men of all classes, of all ages, of all parties, have only one business, only one subject and object—how to help Garibaldi. To live in Turin or Genoa, in Milan or Florence, and not to be Garibaldi-mad is impossible.' The interest in England was scarcely less than in Italy. The audacity of the whole proceeding, a thousand men setting out to overthrow a kingdom and doing it, recalled the triumphs of Drake and Frobisher and appealed to every Englishman. Diplomacy was furious at such an outrage. Russia, Prussia and Austria protested in the strongest terms. But no one moved. Cavour did everything he could think of to keep the ring for Garibaldi. He fought off diplomacy, mobilized every available soldier and concentrated the navy at Cagliari, but the ultimatum from Naples which he expected never came. Some time before he had said that he wanted England to do for the south of Italy what France had done for the north, and England did not disappoint him.[17]

In the meanwhile Garibaldi had landed safely at Marsala at the western extremity of the island, after narrowly escaping from two Neapolitan cruisers, which having just missed him at sea, returned in time to lie off shore and bombard the disembarking troops, until the protests of two English warships in the harbour stopped them. He now set off north-east across the corner of the island for Palermo. At Salemi, Garibaldi proclaimed his dictatorship over the island, nominating Francesco Crispi as pro-dictator. The next day he continued his march. At Calatafimi, his road was barred by a strong force greatly outnumbering him and posted in an admirable position on a terraced hill. It had to be stormed with the bayonet terrace by terrace. As the afternoon wore on exhaustion and losses made Garibaldi's situation almost desperate, until even Nino Bixio, his fiery lieutenant who feared nothing, spoke of the necessity of retreat. It was then that the real greatness of Garibaldi showed itself. He knew victory was vital and he replied, 'Here we make Italy or die'. One last rush and the summit was reached, the Neapolitans broke, and victory was won. Garibaldi had left Quarto on May 5th, he landed on the 11th and won his first battle at Calatafimi on the 15th. Three days later he was in sight of Palermo at Renda. Here he received information that all entrance to Palermo from the west was barred by the main Neapolitan forces and to avoid disaster he turned south and then east. In so doing he eluded a strong force under von Mechel sent out to intercept him, and sent them on a fruitless journey to Corleone. At Gibilrossa, he met La Masa with three thousand Sicilians and after a difficult journey through the mountains arrived where he was least expected, on the east side of the city. On May 27th, he seized the Porta Termini and fighting began in the city. The population rose in support, erecting barricades and joining in the battle, while Lanza, the timid governor, bombarded the city by sea and land. After a three days' battle, Mundy, the English Admiral, induced Lanza to ask for an armistice, offering his flagship as a neutral place for the conference. Terms were arranged, the Neapolitan troops withdrawn, and Garibaldi was left victorious. He was now practically in possession of Sicily but he had one more battle to fight before the island was fully conquered. This was fought at Milazzo on July 20th and Garibaldi's victory left Sicily completely in his hands.

The military occupation of Sicily at once brought the political aspect to the front. Cavour tried the same technique with Garibaldi—gathering the fruits as soon as they fell—as he had found so successful with Napoleon, but the Dictator had other views. He was, moreover, still bitterly incensed with Cavour over the surrender of his birthplace, Nice, to Napoleon, the man who had crushed the Roman Republic. He had appeared at Turin for the opening of Parliament on purpose to indict the government, and had he done so, it is certain that the harmony of the first national Parliament would have been marred by a stormy scene. But ignorant of procedure and scornful of politicians, his attempt to interpellate the Ministry, before the Chamber was properly constituted, was ruled out of order; and before another opportunity presented itself the expedition to Sicily absorbed all his attention. As it was, he was only just stopped from raiding Nice and smashing the ballot boxes. It was not, then, surprising that to Cavour's request for immediate annexation Garibaldi replied with a refusal and when Cavour sent La Farina to Sicily to persuade him, he promptly shipped the new agent back to Genoa. Garibaldi had set his obstinate mind on a single aim. He intended to cross the Straits, conquer Naples, then press on to Rome and evict the French garrison, and crown Victor Emanuel on the Campidoglio. He was going to present Victor Emanuel with a Kingdom and nothing less, and he had no intention of spoiling this glittering gift by handing over piecemeal to the politicians what he had conquered with his sword. As to the political complications which such a programme would arouse, he knew little and cared less. Cavour, though exceedingly annoyed at Garibaldi's obstinacy, nevertheless continued in the policy which had been decided upon with the King at a meeting at Bologna on the eve of the departure of the expedition; to help it all he could while keeping the complicity of the government in the background, always provided that no attack was made on the States of the Church, because this would at once provoke active opposition from Napoleon. Naples, but no further, was Cavour's ultimatum. So a second expedition of reinforcements under Medici, another of Garibaldi's well-tried lieutenants, sailed for Sicily and supplies and munitions were freely provided.

The amazing success of Garibaldi revealed a condition of weakness at Naples which made anything possible, and Napoleon, who, though he wanted Italian independence never wanted Italian unity, saw with dismay that undesirable prospect steadily approaching realization. He now put forward another solution, that of dualism. Italy was to be divided into north and south with the Papacy at Rome set like a jewel between them. The same idea had occurred to Cavour, though probably as a temporary measure—until the southern fruit was fully ripe—but coupled with the necessity of a complete change of system and policy at Naples, and in April, Victor Emanuel had written to

Francis II of Naples proposing co-operation between the two states on these lines, but Francis had rejected all advice. Napoleon now opened negotiations with England, putting forward the new idea and proposing, as a necessary preliminary to negotiation, that the fleets of the two nations should patrol the Straits of Messina and prevent the Dictator crossing to the mainland. At the same time the Emperor brought pressure to bear on Victor Emanuel, if not to forbid, at least to advise Garibaldi not to cross the Straits. The King forwarded an official request to this effect, but enclosed a private note telling Garibaldi to refuse to obey, which he did. Fortunately Cavour found out what was taking place and England turned down the Emperor's suggestions.

The conquest of Naples caused Cavour more anxiety than any other problem he had to face, excepting only the crisis of war or peace in 1859. It was not his plan. It was an improvisation inspired by Mazzini, but not Mazzini the republican but Mazzini the unitarian, for Garibaldi insisted from the first that the expedition must be undertaken in the name of Italy and Victor Emanuel, and Garibaldi's loyalty to the King was absolutely to be relied on; and Mazzini acquiesced. For this reason it seems probable that Cavour's insistence on the dangers of the 'revolution' in his correspondence at this time was not genuine, but had an ulterior purpose. Cavour never feared Mazzini, he was in fact useful to his policy. He was the terrible alternative paraded before Europe when Cavour's programme was not accepted. It was otherwise with Garibaldi. As Cavour once wrote, he had the instincts of a poet, he was also headstrong and obstinate, and carried away by his imagination he was quite capable of pushing on from Naples to Rome and embroiling Italy with France. There was another point. The prestige of the crown. The position of a subject at the head of an army and the idol of the nation, with a kingdom in his gift, was not without dangers. The last phase, as Cavour saw clearly, must then be dominated by the King, not the subject. Victor Emanuel, of course, could come south by sea, but it would be infinitely more impressive if he arrived at the head of his army. These considerations taken together forced two facts on Cavour. Garibaldi must be stopped at Naples and the King must lead his army through the Papal States and bar the road to Rome.

Cavour's first idea was to provoke a palace revolution at Naples, procure the flight of the King and take over the administration before the arrival of Garibaldi. The plan failed completely. Naples, like the rest of southern Italy, would not raise a finger to save the Bourbon but would not fight against him, they just waited for the 'Red Man' as they called Garibaldi. In the meantime in Sicily Garibaldi, having strengthened and reorganized his forces and completed his plans, crossed the Straits without opposition on August 18th and the march upon Naples began. There was no fighting. The southern army either disbanded or surrendered and the Dictator with his troops following on behind him drove forward to the capital. The evening before Garibaldi reached Naples the King and Queen sailed for Gaeta, the fleet refusing to follow them. The next day came the tumultuous entry of Garibaldi. On that same day, September 7th, Cavour sent an ultimatum to Rome, followed at once by the entry of the army into the Papal States. He had prepared the way by a mission to Napoleon, then at Chambéry, whose consent was given. One corps marched on Ancona, scattered the little Papal army at Castelfidardo and laid siege to the city, which surrendered on September 29th. The other corps occupied Umbria. The King joined his army at Ancona and marched south. While these events were taking place, Garibaldi, having collected his troops, left Naples for the Volturno front where the remaining Neapolitan army, more loyal than the southern troops, were concentrated. The battle of the Volturno fought on October 1st ended in a victory for Garibaldi but it checked any idea of an immediate march on Rome. While Garibaldi rested and reorganized his exhausted troops and wrestled with the political chaos, the royal army crossed the Garigliano. On the 26th King and Dictator met at Teano and a few days later after driving together through Naples, the man who had won a kingdom, refusing all offers of reward, sailed back unnoticed to his island home on Caprera.

The political reaction in Europe to the invasion of the Papal States proved less dangerous than Cavour feared. France at once withdrew her Minister from Turin, more to placate French clerical susceptibilities than as a sign of genuine disapproval, and Austria and Russia followed suit. But England was working for peace and the Prussian Minister remained in Italy. England openly approved and Lord John Russell's despatch met with deep and heartfelt gratitude throughout Italy. Cavour's first thought was to obliterate the atmosphere of revolution which surrounded the conquest of the south and regularize the political union of Italy by parliamentary sanction. Electoral lists were hastily prepared and Parliament summoned for January 1861. The last phase of the conquest of the south had been full of difficulty. Garibaldi still refused to allow annexation and had twice written to the King demanding the dismissal of Cavour. Prepared to go to any length to prevent an open dissension between state and dictator Cavour had formally offered his resignation if it would lessen the tension. Victor Emanuel refused to accept it, and he remained in power. The battle of the Volturno at last removed the danger of a forward movement on Rome, and when the Parliament met at Turin for the autumn session the day after the battle, Cavour laid a single clause Bill before the Chamber authorizing the annexation of the south. The Bill was passed without a dissentient voice and the Ministry was given a unanimous vote of confidence and knowing the country was behind him Cavour acted quickly. A plebiscite was taken and Italy became at last a single country.

The first truly national Parliament met at Turin on January 27, 1861. It was opened in person by Victor Emanuel. The address from the throne was brief and when the royal session was over Cavour at once laid before the Chamber a short Bill proclaiming Victor Emanuel King of Italy. He then announced the resignation of the ministry in order that the King might have a free hand in selecting the first government of the united country. Cavour was recalled to power because indispensable, though the King would have liked Ricasoli. A fresh Cabinet was formed, including members representing the new provinces, and then Parliament settled down to work.

The new Chamber of Deputies was profoundly different both in character and composition from any that had preceded it. In size alone it was more than double that of the old Piedmontese Chamber, numbering 443 members against 204, and a special building had had to be erected in Turin to accommodate it. Few of the new members from the south, representing nearly half the Chamber, had any knowledge of constitutional government and small appreciation of the liberal principles which had informed Cavour's policy for the last ten years. Still fewer had any political or even administrative experience and in many cases their claims to election had been based rather on the warmth of their patriotism than their political gifts. Faced with these exceptional features in the Chamber, Cavour thought it desirable to give a lead to Parliament, and through them to the country, on the question occupying every one's thought, the problem of Rome. As to Venice, he was not anxious to deal with it, but in his letters to the King and others he made it clear that he thought any provocation of Austria for 'at least two years' would be madness, as it would take that length of time if not longer to organize the army and navy to be fit to face a campaign. Cavour had already initiated secret negotiations at Rome, which, after a too promising beginning, had been suddenly liquidated, his agent being expelled from the city. He now, first in the Chamber of Deputies and then in the Senate (March 27th, April 9th), made two set speeches upon the subject, laying down the principles upon which he proposed to act. In so doing he traced the line of policy which, after his death two months later, succeeding Ministers for the next fifteen years endeavoured to follow and which became known as the 'Cavourian tradition'.

Cavour began by affirming that Rome, the Eternal City upon which so many centuries of greatness look down, the only city in Italy to which all others gave precedence, must be the capital of the new Kingdom. But if Italy must go to Rome, this could only be by moral means, by negotiation and consent, and not only of the Papacy but also of her eldest daughter, France. This meant the surrender of what remained of the Temporal Power. He then defended two propositions, first that the Temporal Power did not give the Pope independence, and secondly, that the Holy Father would have greater independence without it. Cavour then dealt with the basis upon which negotiations to this end could be undertaken, and summed them up in one word, Liberty. A complete separation between the two powers the State and the Church, a free Church in a free State. To-day, he said, there was complete civil liberty of speech and meeting, there must be likewise religious liberty. It would be necessary, first, to convince the Catholic world of Italian honesty and the reality and fullness of the liberty Italy offered to the Papacy, and then he believed that the Church would bring peace to Italy by accepting the nation's offer.

Cavour was too optimistic. The response for which he hoped never came, and when Italy at last went to Rome ten years later, it was occupied by force not by persuasion. These two speeches were the last of national importance which Cavour ever made. He was absorbed in administrative work. He had much to worry him. The condition of Naples was a growing anxiety. He had sent there the best men he could find but matters seemed to get worse rather than better. Brigandage had broken out and was assuming dangerous proportions, and he had been urged from more than one quarter to proclaim a state of siege, but he had steadily refused. He believed in the virtues of liberty and parliamentary not military government. 'I am the son of liberty', he had recently written to a friend, 'and to her I owe all that I am. If it is necessary to veil her statue it is not for me to do it.' The treatment of the disbanded Garibaldini was another cause of difficulty. Neither the King nor General Fanti had been very generous and the complaints reached Garibaldi, who, furiously angry, came to Turin. A painful scene followed in the Chamber with Cavour. The King patched up the quarrel but Cavour was never the same man after it. His last speech was a plea for concord and oblivion of past differences. At the close of May he had an attack, there was a temporary rally, but another followed, and after that he sank steadily. On June 6th he died. Cavour's death was a terrible calamity.' He held all the threads of national policy in his hands. It is difficult to find any parallel to the loss which Italy sustained. The nearest is perchance that of Abraham Lincoln four years later, whose political career was not without analogous features. Both plunged their country into war, the one to create unity the other to preserve it; the basis of both was their profound love of liberty, and both died when their task was newly completed. Alike, they were without rancour and above party and thought only of their country and died at a moment when their presence seemed vital for a true peace, for of both it might be said that they came with 'healing on their wings', and the noble lines of Walt Whitman, 'O captain, my captain, the fearful trip is done', seem as applicable to Italy's statesman as to the great American who inspired them.

CHAPTER NINE

VENICE WITHOUT VICTORY, 1861-1866

THE geographical unity of Italy, apart from Rome and Venetia, was, at last, a reality. It was now the task of government and people to weld themselves into a unified nation. To appreciate the difficulties of such an undertaking it must be borne in mind that nothing had as yet altered the separatist life of the different states. Piedmont and Tuscany, the Papal States and Naples, still had their individual laws and administration, their peculiar customs and traditions and their varieties of language; for though the cultured classes spoke both Italian and French, they likewise spoke the regional dialect, which differed so widely that to a Piedmontese the speech of a Neapolitan was unintelligible. The amalgamation effected by Napoleon over two-thirds of the peninsula had been only temporary, and although Napoleon's influence was still active in the legal systems, the old life had now been resumed without interruption for forty-five years, since the resettlement at the Congress of Vienna in 1815. Surrounded by a customs barrier, each state was self-contained. There were few railways and none intersecting different states. Piedmont had 850 kilometres, mainly strategical, connecting Genoa, Turin and Alessandria with Milan. There were 200 kilometres in Lombardy and 308 in Tuscany. Naples had two short lines, joining Portici and Caserta with the capital: elsewhere there were none. The difference in the prosperity levels were also very marked, central and southern Italy being far below the north in material wealth. The average of illiteracy was reckoned at 78 per cent, rising to 90 in Naples and Sicily. Schools were few, scattered and of poor quality and in the hands of the Church. An entire new national system of law and administration, education and transport, had to be devised, put in action, and paid for, and to do this in such a way as not to press unfairly on the poorer areas was a task of the utmost difficulty.

The composition of the Chamber of Deputies which had these problems to solve, reflected fairly enough the prevalent feeling in the country. The core of it was the solid block of Piedmontese deputies, around whom gathered supporters from all over Italy. This formed the Right. The Left were Mazzinians and Garibaldini, containing a strong infusion of southern deputies, with an element drawn from

Tuscany and central Italy, all more or less opposed to the predomin-ance of Piedmont, and including in their ranks the group known as the Party of Action, of which Garibaldi was the leader, with a pro-gramme of 'Venice and Rome' as quickly as possible, and by any means. For fifteen years the electorate unfailingly returned a solid Right majority, although during this period 'there were thirteen different Ministries and eight Premiers, and many rifts and jealousies within the party. It would seem that the electors were determined that Italy should be settled on the Cavourian tradition before the alien tradition of the south was allowed to predominate.

The first step taken was to extend the Piedmontese political system throughout Italy, which ensured freedom of speech and association, but which also necessitated drafting officials from Turin all over the country and began the process, known later as 'Piedmontism', which was the cause of so much jealousy. The next step was to decide on the administrative system to be adopted. Cavour had favoured a widespread decentralization, a 'regional' system, and a scheme on this basis was prepared under his direction and submitted to Parliament. But the fear of perpetuating the old regional jealousies and of encour-aging separatism, caused its rejection, and the Chamber adopted the French system, dividing the country into fifty-three departments, called provinces, each under a prefect, directly dependent from the Home Office. Customs and coinage, weights and measures, were quickly unified, and commissions appointed to deal with the new legal code, railways, roads and education. Similar measures were taken with regard to the armed forces. Cavour himself had been engaged just before his death on a scheme for the amalgamation of the two navies, Piedmontese and Neapolitan, and the army chiefs were busy with a similar task based on conscription. All this required time to produce results, and in the meanwhile there was much confusion and discontent over the inevitable dislocation of the accustomed way of life.

As Cavour's successor the King nominated the Baron Ricasoli, already the leader of the government majority in the Chamber and formerly the Dictator of Tuscany. It was an obvious, but hardly a fortunate, choice. Ricasoli had few gifts as a parliamentary Premier. He was a born dictator. Proud and unbendable and lacking tact and finesse, he was devoid, moreover, of that gift of compromise which is essential in parliamentary government. He was, however, a fine speaker, honest and incorruptible, with a clear grasp of essentials. In particular, he was anxious to come to an amicable arrangement with

Rome on the lines laid down by Cavour, and in spite of his predecessor's failure, he reopened negotiations, but he was equally unsuccessful. Another rebuff came from Napoleon, who, on the death of Cavour, perhaps the one man he trusted, at once suspended the arrangement made for the withdrawal of the French troops from Rome, which effectively closed the anticipated opening for trouble in the city and its occupation by the Italian army. Ricasoli sent the President of the Chamber, Urbano Rattazzi, to Paris, to try and influence the Emperor, but he met with no success. Ricasoli was a failure both in his handling of the Chamber and in his relations with the King. His haughty manner and the uncompromising rigidity with which he held to his point of view offended both equally, and after nine months of office he resigned.

Urbano Rattazzi, who followed Ricasoli, was a much more congenial Premier from the King's point of view, to whom he was always obsequiously devoted. A clever, adroit politician, admirable in catching the feeling of the Chamber and trimming his sails thereto, Rattazzi was always something of the intriguer. His name was already coupled with one national calamity, Novara, and it was destined to be linked with two more, Aspromonte and Mentana. The comment of Garibaldi that 'one can always do something with Rattazzi', reveals much. During these first years of the united kingdom the country was under the spell of illusion. It had always been accepted, for example, that unity would lighten greatly the financial burden, whereas the opposite was the fact. Want of money was the fundamental weakness of the new Italy. Union had been expensive. The debts of seven states had to be taken over, and the necessary measures for national defence, administration, education and transport added an enormous burden. Under the old régime, states like Tuscany or the States of the Church had no military or naval expenses, and little was spent on education or transport, but now they had to bear their share of the national expenditure and taxation grew steadily heavier as the expenses increased with development. Another illusion was in regard to the strength of the nation. Italians took it for granted that they were now a Great Power and must do as others did. An imposing army of 350,000 was planned with a navy to match; a national education system and a network of railways were to follow, all this regardless of the financial strain. Yet Italy had scarcely any industries. She had neither coal nor iron, and the armour, guns and machinery of the new navy had to come mainly from England or America, and military equipment from France. The export of oranges and lemons, even with silk and wines and sulphur added, was hardly a sound basis for a Great Power, and until the era of electricity enabled her to use her abundant water supply to provide cheap power, her basic industries were sadly handicapped.

This new and fictitious sense of power increased the impatience of the country for the satisfactory solution of the problems of Rome and Venice. The ease with which the south had been conquered convinced Garibaldi and his more ardent followers that, backed now by a formidable army, all that was needed was a good push to overturn what he termed 'the tottering shanty of Papalism' and little more to incite a massed rising in Venetia and its rapid liberation from Austria. He quickly became restless in his voluntary exile at Caprera. A plot was soon on foot for a rising in Venetia, volunteers began to collect on the borders round Sarnico, and Garibaldi, under cover of opening new branches of the Rifle Shooting Associations, left Caprera and appeared at Brescia, Como and elsewhere. The government was loathe to interfere with the Hero, whose popularity was such as to make him almost independent of official restraint, but they could not ignore the reports of the Prefects as to the imminence of an incursion into the Tyrol or Venetia, and possibly on a hint from Vienna, the arms and volunteers were suddenly seized and the design broken up. Garibaldi at first protested violently, then altered his attitude, probably under royal influence, and went back to Caprera, and the government promptly despatched warships to prevent his return to the mainland.

In appointing Rattazzi to the premiership the King had followed his personal inclination rather than correct constitutional procedure, for Rattazzi was not a member of the Cavourian majority, he belonged to the Left, and in consequence, his influence in the Chamber was at a discount and at any time a determined attack by the majority would have unseated him. He kept his place, in fact, only by underground manipulations, and only so long as no untoward event took place which would consolidate the majority against him. In this difficult position Garibaldi was a terrible embarrassment to the government, and the country had now to pay for its infatuation for the extralegal methods of its Hero and the connivance of the King and government in the events of 1860. Conspiracy had arisen in Italy as the natural reaction of the more daring section of the people against the repressive policy of Metternich. It had been elevated into a gospel by Mazzini, and so long as it was directed against Austria, it was, however futile, a legitimate means of expressing public feeling against a foreign oppressor. But it had lost this character with Garibaldi's invasion of Sicily and became a filibustering expedition, directed against a nomin-ally friendly power, backed by public support and at least the know-ledge of the government. Cavour, unable to stop it, used it as a short cut to his own political ends, but took care to smother it as quickly as possible under the cloak of constituted authority. The support of the King, the temporizing attitude of the government, together with its ultimate assistance, above all the amazing success of the expedition itself, convinced large sections of the country that this was undoubtedly the way to get Rome and Venice. The hand of the government must be forced, then, presented with the *fait accompli* they would gratefully accept it, and Europe would bluster but acquiesce. This feeling could not be eradicated so long as Garibaldi and Mazzini were active in support of it, and it had become so deep-seated that the throne, the parliament and the public were alike infected and fascinated by it.

Garibaldi was so idolized by the public and by all who knew him or had served under him, that he had only to lift his finger and volunteers would hasten to his standard from every corner of Italy and support would come to him from everywhere. But it was no longer a question of opposing the decrepit Bourbon, despised and contemned by every country in Europe, but of attacking Rome defended by French troops or Venetia belonging to Austria, and Rattazzi had good reason to know that both Emperors meant what they said in their warnings against the use of filibustering methods. Garibaldi, however, cared for none of these things. Evading the naval cordon sent to stop him, he reached the mainland and sud-denly appeared in Sicily. Welcomed with effusion by the Governor, the Marquis Pallavicini, recently appointed by Rattazzi, Garibaldi was lodged in the Viceregal Palazzo at Palermo and permitted by the Governor to address the crowd from the balcony. It is doubtful whether at this moment Garibaldi had any definite plan of action in his mind, but the cry of 'Rome or Death' from an unknown voice in the crowd gave him his cue, and on this text he toured the island call-ing for volunteers and arms. The mass of telegrams, letters and despatches which now began to pass to and fro between the Minister of the Interior, who was Rattazzi himself, and officials all over Italy, have been deciphered and published and make curious reading. Though Rattazzi's name will probably always be associated with the humiliation of Aspromonte, which as head of the government could hardly be otherwise, it is nevertheless obvious that he lent no conni-vance to the expedition. He made it unmistakably clear, once Garibaldi's intention to make for Rome became evident, that he must be stopped by all means and at any cost from crossing to the mainland. From all over Italy came telegrams from Prefects or others of the imminent departure of volunteers for Sicily 'secretly and in small groups'. To which the replies were always to stop them. Notices of demonstrations in favour of the expedition came likewise. Amongst more responsible officials there was both weakness and credulity. We find, for instance, General Cugia, in command in Sicily, telegraphing, 'All the captains of trading vessels are accomplices, disembarking volunteers. Civil service nearly all betraying the government, many thinking they are seconding it. It seems true that Mazzini has been in Palermo.' Mazzini never left London. A royal proclamation was issued forbidding the expedition. Orders were sent to General Cugia to concentrate the troops in Sicily between Messina and Catania. Cialdini took the command in Calabria, to block the road to Rome if Garibaldi landed on the continent. Admiral Persano, Minister of Marine, came to Sicily to direct the naval patrol, with strict orders to stop the expedition at all costs. Every precaution seems to have been taken and energetic action urged by Rattazzi.

In spite of this, the cause of all the trouble, Garibaldi himself, went about the island unhindered, no one daring to lay hands on him. When all his arrangements were complete, he seized two ships and crossed unmolested, though two cruisers lay off the port of embarkation (August 24th). Avoiding Reggio, strongly held by royal troops, he withdrew his now famished and weary men, two thousand in all, to the mountains around Aspromonte. Here the troops under Colonel Pallavicini met him. A few volleys were exchanged, and then Garibaldi surrendered, having stopped his men from firing on their fellow Italians, but not before he himself was wounded by an Italian bullet in the heel. He was taken by sea to Varignano, near Spezia. Aspromonte was a wretched business. The wounding of Garibaldi evoking sympathy everywhere, the frantic efforts of the government to stop him from fear of Napoleon, the weakness displayed by those in command, were felt as a bitter humiliation for Italy. Persano as the Minister of Marine was probably most to blame, for his orders were clear, but he would not face the outcry or take the responsibility of having to open fire, and possibly sink, Garibaldi and his ships. He kept out of the way and gave vague orders to his subordinate, Admiral Albini, who followed suit at the critical moment. There was, moreover, a general feeling that it was 1860 over again: that there was an understanding between Rattazzi, the King and

Garibaldi, and that the orders were not meant to be executed. There were too many high interests involved and too much secret intrigue, to permit any serious inquiry, and Rattazzi and the government resigned.

After refusal by his first two choices, Victor Emanuel nominated Carlo Luigi Farini, the former dictator of Emilia, as Premier: but Farini was already suffering from brain trouble and in a short time retired from political life and the premiership devolved upon his Finance Minister, Marco Minghetti. The new President of the Council was born at Bologna and was a disciple of Cavour. He had been a member of the Papal government in 1848, had collaborated with Cavour at the Congress of Paris in 1856, and had been responsible four years later for the scheme of 'regional' administration which had been rejected by the Chamber in favour of centralization. Minghetti was a capable economist and an admirable speaker, moderate and prudent, but lacking strength of character. Incapable of taking a strong line either in the direction of policy or in the control of his colleagues, the bad tendencies already perceptible in the parliamentary system developed throughout his leadership, and opened the road to that decay of sound political life which later discredited the parliamentary system in Italy.

The Piedmontese constitution which had been adopted for united Italy was modelled on the French constitution of 1830, with English influences added. The Premier was nominated by the King, but was not of necessity the leader of the majority in the Chamber, as we have seen in the case of the appointment of Urbano Rattazzi. Nor did his defeat imply a general election and a new party in office, but a change of Cabinet. This produced in Italy, as in France, a rapid succession of Ministries (there were thirteen in the first ten years), great difficulty in carrying through any big programme, and the lack of a sustained and steady national policy. Another weak point in the constitution was the narrowness of the franchise, this, together with the clause excluding illiterates from voting, reduced the electorate to little more than a clique in each constituency. It was estimated that the 443 members were actually elected by about 150,000 voters out of above twenty millions, or about 300 per seat. Thus the great majority of the nation had no direct interest in the parliamentary life of the country. The want of railways and the position of Turin in the extreme north of the peninsula, cut off the majority of members from their constituents whom they seldom saw, and inability to read deprived a large percentage of all political education. Thus when the first novelty of voting had worn off, public interest in politics steadily lessened and instead of being the centre of a network of interest extending throughout the country Parliament became a self-contained organism in which the public took small interest.

Within the Chamber, the party system was weak and undeveloped. It was difficult to procure concerted action on broad party lines and groups partook of the nature of factions. These again were traversed by regional divisions. Under these conditions the course of legislation. was at all times uncertain and accompanied by the inevitable correlatives of faction—secret bargaining and the corrupt use of power and patronage. Local patriotism has always been a strong characteristic of the Italian people and there was a strong regional clannishness amongst members, Tuscans, Piedmontese and Neapolitans working in close corporations. The weakness of Minghetti encouraged this dangerous tendency, of which the most obnoxious sample was the *consorteria*, a group, mainly Tuscan, under the leadership of the new Minister of the Interior, the Florentine Peruzzi, whose policy was founded on jealousy of Piedmont and 'Piedmontism'. 'Italy cannot be governed from Turin' was a favourite dictum and they used the Press to suggest the need to change the capital. This concentration on sectional interests not only created much bitter feeling but led to a neglect or indifference to the real social needs of the country which still further tended to separate Parliament from the thought of the nation.

Meanwhile the government was fully occupied with the two problems of finance and brigandage. The previous Ministry had discovered in the young Quintino Sella, a Finance Minister prepared to face the unpopularity of ruthless taxation and stringent economy. Minghetti, who now took over his portfolio, produced a budget full of financial jugglery which was to bring in vast sums to the treasury. The nation had already subscribed a loan of five hundred million lire and spent it, and Minghetti now relied on large amounts to be saved by departmental economies, dismissal of superfluous officials, and the increase of national wealth due to the efforts of a hardworking people. But palliatives and economies were of little use as the blueprints for public works and the paper schemes for education and finance translated themselves into wage bills and salaries, and the financial position grew steadily worse. As to brigandage, it had now assumed the character of a semi-religious war. The south was garrisoned by an army of ninety thousand and warfare, as bitter and relentless as that waged by General Manhes in the days of Murat, against the same enemy, was being carried on throughout the southern provinces. King

Francis on his expulsion from Gaeta took refuge in the Papal States, and with the support of the Papal authorities organized and encouraged the resistance of the brigands. But the movement was too general and too widespread to be regarded simply as a struggle against bands of brigands. It was a civil war, whose methods degenerated into a savagery which neither gave nor expected quarter. To claim that these half-organized bands were fighting for the return of Francis II or for religion, would be probably an overstatement, but both these motives were present in varying degree. What is certain is that the methods employed by the Piedmontese commanders made them more hated than the Bourbon, and ill calculated to reconcile the south to union. Towns were sacked and burnt, the prisons were overcrowded with suspects, many not brought to trial, and priests and even bishops thrown into prison. Neither men nor women were spared if suspected of harbouring or even sympathizing with the brigands. It is small wonder that for fifty years the south was an unceasing source of expense, vexation and often sullen opposition to Italy, for the union had been enforced at the point of the bayonet, and had the plebiscite been taken in 1863 instead of 1861, it is open to question whether the verdict would not have been reversed in favour of Francis II.

The loyalty of Victor Emanuel had saved constitutional government in Italy, but although he had not the passion for personal rule of his father Charles Albert, he had nevertheless a hankering to mix himself in affairs of state. This tendency had had no chance of developing under strong Ministers such as Cavour and Ricasoli, but with an *intrigant* such as Rattazzi, or a weak character such as Minghetti, the King had small difficulty in initiating a secret policy of his own. Although the problems of Venice and Rome, after Sarnico and Aspromonte, had for the moment dropped into the background, they were always present to the minds of Mazzini and Garibaldi, and moreover, occupied the thought of Victor Emanuel. Garibaldi's change of attitude after Sarnico was undoubtedly due to some assurances as to national policy given to him by the King or Rattazzi, possibly both. They appear to have been connected with a plan to embarrass Austria by a rising in Hungary and Galicia and an attempt to seize Venetia while she was thus occupied elsewhere. Early in 1863 Mazzini got into touch with the King through an old adherent, the engineer Diamilla-Muller, who was sent to London by the government to buy rifles for the National Guard, and who, as a sideline, procured six hundred for Mazzini to be despatched to the Tyrol.

Garibaldi was soon drawn into the conspiracy, which finally developed into a tripartite plan in which Mazzini was to be responsible for a rising of volunteer forces in Venetia, Garibaldi was to organize an expedition into Galicia, while the King was to prepare the support of the royal army, when the movement in Venetia had reached a certain degree of success. The plan came to nothing. Mazzini, as usual, worked indefatigably, until, his patience exhausted, he broke with the King whose constant insistence that they must await the opportune moment, exasperated him beyond bearing, and disgusted with monarchy he declared his fixed intention to resort once more to republicanism.

Garibaldi was equally active and unsuccessful. In the spring of 1864 he suddenly left Caprera on his famous visit to England, giving as a reason the need for medical advice for his injured foot. His reception was magnificent, but his political activities in London, where he resumed his friendship with Mazzini and conferred with Hungarian and Polish refugees, created alarm in diplomatic circles, for none could tell what nefarious schemes might issue from such a reunion. This was probably the reason why his visit was unexpectedly curtailed and he was politely but firmly repatriated in the comfort of the Duke of Sutherland's yacht. He remained at Caprera for two months, during which he made his peace with the King, who was exceedingly angry over the Aspromonte fiasco, by undertaking to take up the threads of the Galician expedition which had the royal consent. In July he left Caprera for Ischia near Naples and set to work collecting arms and enrolling volunteers, but concealed his purpose by an absolute silence. Rumours of an expedition abroad leaked out, however, and reached the Party of Action who strongly disapproved of a movement concerted without their sanction or co-operation, and which involved the absence of Garibaldi from Italy at a moment so fraught with possibilities. So in July 1864 they published a disclaimer in the columns of *Il Diritto*, condemning the proposed expedition and dissociating themselves from a movement 'ordered by Princes and which must serve their interests rather than those of the people'. The exposure of his secret mission annoyed both Garibaldi and the King, but it achieved its object and the idea was abandoned.

Whether or not the discovery of the unauthorized royal intrigues acted as a spur to the energies of the government, the fact remains that very soon afterwards they took up the Roman Question once more. Their intermediary in Paris was the Italian ambassador, Count Pepoli, a cousin of the Emperor. In the most profound secrecy,

Minghetti, the Foreign Secretary the Marquis Visconti Venosta, together with Count Pasolini his predecessor and General La Marmora, met at Pegli on the Italian Riviera and carried through the final negotiations. The Roman Question was a veritable shirt of Nessus to the Emperor; he would have been more than thankful to be rid of it but it clung to him irrevocably. This time, however, he made one more effort to solve the problem by agreeing to the terms of the arrangement made previously with Cavour. Italy was to guarantee the Papal territory from all attack and the Emperor would withdraw his troops within two years. But the sting of the Convention was in the tail, for a secret clause was added that the Italian government would move the capital from Turin within six months. There was a certain ingenuity about this secret provision saving the face of both parties, for it enabled the Italians to claim the transfer of the capital to Florence as a half-way house to its final position on the banks of the Tiber, and the French to interpret it as the definite surrender by Italy of Rome as the capital of the Kingdom.

The Convention of September as it was called had little to commend it. It pleased the *consorteria*, who, to humiliate the Piedmontese, had been advocating the removal of the capital for months. It improved somewhat relations with France, and satisfied the national dignity, irritated at the presence of French troops in Italy, but it was a cruel insult to Turin. It also alarmed and angered Rome, which well knew what to expect when the French garrison was withdrawn. The Convention was announced on the 17th September and on the 21st riots broke out in Turin: the next day they were renewed: the military arrangements were badly mismanaged, the troops firing on the crowd in the Piazza San Carlo and on each other as well. More than fifty were killed. On the 23rd the King requested the resignation of the Ministry and a few days later appointed General La Marmora as Premier. This helped to calm the angry spirit in Turin but the obvious resentment of the populace hurt and saddened Victor Emanuel who withdrew for a time from the city. It was a tragic and thankless ending to the primacy of loyal Turin, which throughout the struggle for unity had borne the burden and heat of the day, giving to Italy the thinkers, the soldiers and the statesman who created her, and sparing neither her sons nor her substance for the unity and independence of the country.

The Church had not hitherto taken the offensive against the spoliation of her possessions and territory by the State, or, as it was widely regarded, the emancipation of her subjects from the ignorance and the oppression of her rule. There had been, nevertheless, a concentration of her forces for the struggle. To meet the dangers around her, a strict subjection to Rome had been imposed on the Bishops, whose hands were at the same time strengthened in their control of the clergy. This was a precautionary measure against internal revolt, in view of the radical condemnation of modern views being prepared in the encyclical *Quanta cura*. There was before the Papacy in this struggle between Church and State, a choice of two paths: either to accept the modern position, and strive to absorb and spiritualize it, as had been done in earlier ages with the crude religions of the barbarians, or to bind her mediaeval robe more closely around her and condemn the principles of the new world. She chose the latter. At the close of 1864 Pius IX published the encyclical, accompanied by a syllabus of eighty modern errors condemned by the Church. Into the furnace of her condemnation the Church threw Socialism, Communism, Bible Societies, freedom of conscience and cult, religious toleration, state education, and the whole prospectus of the Liberal Catholic movement in Europe which sought to reconcile religion with the State. Accepted in Europe as a deliberate attack on Free Government, in Italy it was interpreted as a declaration of war. While it disturbed many sincere Catholics who had hoped to find a *via media* between modern knowledge and the Church's doctrine, it confirmed the anti-clericals in their belief that there could be no compromise with Rome, and hardened them in their determination to assert the supremacy of the State over the claims of the Church.

Quanta cura and the syllabus were, in fact, a declaration of Catholic immobility: the apotheosis of the past. Italy in these years was divided in two. On one side stood the Italy of history, whose dominant tradition and atmosphere was religious, with its host of cathedrals and churches, convents and monasteries, set amid the lavish beauty of the land; the Italy of religious art, with its endless Madonnas and Saints and Angels; the Italy of faith and devotion, but also of superstition and ignorance, and above all, poverty. From this basis rose the hierarchy of religion, penetrating every phase of life and crowned with the pomp and splendour of Pontifical Rome. On the other side stood the new Italy, a blend of pride in her new nationality, of thirst for power and greatness, and grim determination to eradicate the predominance of priest and monk and seat her King in the Eternal City. Between these two aspects of the national life no compromise could as yet be found. The outstanding feature of her new political life was prodigality. Much of it was vital and necessary, but it was conceived in a grandiose spirit which fitted ill with her narrow resources. Millions were voted for railways and arsenals, docks and harbours. More millions were spent on her large conscript army and still more on her new navy of ironclads, whose pride of place was given to the *Re d'Italia*, armoured and engined in America and fitted with the latest of Armstrong's guns.

To meet this abnormal expenditure, the receipts from the budget were totally inadequate. A series of loans had to be floated, increasing the national debt to ruinous proportions. Taxation was steadily increased, but nothing seemed to make an impression on the annual deficit. In such circumstances the reputed wealth of the Church was a sore temptation to the harassed government. Already greedy eyes had been cast in this direction and tentative efforts made to tap this unexploited source of wealth. Appointments to vacant episcopal sees were delayed and the incomes transferred to the Treasury. In 1864 a report to Parliament revealed that no less than a hundred and eight sees were empty. The next year a Bill for the suppression of the religious orders was prepared, but was opposed by the extremists of the Left as not sufficiently comprehensive. Its introduction caused a storm of protest in the country and it was withdrawn. But in 1866, under the financial pressure of the war with Austria, a thoroughgoing Bill was carried through by which 2,382 monasteries and convents, housing 29,000 religious, were suppressed, their property confiscated, and the inmates pensioned off at the rate of about fourpence a day. A few, very few, were spared. Monte Cassino, the cradle of Western monasticism, was saved by an effort. A white robed monk still conducts tourists from Florence through the Certosa di Val d'Ema, where the past generations of the Ricasoli family lie interred, but to-day the most famous are just show places, and few visitors can have escaped a feeling of regret and sadness as a government official leads them through the silent emptiness of what were once amongst the most revered shrines in Christendom.

The transfer of the capital from Turin to Florence took place in the early months of 1865. To move the royal household, the two houses of Parliament, together with all the government officials and their staffs, was a long and most troublesome proceeding. Florence was ill prepared for such an invasion, and large sums had to be spent and much inconvenience caused before it was completed. It coincided, moreover, with a diplomatic crisis of the greatest delicacy and of critical importance to Italy, the growing friction, and all that that implied, between Prussia and Austria. The change of capital was accompanied by a general election. The new Chamber was no improvement, the Left making a vigorous bid to force La Marmora to resign. His Finance Minister and others left the Cabinet, but the King would hear of no other Prime Minister and the Ministry was reconstituted. The financial position was almost desperate: rank extravagance in the departments, notably the War Office, for which La Marmora had the utmost difficulty in finding a Minister, ugly cases of peculation amongst officials, brought demands for public inquiry and drastic economies in the armed forces. But this latter was the one thing that had to be avoided, in view of the possibility of war between Austria and Prussia, for this would at last open a road to the recovery of Venetia.

The first definite approach to good relations with Prussia, whose position *vis-à-vis* to Austria was closely analogous to that of Italy, had been made by Cavour, when in 1861 he had sent General La Marmora to Berlin to congratulate the new King William I on his accession. The result had been a special mission under General von Bonin to Turin, which was present at the Royal Session which proclaimed Victor Emanuel King of Italy. In 1863 and 1864 diplomatic Europe had been convulsed over the Schleswig-Holstein question, which had ended in a joint attack on Denmark by Prussia and Austria, the seizure of the two duchies, and their partition between the victors. But the robbers had quarrelled over the spoil and it now looked as if there would be war between them. This, in fact, was Bismarck's objective but it was contingent upon two conditions, the neutrality of France and alliance with Italy. To Italy, war between Austria and Prussia would be an opportunity for the recovery of Venetia such as hardly any other combination could present, for not only did an alliance with Prussia impose a war on two fronts upon Austria, but success would mean the recovery of Venetia without any obligation being incurred towards France. It would be a situation almost as favourable as 1848, but now Italy with a large army at her disposal had taken the place of Piedmont. To Prussia, the Italian alliance had equal value, for an Italian victory could in no way embarrass Prussia, and whatever the issue on the Italian front might be, Italy would immobilize a large Austrian force and create for her all the difficulties of a war on two fronts, leaving Prussia to deal with, at most, two-thirds of the Austrian strength.

The unknown quantity was Napoleon. If France joined Austria the war would not take place, for it would be Prussia not Austria who would then have the double front to defend, and Italy would certainly not oppose Napoleon. Even if France remained neutral, but placed a veto on an Italian alliance with Prussia, Bismarck's position would be jeopardized, for she must face the concentrated power of Austria instead of only a part of it. The first opening move was made by Prussia whose Minister at Turin, Count Usedom, in an interview with La Marmora on August 4th put the plain question, 'What would the attitude of Italy be in the probable event of a war between Prussia and Austria?' La Marmora's reply was very cautious. If, he said, Prussia seriously contemplated making war on Austria, and if she made Italy a serious and formal proposal, they would examine it: but if the Italian reply was to be used merely to exert diplomatic pressure on Austria, the proposal would not be considered. When a few days later the Prussian Minister assured La Marmora that Prussia had decided to make war on Austria, La Marmora replied that no pledge could be taken until they knew the attitude of Napoleon, which was as necessary for Prussia as for Italy. Still persistent in his attempt to get Italy to make a premature declaration, Usedom a week later insisted that he knew for certain that accord with Austria was now impossible, that if Italy now promised her alliance with Prussia, Venice was in her hands. The next day La Marmora received the notice of the Convention of Gastein, by which a settlement of their difficulties and mutual concord had been established between the two German Powers. Usedom hurriedly left Turin and La Marmora did not see him for two months.

Few knowledgeable persons regarded the Convention of Gastein as a permanent settlement. The question of hegemony in Germany had to be settled between the two rival Powers. But it suited Bismarck. The military preparations were not complete and it was necessary to assure himself that France would remain neutral and that the Emperor would place no veto on a Prussian alliance with Italy. So Bismarck paid his visit to Napoleon at Biarritz. It was successful, France would be neutral and Italy was free to do as she liked at her own risk, for no support would come from Paris. At the same time La Marmora sent to Vienna a special agent to discover whether Venetia was for sale, suggesting a thousand million lire, but all suggestions of such a kind were at once turned down and the mission was abortive. He then again took up the threads with Berlin. Bismarck, once sure of France, wasted no time. In January, a deputation arrived from William I with the Grand Collar of the Order of the Black Eagle for the King, together with a request to send in the greatest secrecy to Berlin, a general in the confidence of the government to confer with the Prussian authorities in preparation for war with Austria. This was followed by a Treaty of Commerce between the two nations, which a year previously Bismarck had refused. In March, General Govone was sent to Berlin. An alliance was a foregone conclusion, for as La Marmora said, no Italian government would last a week which refused to try and seize Venetia the moment Austria was engaged with another Power, but it was necessary to be wary. Italy had had one Villafranca and she did not want a second. The treaty must be offensive and defensive and there must be no loophole which would enable Prussia to withdraw at a critical moment and leave Italy to face the full strength of an exasperated Austria. Bismarck tried hard to induce La Marmora to sign a treaty of alliance at once, to anticipate any private arrangement with Austria which would make war unnecessary for Italy, but he refused. War with Austria was not popular in Germany and stiff opposition came from the King and the Court. England was urging peace and offering mediation, and Bismarck was almost at his wits' end to find a *casus belli*. He suggested that if Italy would begin the war, he could then force the hands of the King. But La Marmora refused again. Finally on March 27th the terms of the Offensive and Defensive Treaty arrived at Turin. Italy was to declare war immediately *after* hostilities commenced between Prussia and Austria. There was to be no separate peace. Italy was to get Venetia but not the Trentino, which was within the Germanic Confederation, and Prussia was to get a territorial equivalent. If the Austrian fleet left the Adriatic, the Italian fleet was to proceed to the Baltic. The terms were accepted. Full powers were given to Govone at Berlin and the treaty was signed on April 8th.

The relations of Austria and Prussia were alive with mutual suspicion but both denied any aggressive intentions, and having received Bismarck's official disclaimer, Vienna now proposed simultaneous disarmament. This proposal was at once supported by all parties anxious for peace, and Bismarck found it impossible to refuse, and both sides called a halt. Almost at the same moment Austria accused Italy of strengthening her forces on the Venetian border; the charge was based on a misconception, for the troops observed returning to Bologna were, in fact, normal garrison cavalry regiments recalled from Naples as no longer required, but Austria at once reinforced her Venetian troops. The information received by La Marmora of the steady despatch of large reinforcements into Venetia and the need to take defensive steps was clarified on April 26th by a letter from the

Foreign Minister at Vienna to Bismarck, telegraphed from Berlin. In this, after expressing his satisfaction at the resumed peaceful relations with Prussia, he went on to say that as Italy had put her army in a condition to attack Venetia, Austria was obliged to call up the reserves and put her Italian army on a war footing. This letter, welcomed at Florence as meaning an Austrian attack on Italy, which would not only bring the terms of the Prussian Treaty into force but would bring over France to the Italian side, decided La Marmora on immediate action and on April 27th he ordered mobilization.

But precisely at this moment the bellicose attitude of Italy received a severe setback. Instead of approving her action Napoleon disapproved, and worse than this, the one thing La Marmora had always feared, that at the last minute Prussia would draw back and leave Italy to face Austria alone, seemed about to be realized. On May 2nd La Marmora received a despatch from Govone reporting an interview with Bismarck in which he told him that 'the King would refuse to engage himself to declare war on Austria immediately it broke out in Italy, that he does not interpret the treaty in this sense, nor does he believe that this obligation was reciprocal according to the literal interpretation of the text'. But Bismarck could not refuse to honour his own signature to the treaty, and two days later came reassuring news. Partial mobilization was ordered, and an attack on Italy by Austria would mean war with Prussia, and Italy at once declared herself determined not to take the initiative. Austria had failed to detach Prussia from Italy, as no doubt was her real objective, and a war on two fronts now appeared imminent. She made one last desperate effort to save herself, offering to cede Venetia for a definite guarantee of Italian neutrality. It was a sore temptation to Italy, a less honourable Premier might have found some way to accept it, but La Marmora was loyal to the treaty and refused. As usual, Napoleon had been hankering after a congress but both Italy and Prussia had rejected it, now, as a last minute solution it was put forward again by England, France and Russia; it was wrecked as in 1859 by Austria, who refused the three suggested bases, the cession of Venetia, decision by universal suffrage in the Duchies, and Federal reform. On June 16th Prussia declared war on Austria and Italy four days later did the same.

Opinion as to the outcome of the war was to prove very wide of the mark. In France, popular favour ran to Prussia, but Napoleon expected a long war ending in the victory of Austria and an Italian conquest of Venetia, leaving France the arbiter of Europe. In England, it was believed that Italy would defeat Austria but that Prussia would be beaten. The Italians were very confident. Their fleet, especially in ironclads, was more powerful than that of Austria and her new conscript army far outnumbered the force which a divided Austria could bring against her. The army of nearly a quarter of a million men was divided into three groups. In the north, around Como, was Garibaldi with 30,000 volunteers, with much the same task as in 1859, to overrun the Tyrol and Trentino. Along the Mincio lay the main army under the King and La Marmora (who was now replaced as Premier by Ricasoli) numbering 130,000 men, while at right angles to this force along the valley of the Po, Cialdini commanded an army of 70,000 ready to advance into Venetia. Though of imposing proportions the Italian army was weak in the higher branches of staff work and intelligence: the quality of the conscripts was untested, and above all, it lacked unity of command. The relations between the two commanders was so delicately adjusted that La Marmora could give no orders to Cialdini but only invite him to alter his dispositions. The Austrian army under the Archduke Albert numbered 130,000, but from this the fortress garrisons and troops to keep order had to be deducted, and it is doubtful if he had even half the strength of the force opposed to him.

On June 24th, four days after the declaration of war, the main Italian army advanced in seven columns to the Mincio. No opposition was expected for they believed the Austrians to be behind the Adige, whereas the previous day the Archduke had advanced his main force and seized the high ground of Sommacampagna, and now occupied a strong, compact, crescent-shaped front of fifteen kilometres, with ninety thousand men. Thus in the second battle of Custoza the role of the two armies was exactly reversed, the Austrians defending the high ground above and beyond the river, while the Italians attacked; whereas in 1848 it was the Austrians who attacked and the Italians who defended. In both the Austrians were the victors. The difficulties of the terrain made a simultaneous advance of the Italian columns impossible, and the Austrians, with the advantage of fighting on interior lines, which largely discounted the enemy's superior numbers, and in a position overlooking his advance, were enabled to deal with his columns in detail. The fighting lasted all day, but La Marmora's failure to exploit his numerical superiority and to bring his reserves into action at the right time and place, made it possible for the Archduke to have local superiority wherever it was needed. In the evening after long hours of confused fighting the Italians withdrew across the river. The Italians lost about 8,000 men; half of them prisoners, with 700 killed and over 3,000 wounded. The Austrians lost more killed and wounded but only 1,000 were taken prisoner.

Custoza was neither a victory nor a defeat, for the Austrians made no attempt to cross the Mincio in force, but its effects were a moral disaster for Italy, and a striking example of incompetent leadership. Owing to defective intelligence work the vigorous Austrian defence had all the elements of surprise. Early in the engagement one Italian division gave way badly, and as they streamed back to the bridge where the King and La Marmora were posted, the latter seems to have lost his head and believed the whole army was in retreat. At midday he left Valeggio and galloped twenty miles to Goito looking for reserves to cover the retirement. Corps and divisional commanders were left without orders or directions, and knew nothing of what was taking place elsewhere. For most of the day the army fought on the initiative of individual commanders. Cialdini received no word of what was happening until he heard that the army was in full retreat and was urged to fall back on Modena to protect the capital. Not content with recrossing the Mincio La Marmora fell back to Cremona and took up a defensive position behind the Oglio. This ended the first phase of the campaign. In the meanwhile everything went well for Prussia and on July 3rd came the great victory of Sadowa which decided the war. The Archduke Albert with the bulk of his forces was hastily recalled and unable to defend Venetia Austria prepared to surrender it to France for restitution to Italy. By this time the Italian army had rallied. La Marmora resigned his command and Cialdini replaced him and the army crossed the Po and without opposition occupied Padua and Vicenza and by July 25th the whole force was pressing steadily forwards.

Custoza was a cruel blow to Italy but the country had still hopes of a great naval victory which would offset the military failure. The fleet was at Taranto, where Admiral Persano was still making ready to put to sea. Urged to take action, he steamed up the coast to Ancona and awaited further reinforcements. Here he remained at anchor until peremptory orders, coupled with the threat of replacing him, brought in person by Depretis, the Minister of Marine, forced him to put to sea with the intention of seizing the strongly defended island of Lissa. News of the attack on Lissa reached the Austrian Admiral Tegethof, at Pola, by telegraph. Tegethof was a Dane and a bold sailor, he at once put to sea and aware of his inferiority in gun power and armour gave orders to use the ram if possible. Persano was still engaged in bombarding Lissa when the approach of the Austrian fleet was signalled. He drew up his ships in a double line broadside on to the enemy, and at the last moment left his flagship, the *Re d'Italia*, and went on board the turretship *Affondatore*, without apprising the fleet of his change of ship. The orders of the Austrian admiral were carried out. With Tegethof on his flagship, the *Max*, leading, the fleet broke the Italian line, flung it into confusion, and in the mêlée that followed the *Max* rammed and sank the *Re d'Italia* with the loss of over four hundred of her crew. Another Italian ironclad, the *Palestro*, was rammed, set on fire, and blew up. No Austrian ship was lost. The main action lasted about an hour, after which the two fleets disengaged and Tegethof, having steamed right through the Italian lines, reformed his ships between Lissa and the adjacent island of Lesina. But Persano made no attempt to renew the battle and retired to Ancona, where a few days later the *Affondatore* sank at her moorings. In spite of the equivocal character of Persano's first despatches, which seemed to imply a victory, the truth was soon known and with a sense of bitter humiliation Italy realized that, like Custoza, Lissa was a national disaster. Persano was afterwards tried for cowardice and incompetence. Though exonerated from the first charge he was dismissed the service without pension, and ended his days dependent on the King's generosity. Custoza and Lissa were closely parallel. In both there was superiority in numbers rendered useless by incompetence in the higher command. Lissa was fought on July 20th and on the 26th Bismarck, ignoring the terms of the alliance, signed an armistice with Austria without consulting his ally. Austria at once reinforced her Italian front with all available troops and Cialdini found himself facing three hundred thousand men. Unsupported by Bismarck Italy had to submit. The Trentino was evacuated, and Venetia, handed over to France, was retroceded to Italy at second hand.[18]

Defeated on land and sea, 1866 was a black year for the national pride of Italy. She strove to forget her wounded spirit in an outburst of rejoicing for the recovery of Venetia and the restoration of the iron crown of Lombardy which the Emperor returned to Victor Emanuel. But even so her troubles were not ended. In September rebellion broke out in Palermo and for six days the city was in the hands of the mob. The mania for immediate unification regardless of the deep-seated mode of life of the people, which characterized Italian legislation during these years, was disastrous in Sicily. The new provincial system upset the traditional economy of the island: hatred of conscription drove the peasants to the hills as brigands, whilst the wholesale dissolution of the convents and monasteries outraged the religious bond which still existed between the Church and the people. Poverty, ignorance and superstition played their inevitable part and the familiar methods of insurrection provided the means of rebellion. Troops had to be poured into the island, a military régime set up and the miserable tale of executions, imprisonments and repression, repeated once more. It was a tragic ending to a disastrous year relieved only by the final solution of the problem of Venice and her return at last to Italy. It was a great compensation, but the methods by which it was achieved gave small cause for satisfaction.

CHAPTER TEN

ROME AT LAST, 1866-1870

THE Peace of Prague which ended the war of 1866 left Italy in a very similar position to that in which she found herself after Villafranca in 1859. She had won Venice, as she had previously won Lombardy, by the help of an ally stronger than herself; but just as Napoleon had left Mantua and Peschiera in Austria's hands, giving her direct access to her lost province, so now the lack of support from Prussia left Italy once again in a weak strategic position which imperilled her safety and made her task in 1915 one of enormous difficulty. It was the policy of Bismarck, once Austria was defeated, to avoid creating a spirit of *revanche* and to give the defeated enemy as generous terms as possible. So he gave Italy no support over the Tyrol or the Trentino and allowed Austria, not only to retain both, but to secure a strategic frontier which dominated the entire boundary of northern Italy. With the deep wedge of the Trentino on the west, and Istria and the valley of the Isonzo in her hands, Austria threatened the Venetian plain and the Po valley from east and west, while her possession of the commanding ridges from Monte Nevoso to the Brenner gave her an almost impregnable southern frontier. It was not, however, until fifty years had passed that the strategic weakness of her northern boundary became a national danger to Italy.

The recovery of Venetia left Italy with her last problem, Rome, and in December 1866, in accordance with the terms of the September Convention, the last French troops left the city and Italy became responsible for safeguarding the Papal frontier. The wolves were set to guard the fold. Rome, however, was not undefended. To keep internal order the Pope had been permitted to enroll an army of thirteen thousand men, commanded by General Kanzler. Part of this force, the Papal Zouaves, were recruited from all over Europe. In addition, Napoleon had sanctioned the formation of a body of French troops known as the Légion d'Antibes. Such a force was capable of repelling incursions by volunteer bands but could offer no serious resistance to the Italian army. It was hardly to be expected that Garibaldi and the Party of Action would respect the new situation for very long, and an unauthorized attempt on Rome was regarded almost as inevitable. Ricasoli must have been well aware of this danger, and in

order to forestall it he determined once more to endeavour to come
to an understanding with the Vatican. He had resigned the premiership in 1862 after the failure of his first effort at conciliation, Rattazzi
had followed him and Aspromonte had followed Rattazzi. The same
series of events were now to be repeated, with Mentana replacing
Aspromonte.

Ricasoli was profoundly distressed over the widening breach
between Italy and Rome. He was a religious man, and realized how
deep were the roots of the Catholic Faith in the country, and he was
determined that, if generous concessions would win over Rome to
work with, not against, the new Kingdom, he would make them.
As a preparatory step he sent to Rome the Councillor of State,
Tonello, nominally to arrange for the appointment of bishops to the
vacant sees, but in reality to open the political question. In the meantime he prepared his Free Church Bill. The mission of Tonello met
with small success. Agreement was effected in the appointment of
fourteen bishops but all idea of co-operation between the two Powers,
Rome summarily rejected. Then Ricasoli brought forward his Bill.
It was Cavourian in principle, embodying the separation of Church
and State on the basis of mutual freedom. The State would surrender
the *exequatur* and the *placet*, giving Rome complete liberty in the
appointment of bishops.[19] He offered to put the sale of the Church
lands into the hands of the Episcopacy who were to hand over a
stipulated proportion to the State. The Church was to be disestablished
but to possess a freedom such as it possessed in no other country in
Europe. This implied that the first clause in the Constitution, personally insisted upon by Charles Albert in 1847, that the religion of the
State was 'Catholic, Roman and Apostolic', was to be abrogated.
When these views became known the opposition in the Chamber
became intense. The policy of surrender infuriated the anti-clericals
as much as the separation of Church and State offended the Vatican.
It was quickly obvious that the Bill was doomed, and Ricasoli, realizing
the strength of the opposition, induced the King to dissolve Parliament. The new elections were fought with unusual bitterness. Garibaldi was brought in to make speeches in Venetia, where he
denounced Pope and priests with all his accustomed vehemence.
Ricasoli might have known that with the hopelessly narrow franchise
the country had no chance of expressing its opinion. The elections
were in the hands of the sitting members, the prefects, who took their
orders from the Home Office, and the civil service, and with the
weight of the Church thrown against him, the result was a foregone

conclusion. The new Chamber proved as adverse to the Bill as its predecessor and Ricasoli, in despair of passing it, resigned. The King, as five years before, nominated R1ttazzi as his successor (April 1867).

Rattazzi's third and last premiership was no more fortunate for the country than those which preceded it. The Cabinet, composed of new men of no outstanding quality, was completed by the middle of April. Rattazzi himself held the critical office, that for Home Affairs, and the Marquis Visconti-Venosta, the ambassador at Constantinople, was destined for the Foreign Office, but the brief duration of the Ministry prevented his arriving in time to take part in it. The Cabinet, however, contained one straightforward member not afraid to speak his mind, General Genova di Revel, the younger brother of the old leader of the Right in the Piedmontese Parliament. We get an insight into the general situation and the official attitude of the government in an order issued by General Revel to the Commandants at Florence and Naples on April 16th.

This Ministry is informed that the insurrectionary party may be preparing attempts at invasion in the territories still subject to Rome. Your Excellency is therefore warned to make such dispositions that, if such attempts materialize, they shall be stopped at all costs, it being the firm intention and duty of the Government scrupulously to respect the Convention of September 1864. I believe it opportune to add that, one of the means by which the individuals of this party hope to facilitate the execution of their plans, is to get the idea circulated and believed that the Government, although declaring that it is hostile to their designs, is secretly in favour of them. It is therefore necessary that the Commandants and officers under Your Excellency's command should be warned of this, so as not to be deceived: rather, if such rumours circulate it will be necessary to trace their origin in order to discover the true agents of the party. This Ministry likewise warns V.E.* as to the need for careful disposition of the troops guarding the frontier, for it might happen that individuals of this party, having created some disturbance within the Papal boundary, should then appeal to our troops to intervene. The commanding officers on the frontier should be warned against this trick, since on no account are they to cross the boundary.   * V.E. = Vostra Excellenza.

This correct official attitude was unfortunately undermined by an unofficial attitude, inspired or winked at by Rattazzi himself, which before long created an impossible situation between the army and the volunteers, which reduced the frontier guard to an ineffective demonstration.

The Convention of September provided this solitary satisfaction, that there were now no foreign troops in Italy; but it denied her any opportunity of profiting thereby to complete her unity, for she must now keep herself and every one else from touching the sacred ground of the Papal territory. There was, of course, an underlying plan of campaign, to provoke a revolution in Rome and then occupy it to restore order; the same method as Cavour employed unsuccessfully at Naples in 1860, for the 'Cavourian tradition', which still inspired the government, included the bad side as well as the good of their model, though they failed to improve on the one or to emulate successfully the other. The new responsibilities of the government produced, however, no weakening or change of plan in the two men from whose influence most danger was to be anticipated, Garibaldi and Mazzini. Both were set on going to Rome with or without the government, but their purposes in so doing were different. Mazzini, who had now gone back to an uncompromising republicanism, full of contempt and bitterness towards Napoleon and Victor Emanuel alike, meant Rome to be the springboard for the declaration of a republic; Garibaldi, whose simple directness of temperament saw no further than cutting the Gordian knot of the political *imbroglio* by direct action, wished to leave all political issues aside until Rome belonged to Italy, and refused to take what Mazzini termed 'the republican initiative'. This divergence of view is made clear in their correspondence.

In a letter dated the 10th of June, 1867, Mazzini writes, 'Garibaldi, one thing Italy demands from you and me before we die: and it is a republican initiative. This we must give to Italy from Rome. You are a Roman general, but republican, and charged to hold high the banner of the Republic. I was a triumvir. Neither you nor I have surrendered: we have the right and duty to continue 1849'; and Garibaldi answers, 'I think we ruin the Roman affair by imposing a political programme. Let the child be born; once born it will be baptized and we will baptize it. The urge to-day is to ruin the Papal Government. Let us both then work together to that end.' The same note is struck in other letters of Mazzini written at this time. To the 'brothers at Genoa,' he says, 'for us republicans to carry the monarchy of Custoza and Lissa to the Campidoglio, is, in truth, too much', and to his emissary at Turin, 'I work now only for the Republic. If the Piedmontese understood their mission they would unite with me to begin the republican initiative from Rome. To-day 150,000 lire would ensure it.' Money, as usual, is the crying need, and in an unexpected appeal to Bismarck, he raises his terms for services yet to be rendered though he can offer no security. 'I abhor the Emperor', he writes, 'and the supremacy which France exercises in Europe. I believe that an alliance with her against Prussia, to whose victories we owe Venetia, would be a crime that would stain our young Italian banner. I think that there is need for a strategic alliance between Prussia and our Party of Action. The Prussian Government must furnish us with two million lire and two thousand needle guns. I pledge myself, on my honour, with such means to destroy every possibility of alliance between Italy and the Emperor, and to ruin the government if it persists.' It was a dangerous propaganda. The House of Savoy had already its enemies and the next few months would increase them. The scandal of the King's private life, the hated veto of Napoleon and the reputed subservience of the King, did little to strengthen the House of Savoy on the throne of Italy and of the many seeds sown haphazard by Mazzini some were sure to germinate.

The opening session of the new Chamber, which lasted until the beginning of August, was chiefly occupied with finance. The army estimates and the problems connected with the sale of Church property involved in the dissolution of the monasteries, being the principal subjects of discussion. Revel, the Minister for War, was forced to reduce his estimates from 150 million lire, his original minimum, to 134, and the State finally undertook the sale of ecclesiastical property. It was not long, however, before the volunteer movement began to attract attention. During this summer of 1867 Rome was crowded with foreign clergy and delegates assembled to celebrate the eighteenth centenary of the martyrdom of S. Peter and S. Paul, and the occasion was used by Garibaldi for a violent attack on the Church, this 'nest of vipers' as he termed Rome, which he declared his intention of cleansing. There were hundreds of volunteers only waiting for the word as to when and where to assemble, and the encouragement given in the speeches of Garibaldi and the clear indication of his intention to march on Rome, began the process. In the middle of June some two hundred young men were assembled at Terni where a deposit of arms was stored. It was discovered by the military, the arms were seized, and though the volunteers quickly dispersed, seventy-two were arrested. Almost at the same time great excitement was caused and given excessive prominence in the Press, over a visit of a prominent French general, Dumont, to Rome, where at the request of the Papal authorities he inspected the Légion d'Antibes. This action by a highly placed officer, retaining his status as a general of the French regular army, was a bad diplomatic blunder, for it thereby recognized the national character of the Legion as part of the French army, and in so doing violated the terms of the Convention of September.

In response to questions in the Chamber Rattazzi replied that the government had protested to Paris regarding the general's action: France, he said, had recognized the irregularity of such conduct and had promised to remedy it, declaring, however (to escape its own responsibility) that the general had gone to Rome on his own initiative, without any mandate from the government, having imprudently acquiesced in the request of the Roman authorities. The French government had, moreover, admitted that such an action was not consonant with the loyal and absolute execution of the Convention. This incident, Rattazzi added, should make Italy more than ever careful to avoid any infringement of the Convention, and the government was determined to do so. 'It is necessary', he concluded, 'that from this bench there should be a solemn, authoritative, pronouncement that those who impute to the government a secret connivance with any attempt on Roman territory, not only speak falsely but do the greatest injury to the government of the country.' The discussion which followed closed with the acceptance of the Cavourian maxim that Italy must go to Rome, but by moral means, a method which the Left was at the time doing its best to replace by a volunteer expeditionary force under the command of Garibaldi.

The firm statement of Rattazzi, that the government was determined to uphold the terms of the Convention, backed as it was by the arrest of the seventy-two volunteers, calmed their ardour for a time, and during the summer there was a marked cessation of their activity. But below the surface an organization was at work, a repetition of that which preceded the expedition of Garibaldi and the Thousand in 1860. At the head of it, as before, was Crispi, Garibaldi's organizing brain, together with Bertani and others of the same stamp. The Deputies of the Left were, of course, in sympathy, and when the Chamber rose at the beginning of August, they departed to their constituencies full of ardour for the volunteer movement. It was just another conspiracy to force the hands of the government, but even more elaborate and successful than before, though the outcome was otherwise. More important than the help of individual deputies was that of the permanent officials, in whose hands was the real power. Two of these, Monzani, the secretary-general for the Home Office, the senior permanent official under Rattazzi himself, and Melegari, who held a similar post at the Ministry of Marine, were ardent Garibaldini. It was Monzani from whom the prefects, sub-prefects and the officials of the railways and telegraphs took their orders, and received promotion or dismissal, and his word was law. From Melegari went orders to all harbour and dockyard officials, and these two played a vital part in subsequent events.

In August the volunteer movement began in earnest on both sides of the border. There was already a national committee in Rome working for a revolution from within and at Rattazzi's personal request a Major Ghirelli had been given a year's leave and sent to Rome to form a Roman Legion to start it. There were committees all over the country, protected by the Deputies of the Left, enrolling volunteers, collecting arms and munitions. The Prefects and railway officials were under orders from Monzani to provide free transport and passes to volunteers. Secret deposits of arms were established both on the frontier and in Roman territory. As to Garibaldi, he did as he pleased. 'Italy is made', wrote Revel, the one man in the Cabinet with a mind of his own, 'but can this be called a state when it lacks a government superior to the individuals within it? Here is Garibaldi, a Deputy who will not take the oath, a citizen who gives no heed to the laws. We have reached a point when a private individual can do as he likes, can prepare a war against a neighbouring state which the government has pledged itself to respect! Is this a government?'

The first week in September Garibaldi suddenly left Italy for the Peace Conference at Geneva. He was hardly a success, he was hissed, according to Revel. A week later he was back in Italy, now determined to push matters to extremes and planning to join the volunteers at the frontier.[20] The moment was critical and at a Cabinet meeting Revel proposed boldly to arrest him. The members hesitated, dreading the unpopularity of such an action, but in a talk afterwards with Revel, Rattazzi agreed. Revel had everything ready and Garibaldi was arrested in bed at Sinalunga on his way to Terni. He was taken to Alessandria, then to Genoa and finally deposited once more under naval guard at Caprera. The whole proceedings were more like a triumphal journey than an arrest. At every stop functionaries of all kinds and groups of enthusiastic volunteers were on the platform to greet him. At Alessandria Garibaldi addressed the crowd, and he wrote to Crispi that if he had but said the word the whole garrison would have followed him to a man. The tactful conduct of Captain Incisa of the *Esploratore*, who transferred him from Genoa to Caprera, prevented trouble at the port, helped by Garibaldi himself, who assured the crowd that he was returning of his own freewill and not under compulsion.

The temporary absence of Garibaldi made little difference to the general progress of the volunteer movement, now left in charge of his son Menotti. The method was simple and effective. The volunteers arrived at the frontier unarmed, and were thus free from interference by the troops on guard. They then crossed the boundary and were armed and organized into bands at one of the secret stores of arms, or else crossed by night in an unguarded spot with arms already provided on Italian soil. The first band crossed on September 28th, four days after Garibaldi's arrest. There was little co-ordination and isolated groups of volunteers skirmished with the Papalini without any effective result throughout the first half of October.

Up to the end of September the policy of Rattazzi, at least outwardly, had been loyal to the Convention, though there was always an underlying suspicion of his possible duplicity amongst those who knew him best. On the 21st an article had appeared in the Official Gazette warning the public that if any tried to violate the frontier, and thus infringe the country's pledged word, the Ministry would not allow it; and three days later it announced the arrest of Garibaldi as a proof of its determination to do its duty. But the first week in October Rattazzi changed direction. He was politically dependent on the support of the Left, and the influence of Crispi over him was strong. Equally so was that of his own wife, formerly Marie de Solms, a distant cousin of Napoleon's and a well-known romantic writer. She urged him on to rival Cavour and he was not averse. After the arrest of Garibaldi, in Rattazzi's absence from home, his house was violently attacked, one of the guards killed and two wounded. This too had happened to Cavour. Then came a letter from Garibaldi to Crispi, passed on doubtless to Rattazzi, in which he said, 'I see but one way to satisfy the nation. To invade Rome with the Italian army and at once. I will pardon the misery of Italy but not its degradation, and to-day not only the nation but the army feels outraged. Let the government consider this and it will be persuaded that a few days of energy will settle everything and satisfy the entire nation, and if there are threats from abroad of stopping us, the very women and children will rise and the world will see a revolution of a people such as it has never seen yet.' Perhaps this was the final straw; anyway on October 6th Crispi entered in his diary, 'Rattazzi enters into the system', and the same day in a letter of Dina to Castelli, he says, 'It is the policy *à la* Cavour. Rattazzi has assured me that he will

intervene at Rome. I hope he means it.' There was no more interference with the volunteers. Revel himself saw on Rattazzi's desk a
demand for free transport for six hundred volunteers from Genoa to
Terni, signed by the Director General of Public Security.

After the attack on Rattazzi's house the Court became alarmed,
demanding the concentration of cavalry and artillery in the capital.
But Revel had no opinion of the bellicose temper of the Florentines
and calmed the Court, but he gave exact orders to the four battalions
as to their actions at the first sign of disturbance. Nevertheless the
public agitation grew. The Press were in the van. The journals were
full of accounts of insurrections in the Papal States repressed by the
Zouaves, which were inventions to disturb the country. 'All lies!
Revolutionary inventions!' wrote Revel. Before the situation grew
worse Rattazzi made a final effort to induce the Papacy to give way.
The Canon Ortalda went to Rome with a letter written by Revel.
The government, he said, would leave the Pope Rome and Civitavecchia: would take over the public debt: and guarantee tranquillity
by occupying the provinces. It was quite useless, the Canon obtained
nothing. On October 17th Revel and Rattazzi had a private audience
with the King. The outcome was a telegram to Count Nigra, Italian
Ambassador at Paris, ordering him to go at once to Napoleon at
Biarritz and expose the situation. The government, he was to say,
could no longer control the situation. They proposed to enter the
provinces, to disarm the volunteers, restore tranquillity and respect
the Papal independence. They would not enter either Rome or
Civitavecchia unless requested so to do by the Roman government.
Afterwards the troops would be withdrawn. Revel then explained
that he had already given all the necessary military orders to carry out
these arrangements at the shortest notice. It happened that the same
evening there was a Cabinet meeting. Rattazzi asked Revel to
explain his proposals. He did so. His scheme was rejected, and he
then and there resigned and left the room. This ruined the Ministry,
and on the receipt two days later of threatening despatches from Paris,
the Cabinet resigned in a body (October 19th).

Events now moved with startling rapidity. The country was without a government and while Cialdini tried unsuccessfully to form
a Cabinet, Garibaldi acted. The same day that Rattazzi resigned,
evading the naval patrols, he escaped to the mainland and on the
22nd appeared at Florence. All attempts on the part of Crispi and his
friends to restrain him were useless, and that same day he went
through by train to the frontier. Official attempts to stop him failed

completely, the telegrams being obviously delayed on purpose until his train had passed through. The next day he crossed the frontier at Porto Carese with seven thousand men. The one chance of a successful occupation of Rome by Italy in 1867, lay in a spontaneous and effective rising within the city. Had the Romans revealed the same spirit as the Palermitans of 1860, Rome might have been won with the tacit consent of Napoleon. But nothing was less calculated to inspire such a movement than the presence of Garibaldi as the *deus ex machina*. In 1860 at Palermo Garibaldi was a legend, an invincible fate. Did he not shake the Bourbon bullets, unharmed, from his poncho? Besides, the Palermitans had a real hatred of their government, a rebellious spirit, and an effective technique of street fighting. Rome was profoundly different. For centuries the Romans had lived in the ambit of Papal influence and had, as it were, absorbed a clerical mentality. Their interests, their amusements and recreations, were based on ecclesiastical functions, and they loved the pomp and circumstance of Catholic ritual. Their gossip circled round the intrigues of the Papal court, their scandal was ripe with the reputed peccadilloes of Canons and Cardinals. The Church amused them, employed them and fed them, and to her they looked alike for consolation in trouble and material help in times of stress. They were, moreover, fond of Pio Nono, and if they were jealous of their right to criticize the Papacy, this was merely the obverse of their devotion. Self-contained, unambitious, content with their government of priests, proud of their unique city, they asked for no more than to be left alone. What support were such a people likely to give to Garibaldi, with his flaming denunciations of the Papacy, his hatred of priests and monks, who described the Eternal City as a 'tank full of vipers'?

Nevertheless, on the night of the 22nd an attempt to master the city was made. A bomb blew up part of the Zouaves' barracks: a gate was seized, and if the people had risen success might have been achieved. But they did not. Kanzler recaptured the gate, quelled the few demonstrations, and restored order. The next day there was a partial rising in the Trastevere, always the storm centre of the city, but it came to nothing. The same night a small detachment of Garibaldini, led by two of the devoted Cairoli brothers, both of whom were killed, attempted to bring a boatload of arms to the city by water; but they waited at the appointed place in vain. They retired to the villa Glori where they were attacked and the survivors dispersed. So ended the revolt of Rome. Garibaldi, undeterred by the Roman fiasco, pressed on. On the 25th he captured Monte Rotondo, but it was expensive and delayed him longer than he could afford. The next day he was within a few miles of the city but here his advance stopped. It was impossible to seize Rome without artillery and with but a few thousand tired and wayworn troops. He decided to make for Tivoli where he hoped to be joined by Nicotera. The decision was fatal. The Garibaldini always went forward not back. Demoralization set in: the troops began to slip away. Two thousand, it was said, disbanded before he reached Mentana on the 27th. Here he was trapped by the Papalini, supported by the French, across whose front he had to march to reach Tivoli. There is one force more powerful than patriotism, religious fanaticism; the power that Cromwell evoked to crush the gallant cavaliers of Charles I. These Papal forces were of this type. Moved by devotion to their faith, the main body of the Zouaves had come from Ireland and Canada, from Belgium and Spain and France, to defend the Pope. They fought with staunch determination, as did the Garibaldini, but the latter were no longer flushed with victory and they lacked the genius of the old leadership, for neither Garibaldi nor his volunteers were of quite the same stamp as the heroes of the Thousand. As evening fell the defeat of Garibaldi was complete. He left the field with his scattered forces and recrossed the frontier where he was arrested and sent back to Caprera.

The failure of the rising in Rome, whose success might have induced Napoleon to let things take their course, and the incursion of Garibaldi in flagrant contempt of the Convention of September, decided the Emperor on action. He had hesitated long, but the day before Mentana the French troops at last sailed from Toulon. The pride of Victor Emanuel was roused, and he telegraphed that if they landed in Italy the royal army would cross the frontier, and at the information of their disembarkation at Civita Vecchia the Italians occupied Viterbo and Velletri. The French troops reached Rome on October 30th. The Italian action was but a gesture. Two days before General Menabrea had formed a new Cabinet. He had no sympathy with Garibaldi's action. He refused to allow any more volunteers to cross the border, confiscated supplies, and on the 31st recalled the Italian troops from Papal territory. There was to be no war with France. The bitterness felt at Garibaldi's defeat was intensified by the tactless boast of the French commander that 'the *chassepots* had done marvels', and the subsequent debate in the French Chamber, which upheld the action of the government, coupled with Rouher's grandiloquent *'jamais'*, that the Italians should *never* get Rome, added anger to humiliation. Mentana cancelled all Italy's gratitude for what the

Emperor had done for her in 1859 and almost with a sense of shame, the country realized its weakness and inability to defy the dictation of its powerful neighbour.

When the excitement over Mentana died down and the hopes of Rome faded, the country turned back wearily to the chronic struggle with the financial deficit. The new Premier, Menabrea, a distinguished engineer, had been one of the reactionary stalwarts of the old Piedmontese Right. At the time of Cavour's formation of his centre party, Menabrea had accused him of wishing to 'sail to other shores' and had received the reply that the new party had no such intentions but they intended to sail 'in the direction of the prow not of the poop'. Menabrea was still a rigid conservative and his Ministry gave Italy her first lesson in restricted liberty. His first Cabinet did not last long. After a month of furious debates arising out of Mentana and the policy of Rattazzi's government, the Chamber gave him a vote of confidence by only two votes and he resigned. He then remodelled the Cabinet which held on its troubled course until December 1869. The new Finance Minister, Cambray-Digny, was bent on economy. He farmed out the State Tobacco Monopoly for a hundred and fifty millions in cash, and at last imposed the much debated and greatly hated grist-tax, an excise on all corn that passed through the mill. By such means the increase in debt was checked but the State was still far from establishing an equilibrium.

Whilst the Chamber wrestled with the financial problem the more moderate opinion in the country, both in Parliament and outside it, was seriously concerned by the danger to Italy's reputation for trustworthiness, revealed by the conduct of government officials in the events which culminated in Mentana. In this Menabrea fully agreed, and promptly exposed what had taken place by the publication of a long series of telegrams received or sent by officials in the critical months of 1867. The revelation was disturbing. Public money, naval stores, rifles and ammunition, the free use of trains and telegraph, had been put without stint at the service of the volunteers, while at the same moment the government was loudly expressing its determination to uphold the nation's honour by the firm maintenance of the obligations involved in the Convention of September. Equally prejudicial to the best interest of the Kingdom had been the attitude of the Press, which, carried away by the publicity value of an attack on Rome by Garibaldi, and ignorant or indifferent to the pledge to protect the Papal frontier, as well as to the international dangers involved, had systematically published all the baseless rumours best calculated to excite public opinion. 'Is there a journal', wrote Revel, 'that openly defends our political loyalty to treaties? Not one.' The whole business was thoroughly discreditable. Ministers, deputies, permanent officials, were alike implicated, and the reaction against this abuse of liberty was a healthy sign, but it could not disguise the fact that the national conscience had not yet grasped the conception of national honour as the first charge on government action. The policy of repression which followed, the Press prosecutions and the police inquisitions, the confiscation of documents and the dissolution of democratic societies, did not, however, commend itself to the best elements in the country. They probably knew that the real culprits went unscathed. However, if the means employed were to be condemned, as they certainly were, they at least made it clear that the end, the possession of Rome, was one which in one way or another the country was determined to realize.

It was here that Menabrea was weak. He showed an almost complete indifference to the Roman question and certainly would not have allowed it to become either a cause of internal agitation or even of diplomatic protest. Perhaps he shared the curious idea of Ricasoli who, at one time, thought of using Rome (when they entered it) as a kind of capital *emerita*, for use on state occasions, whilst the government of the country was carried on from Florence. What finally ruined the Ministry, however, was not Rome but the scandal which arose over the farming out of the Tobacco Monopoly. Shares in the bank which found the money for the government became a very profitable investment, and the Right was openly charged by a deputy of the Left, Lobbia, of speculating in them. Both Ministers and members were accused of being implicated and the royal family itself was not exempted. A few days later Lobbia was found stabbed. The inference was obvious, and though Menabrea fought off the charges for a time, the reputation of the Ministry was ruined and in December 1869 Menabrea resigned.

The appointment of his successor was a matter of more than usual difficulty. The generally accepted candidate was Giovanni Lanza, an opponent of Menabrea whose election as President of the Chamber by forty votes over the government nominee had been the immediate cause of Menabrea's resignation. Lanza was a Piedmontese of the old school whose parliamentary experience dated back for twenty years. A doctor by profession, neither brilliant nor wealthy, whose reputation for sterling honesty was his principal asset, he was acceptable to the moderates on both sides of the Chamber. The difficulty arose with the King, who had a partiality for Ministers drawn from the Court circle, so that he himself was kept in close touch with policy. Menabrea, for example, was a personal A.D.C. to the King and the two most prominent members of his late Cabinet, Cambray-Digny and the Marquis Gualterio, were respectively Grand Master of Ceremonies and Minister of the Royal Household. Lanza came from another stratum of society, whose wife, in reply to his letter announcing that the King had offered him the premiership, could write from her farm in the historic village of Roncaglia, where once Frederic Barbarossa parleyed with the rebellious communes, 'The stock is increased by a fine bull calf. The vinegar is made. The white wine is turned and I do not think it will be necessary to turn it again as it is very sweet.' The King offered Lanza the Presidency of a Coalition Cabinet to include the three ex-ministers mentioned. He not only refused but demanded the dismissal of all three ex-ministers from their Court appointments as a necessary condition of forming a new Cabinet. He did not intend to have a *camarilla* hostile to him at Court. The struggle was prolonged but Lanza was victorious. The ex-ministers withdrew from Court and Lanza formed his Cabinet, with Sella as Finance Minister and Visconti Venosta at the Foreign Office, while he himself took charge of the Ministry for Internal Affairs.

Once again the first place had to be given to rigid economy, Lanza pledging himself that all public grants should be expended 'with the parsimony of a miser', while Sella, not to be outdone, promised that all expenses should be 'cut to the bone'. It was their joint opinion that the country could stand no more taxation, and they relied for economy chiefly on a ruthless cutting down of the Army and Navy Estimates. The Ministry had hardly settled down, however, before the country was upset by a scattered series of futile outbreaks. It was Mazzini's last effort before the winning of Rome robbed him of his principal weapon against the monarchy. After the conquest of Venice he had started yet another organization, the Universal Republican Alliance, whose objective was Rome, the Trentino and Istria, and of which he wrote, 'The Republic is the word of order for all: Rome the objective: insurrection and national war to the invader, the means'. There were groups of his *affigliati* throughout the country and the republican idea had even penetrated into the army. One of Mazzini's circulars fell into the hands of the government, and thus forewarned, the officials easily controlled the weak efforts of the movement, but at Genoa, Padua, Ravenna and elsewhere attempts were made without the least success. At Pavia a sergeant was killed and two soldiers wounded, and a corporal who had joined the malcontents was tried and shot. In the south trouble was caused by Ricciotti and Menotti Garibaldi, who having obtained a concession from the government for constructing a railway tunnel in Calabria used their isolated situation to stir up republican ardour. It was all very futile and useless, but with the sporadic brigandage still alive in the south and the terrorism which was endemic in the Romagna it revealed a state of unrest which distressed all who had the true interests of the country at heart.

Another source of uneasiness to the Ministry was the Oecumenical Council which met in Rome during the first half of 1870 to promulgate the doctrine of Papal Infallibility. Thoughtful people in Italy feared the extension of the doctrine from spiritual matters to the possession of the Temporal Power, making its retention thereby an article of faith. Lanza sent the Deputy Domenico Berti to Rome to get in touch with the more moderate Bishops and at the same time to keep the Ministry informed of the course of the Council's deliberations. The Dogma, restricted, however, to matters of faith and morals, was promulgated on July 18th and though it raised great controversies throughout Europe, had no direct bearing upon the problem of Rome. There was, nevertheless, a political programme beneath the spiritual surface of the Dogma. Throughout it was the work of the Jesuits who claimed the supreme dominance of the Faith over the State. Infallibility was the consecration of the absolute authority of the Church over Society, involving the subjection of civil and political rights to an infallible Pope. It was a claim in complete contradiction to the system of modern civilization and a challenge to every Catholic State and it did much to sap their resistance to the extinction of the Temporal Power and the entry of Italy into Rome.

Lanza had a desperate struggle over the reduction of the Army Estimates, especially in the Senate, where General Cialdini, voicing not only the opinion of the Generals but also of the King, put up a bitter opposition. He was accused of imperilling the national security, of disorganizing the whole system of national defence and reducing the armed forces of the Kingdom below safety point. Though the Bill was passed, its provisions were never executed, for the outbreak of the Franco-Prussian war in July reversed the whole situation, and before long Lanza had to enlarge instead of reduce the army and, moreover, demand an appropriation of forty millions in excess of his original estimates. In the preceding summer Napoleon had approached both Austria and Italy with the suggestion of a triple alliance. But Menabrea, who was then Premier, had cut short the negotiations by insisting that the settlement made after the war of 1866 should not be disturbed. The Italian government had quickly perceived that Napoleon had a war with Prussia in view, and they were unwilling, as well as unprepared, to fight their former ally. Then came Mentana, which ruined any hope of public support for a French alliance and the subject was dropped.

In May 1870 when war with Prussia was becoming inevitable Napoleon revived the question of a triple alliance. Italy demanded the withdrawal of the French garrison and a free hand with Rome, and the Emperor, still under the clerical influence of the Empress and Grammont, ruined his chance of help from Italy by a refusal; so when the war broke out in July, Italy announced her neutrality. In August when complete disaster threatened, Napoleon made his last bid for Italian help, sending the Prince Napoleon to beg sixty thousand men from the government of his father-in-law. But it was impossible. The scales of victory were already heavily tilted against France. What troops Italy had were on the Roman frontier: her financial condition was parlous, and though the generous heart of Victor Emanuel urged the Ministry to the help of Napoleon, Lanza and Sella were immovable, and the Prince returned empty handed. Not the least curious example of Italian feeling at this time was revealed in the conduct of Mazzini, who reopened his correspondence with Bismarck, this time offering three thousand men to fight for Prussia. A ship was to be sent and the contingent was to be treated as part of the German army. This was in July 1870. An emissary arrived but the negotiations were brief, for the Italian government came into possession of the correspondence. The authorities were warned, and in August Mazzini was arrested at Palermo and interned at Gaeta. Then came the disaster of Sedan and the proclamation of the republic, and Mazzini's three thousand turned Garibaldini and joined the force commanded by Garibaldi in France to fight *against* the Prussians.

On the last day of July the Italian government called up two classes of the army. Two days later word came from France that the government was to recall the Rome garrison at once, and the terms of the Convention of September were to be brought back into force, and Lanza accepted these conditions. On August 10th two more classes were called to the colours and on the 16th Parliament was summoned, having already risen for the summer vacation, and on the

19th the Ministry asked for an extraordinary grant of forty millions. The same day the last French troops sailed for France. By now General Raffaele Cadorna was in command of thirty thousand men on the frontier and the presence of this imposing force guarding the Papal State exasperated the impatient Deputies of the Left and the debate on the forty millions developed into a violent attack on the whole policy of the government. They were accused of betraying the nation, of sacrificing the national aspirations and of using the army as a police force to guard the Pope. 'If *you* will not go to Rome', cried the deputy Mellana, 'at least let *us* go, this attitude of yours thwarts the revolution.' Which was precisely what Lanza intended to do. The speech of the Foreign Secretary, Visconti Venosta, full of discreet reservations, was no help. Finally, after a stormy sitting, Lanza replied, and without disclosing the policy of the Ministry, gave sufficient reassurances of his intention to go to Rome to obtain a vote of confidence by 214 votes against 152.

The policy of Lanza was both wise and prudent. He laid down three necessary pre-conditions before he took action: to prevent any untoward demonstration by the volunteers; to win in advance the consent of Catholic Europe; and by the presence of an overwhelming force to prevent, if possible, any bloodshed. To these might also be added a further effort to induce the Pope to speak the word of peace to Italy. Mazzini was already safely interned at Gaeta. Strict surveillance was ordered regarding Garibaldi, and no laxity was permitted amongst functionaries in the matter of passes and transport to volunteers. There was, Lanza knew, one saving clause in the Convention of September which might give him the opening he required, for it contained a phrase, inserted by Italy and accepted by the Emperor, that 'in the case of extraordinary events both of the contracting parties would resume their freedom of action'. Having scotched as far as might be the danger of extra-legal efforts from within, Lanza on August 29th circulated a memorandum amongst the Powers insisting on the necessity of the immediate occupation of Rome. Four days later the 'extraordinary events' materialized, Sedan, the surrender of Napoleon, and two days later (September 4th) the proclamation of the Republic. The Convention of September was dead and Italy at last had a free hand. But Lanza, cautious as ever, refused to be stampeded. On September 7th he circularized the Powers again, this time giving in outline the steps which the government proposed to take to ensure the freedom and spiritual independence of the Papacy when Rome passed to Italy. At the same time he sent Count Ponza di San Martino with a final appeal to the Pope. The response of the Powers was most gratifying. They were satisfied that the Papal independence would be preserved, and convinced that the occupation of Rome was now inevitable. Not a single Power protested. Spain, Austria, Germany, even France, recognized that the hour had struck for the fall of the Temporal Power and that Rome must be the capital of the new Italy. The Pope, as before, rejected all compromise, he would yield only to force.

This phase coincided with Prince Napoleon's last desperate appeal for help, and the chivalrous nature of Victor Emanuel revolted at the thought that so cold blooded a reason as mere want of money, should prove an insurmountable barrier to giving, to one who had done so much for Italy, the instant help in his hour of need which his generous heart prompted. In his anger and bitterness he turned against Lanza and so strongly and openly did he express his feelings that Lanza sent in his resignation, having, as he said in his letter, 'no longer the heart to remain at the head of the government after the repeated manifestations of the King's distrust and dissatisfaction shown to him both when alone and in the presence of his colleagues'. Victor Emanuel realized his mistake and a reconciliation took place at once and Lanza continued as Premier. The restored relations with the King, the response of Catholic Europe, and the telegrams received from all over Italy urging the government to action, cleared the way for the final operations. On September 11th Cadorna crossed the frontier and on the 19th the army was in position before the city, and a last minute appeal to General Kanzler to avoid bloodshed having been rejected, the next day Cadorna attacked. The artillery breached the walls near the Porta Pia and the troops stormed into the city, but the Zouaves fought with courage and determination and the losses on both sides would have been far heavier had not Kanzler surrendered, in obedience to the orders of the Pope, when honour was satisfied.

Order was quickly restored in the city and at the request of Cardinal Antonelli both the Leonine City and the Castle S. Angelo were occupied by Italian troops. The King did not come at once to Rome but appointed General La Marmora as King's Lieutenant. As soon as possible a plebiscite was held which gave an overwhelming vote for union with Italy, and it is interesting to note that it was taken even in the Vatican itself, which, doubtless, made a handsome contribution to the fifteen hundred negatives which made up the sum total of the opposition. The consolidation of Rome as the capital of Italy was not however accomplished without a period of stress and uneasiness for the government. The bitter complaints and recriminations of the Pope broadcast over the Catholic world produced, as was to be expected, a chorus of protests and appeals against such an outrage.[21] But the Catholic governments were content to await events before contemplating action. The wise and clever policy of Lanza had put them in an awkward position, for not only had they known beforehand the general lines of his policy and had not protested, but he had offered to make the conditions to be established regarding Papal independence a matter of international agreement, recognizing the world-wide interest in the question. Of the alternatives thus offered of either sharing the responsibility or of being in a position to throw all the blame on Italy, they chose the latter, and thus Italy was enabled to arrange matters without foreign interference.

There was great impatience for the official occupation of the national capital. It did not matter, the Deputies declared, if the King had no palace and the Chamber was unfurnished, the essential was to have King and Parliament in Rome. But Lanza insisted on an effective entrance, and would promise no more than that the capital should be transferred within six months. On October 9th the King issued a general amnesty and Mazzini was released with the rest. This was followed by the dissolution of Parliament and a general election and the new Parliament met at Florence on December 5, 1870. Its main task was the settlement of the relations with the Papacy. The Law of Guarantees, promulgated on May 13, 1871, gave to the Papacy full liberty in its spiritual authority and jurisdiction: freedom of communication between Rome and all the members of the Church: liberty of association and reunion: liberty of appointment to all ecclesiastical offices and liberty of teaching. The Pope retained the full prerogatives of sovereignty and received an annual grant of £129,000, a sum equal to that assigned to him in the last Papal budget. He retained, free of all taxation and government interference, the Vatican, S. John Lateran and his Villa at Castel Gandolfo and the buildings hitherto reserved for Councils and Conclaves. Only his summer residence in Rome, the Quirinale, was excepted, for it was chosen as the Residence of the King. Though the Papacy had lost its temporal power, it retained all its spiritual authority and its position as Head of the Catholic Church with its prestige and dignity undiminished, and it was even more fully independent spiritually, freed as it was from the trammels of the civil power.

The weak point in the Law of Guarantees lay in the fact that it was unilateral. The Papacy had no hand in it. The Pope refused to accept or even recognize it. He regarded it as coming from a usurping government. He ignored the annual grant and closed the Vatican, declaring himself a prisoner. Henceforth there was always a doubt on the question of possession. What the State had given it could reclaim, and, in fact, after the death of Pius IX when there was uncertainty as to whether the Conclave would not assemble elsewhere than in Rome, Crispi threatened that if the Vatican was vacated the State would occupy it, which revealed the uncertainty of the Church's tenure. In November the Pope issued a violent protest against the acts of the 'subalpine Government', for he would not even say the word 'Italian', declaring once more that the Temporal Power was essential to the liberty and effective functioning of the Church.

On June 30th the government was transferred to Rome. The Senate was installed in the Palazzo Madama, previously the Roman Custom House, and the Deputies in that of Montecitorio. Two days later Victor Emanuel took up his residence at the Quirinale, and on November 27th Parliament was formally opened by the King. The Risorgimento was over. A new Italy had arisen, free, independent and united, under a constitutional government with her King in the Eternal City. It had taken fifty years to achieve, if we date it from the risings of 1820 to 1821 when both North and South first demanded a Constitution. Nothing is perhaps more remarkable about this long struggle than the pertinacity with which Italy clung to her ideal and the amazing resilience of the national spirit in the face of disappointment, defeat and failure. Every resource was called into action. Poets and writers, politicians and orators, kept alive the struggle even in the darkest hours. The one free Kingdom, Piedmont, found soldiers and statesmen and the royal house for Italy. Led by her Kings she fought and lost and fought again. Conspirators and filibusters, inspired by Mazzini and Garibaldi, with utterly inadequate resources and by the most unprincipled methods, yet filled with the highest aims and the purest spirit of self-sacrifice, flung themselves into the struggle defying governments and armies alike. Every one had to help; France and England and Prussia had all to make their contribution. Exiles carried the cry of liberty and independence across the world, irritating governments, causing trouble everywhere, but never ceasing to protest and conspire. When men were wanted they arrived. Venice found her Manin, Tuscany her Ricasoli, Piedmont her Cavour. Defeats were merely postponements. The whole movement was alive with paradoxes and contradictions. Mazzini quarrelled with Garibaldi and both hated Cavour. Victor Emanuel intrigued with

Mazzini, conspired with Garibaldi and submitted with an ill grace to the genius of Cavour. Yet all were working for the same end. 'With the affection of a son, the faith of a Catholic and the honour of a King' Victor Emanuel despoiled the Pope of Rome, and he meant it all. And yet from Pope and King, from poets and conspirators, from all who fought and struggled and suffered, we seem to hear the same refrain alike in defeat and victory, Italy, my Italy!

CHAPTER ELEVEN

THE NEW ITALY: TO THE FALL OF
CRISPI, 1871-1896

THE occupation of Rome made no change in the government, save that it brought Lanza the Collar of the Annunciata, an honour he would fain have refused from a sense of social inequality, but was persuaded to accept. He remained in office for another two years. Two important measures were introduced in his last period. The first, which was unsuccessful, was a Bill for the reorganization of the Provincial and Communal administration. Ever since the introduction of the centralized system its working had been unsatisfactory. Several tentative efforts had been made to improve it without success. The trouble with the existing system was that nobody would mind their own business. 'We have sixty-eight little Parliaments', wrote the Senator Jacini, an expert on the question, 'called Provincial Councils, which busy themselves with such questions as Garibaldi's Million Rifle Fund, the Tobacco Scandal and the Roman question, and at the same time we have a National Parliament which has the right to occupy itself with the smallest details of local administration'. Lanza's Bill defined their powers and their relations with the central government, and endeavoured to remove the overlapping which everywhere complicated local administration. Unfortunately, there was a political motive at the back of the deputies' determination not to alter the existing system, for since the appointment of the Syndic of the smallest Commune, as of Provincial councillors, depended directly from the Home Office, it was in the interest of individual deputies to get men of the right colour appointed, and this led to perpetual wire pulling, and the Bill was rejected. The other measure was the application of the Law on Religious Corporations to those existing in Rome. It was a thorny question and the cause of strong clerical opposition, but he carried it through and removed one more difficulty from the path of his successors. It was over a financial question that the Ministry was finally defeated in June 1873 and Lanza resigned. He was weary of office and overstrained. Acknowledging the King's acceptance of his resignation he wrote, 'I repeat the words of old Simeon, *Nunc dimitte servum tuum . . .*' and the King replied, 'I fear that in singing the *Nunc Dimittis* you are mixing it with *Alleluias*. My friendship for you, and equally yours for me, will last until the valley of Jehoshaphat.'

The fall of Lanza brought Minghetti once more to power, and his Ministry, the last of the Right, covered the three years from 1873 to 1876. Sella joined it, and together they made a final desperate but successful attack on the adverse balance. Italy was gratified during these years by Victor Emanuel's visit to Vienna and Berlin, which was returned in the autumn of 1875 by Franz Joseph's visit to Venice and that of the German Emperor to Milan, the delicate relations of King and Pope making it inadvisable for either monarch to come to Rome. In March 1876 Minghetti announced the balancing of the budget, but though received with general satisfaction, it was the cause of his fall. Sella had employed the utmost severity in the application of taxation, especially in that of the hated grist tax. If Cambray-Digny had scourged the taxpayers with whips, Sella had chastised them with scorpions and extracted the last ounce of profit for the Exchequer. His methods had disgusted the moderates who withdrew their support, and the Left seized the opportunity for a vote of censure, which was carried, and the Right, after fifteen years of office, was driven from power.

The fall of the Right on the 18th March, 1876, was regarded by the more thoughtful element in the country as little less than a disaster. They embodied an ideal and a tradition which enshrined all that was best in the national thought. None of them since Cavour were great statesmen, but they had united Italy, given her Rome, settled the basis of her new life and set a high personal standard in political life. Their work throughout had been constructive and with the winning of Rome as capital, it was finished. What was now needed was a period of consolidation, of steady government, facing boldly the social problems with which the Right had had no time to deal. Nevertheless, a good beginning had been made, and the fruits of the lavish expenditure after 1860 were beginning to reveal themselves. Railway construction, for instance, had risen from 1,500 kilometres to 6,500, and the trunk lines were almost completed, now stretching from Turin to Brindisi. Fourteen hundred kilometres of new roads, mostly in the south, had been opened. The telegraph service had been twice doubled, and great improvements made in the harbour works at Genoa, Livorno, Naples and Brindisi. Negotiations were on foot for the passage of goods and passenger traffic from central Europe to Brindisi for trade with the East, which, with the opening of the Suez Canal, promised a great future for Italy.

Italy, in fact, was a rapidly changing country. The old mode of life was disappearing and with it the men who had brought about the new nationality. Mazzini died in 1872, saddened at the failure of his republican propaganda and at the inability of the people to rise to the full stature of his lofty moral ideal, haunted by the ever present doubt—

> Are this and this and this the shining ones
> Meet for the Shining City?

Rattazzi died in 1873 and his mantle of leadership of the Left descended on Agostino Depretis. Napoleon III died during the same year. Abroad, Italy's new position was recognized, and her handling of the Roman question generally accepted as wise and generous. As all opposition parties, when power comes within their grasp, the Left had been lavish of promises. Taxation was to be lightened, the grist tax abolished, higher wages and better conditions, a widened franchise, were all, at last, to be realized. When the shock of the fall of the Right was past, there was a wave of hope and enthusiasm for the new government, but it did not last long. On March 28, 1876, the new Cabinet was announced: Depretis, President of the Council and Minister of Finance; Amedeo Melegari, Foreign Affairs; Giovanni Nicotera, the Home Office; and Mancini, Justice, with Giuseppe Zanardelli in charge of Public Works. The record of most of the new government was not reassuring. They were mainly converted Garibaldini nurtured in the creed of conspiracy and extra-legal methods. They had no tradition behind them and lacked any unifying moral principle. The first act of Depretis was to confirm his position by a general election. Giovanni Nicotera, upon whom as Minister for Internal Affairs the working of the election mainly fell, was a violent person of an authoritarian type, perfectly shameless in his application of government pressure to secure a large majority. By threats of dismissal or promises of promotion, or, if necessary, the removal of recalcitrant officials, he obtained a resounding success, four-fifths of the new Chamber professing loyalty to the Left. Lanza was re-elected but Sella and Minghetti were both defeated.

Up till 1876 the two party system, at least in name, had been kept in being, but the Chamber was now inundated with new men, devoid of any political experience and often inspired more by personal aims of advancement or profit than by any sound principles of party loyalty. The election was, in fact, the crucial test of the success or failure of parliamentary government in Italy. Had it resulted in a compact and effective opposition, containing the best elements of the

Right, it would have steadied and restrained all tendencies to violence and disorganization and forced the Cabinet to produce a sound programme. But the best men were defeated and the Right dissolved, and in its place was an unwieldy and unorganized majority, tending at once to split into fragments, which made support and opposition equally incalculable, so that its very success proved a greater embarrassment to the Ministry than the presence of a genuine opposition would have produced. When the Chamber assembled the weakness of the government quickly became apparent, for Depretis not only announced his intention to retain every penny of the revenue, which meant no lightening of taxation, but he failed to produce a definite programme of his own, being content for the most part to carry on with that left-over from the preceding Ministry. Commissions were appointed to deal with the more difficult problems, such as the grist tax; a sliding scale was introduced in the lower categories of the income tax, which gave some relief to those with small incomes; in educational matters, religious instruction was made optional, and school attendance compulsory between the ages of six and nine, which, however, was more honoured in the breach than the observance for many of the smaller communes were quite unable to find the money either to build school houses or to pay for teachers. What credit the Ministry obtained from these reforms was more than outweighed by the public irritation over the restrictive activities of Nicotera. Both Mazzinians and clericals were busy making trouble, both alike working up public feeling against the government, and Nicotera in reply, suppressed newspapers, prohibited public meetings and sent strikers to the penal settlements, with a disregard for the law on liberty of association and free speech which profoundly disturbed the public. When to this was added charges of corruption and of violating the secrecy of the telegraph in the interests of his own newspapers, the Ministry was compelled to resign (December 1877). Depretis was not replaced but reconstructed the Cabinet, substituting Crispi for Nicotera.

The second Ministry of Depretis was scarcely formed when the country was plunged into grief by the almost simultaneous death of Victor Emanuel and Pope Pius IX (January to February 1878). Between the two great protagonists of Italian unity there was a deep personal regard despite the political gulf which separated them. Victor Emanuel had his faults, but he was every inch a King, a born soldier and a loyal friend. His strong political good sense was often a real help to his Ministers, and though his proud nature resented dictation from any one, even Cavour and Ricasoli, whose own strength of character too often clashed with his, bore witness to the King's loyalty and judgement. No greater contrast could well be found, both in appearance and character, than that between Pio Nono and Victor Emanuel. Pius had the good looks and the personal charm which the King lacked. His early liberalism came from his heart not his head, and the Roman Republic of 1849 cured him of it for ever. Moreover, he had men beside him like Cardinal Antonelli, with all the traditional rigidity of Romanism, who saw to it that he never wandered from the narrow path again. The quarrel with Italy was not with the King but with democracy, for the Catholic Church is a hierarchy with a creed of absolutism, and it would make no compromise with popular government in Italy; nor is it uninstructive to observe that the *non possumus* attitude the Church adopted, was maintained steadily for fifty years until democracy was swept away by Fascism and Rome had a Dictator to deal with. Then, and only then, did she consent to come to terms.

King Humbert, who succeeded his father, was a brave soldier like all his race, as he had proved on the field of Custoza in 1866, but his political tendencies were as yet an unknown quantity. His Queen, Margherita of Savoy, was one of the jewels of the new Italy, whose beauty and gracious manner did much to make the royal house popular and left a memory still treasured in Italy. The election of the new Pope was viewed with some trepidation, and there were rumours that the Conclave would be held outside Italy, but, as already mentioned, the firm attitude of Crispi, who threatened to occupy the Vatican if the Cardinals vacated it, and at the same time guaranteed absolute liberty and safety if the Conclave was held as usual in Rome, sufficed to prevent any unaccustomed procedure and after a brief conclave Cardinal Pecci was elected. He took the title of Leo XIII. The perfect tranquillity in which the election was held was a good omen for the future, and the government had good reason to be grateful to Crispi for his able handling of what might have been a difficult situation.

Crispi's influence had already strengthened the Ministry, when a most scandalous sample of political revenge drove him to resignation. His predecessor, Nicotera, out of jealousy and bitterness at his loss of office, unearthed an incident in Crispi's private life, similar to that brought against Parnell, and induced the editor of *Il Piccolo* to publish it. The result was much moral indignation and Crispi's retirement for some years from public life. Political leaders were not easy to find in the ranks of the Left, and the new King had some difficulty in discovering a successor to Depretis, who resigned with the retirement of Crispi. He finally nominated Benedetto Cairoli, a name dear to the nation, for he was the only survivor of five brothers, the rest of whom had given their lives for Italy. Cairoli was a better patriot than statesman. Uncomplimentary remarks were made by his opponents as to his political capacities and he was certainly unfortunate. He held power twice and each time Italy received a setback. He had absorbed the lofty moral ideals of Mazzini, and applied to international politics the high standard of his own personal life. Faced with the competition of such masters of craft as Bismarck and Disraeli, Italy's aspirations found small chance of fulfilment under the leadership of a man to whom clean hands were of far greater importance than full pockets. Cairoli's Ministry took office in March 1878, on the eve of the Congress of Berlin, which opened in June. His Foreign Minister was Count Corti, a very· reserved man and an indifferent speaker. Zanardelli took the Home Office.

The foreign policy of the new Italy was entirely unaggressive, and the reorganization of her army and navy, upon which she was spending large sums, was purely defensive. Her relations with France and Austria, which three years previously had been satisfactory, had since deteriorated, and in the autumn of 1877 Depretis had sent Crispi on a tour of the European capitals, partly for general information but also with a definite idea of sounding Berlin as to an alliance which would safeguard Italy against an attack either by France or Austria. The reply of Bismarck was yes, as to France, but no, as to Austria, and the proposal went no further. At Vienna, Crispi found the government greatly annoyed at the irredentist activity of Italy in the Tyrol. France, he found full of suspicion, strengthened by his visit to Berlin, that Italy was preparing an attack on France in alliance with Germany. England, on the other hand, was friendly, and suggested discussions for a joint understanding on Mediterranean problems of interest to both countries. But no proposals of advantage to Italian interests seem to have been put forward for consideration at the forthcoming Congress. Such was the position when Cairoli took office. His handling of the situation was very weak. The English suggestions, which might have given Italy a useful backing, were allowed to lapse, and no check was put upon the agitation going on in the Tyrol. Zanardelli, into whose province such matters came, was a great believer in liberty, whose motto was 'repress but not prevent', in other words to allow unlimited agitation until it resulted in action, and only then to stop it. So the republicans held meetings and cheered for the republic, and the irredentists fulminated against Austrian oppression, without the least interference by the government. Thus, when the Congress opened, and Italy made her debut as a European power, she was without support, with at least two powers, France and Austria, irritated, if not hostile, towards her.

Count Corti went to Berlin without experience of a Congress, without previous contact with the plenipotentiaries he was to meet, and under the depressing influence of the successive dicta of the new Italy's Foreign Ministers: that of Visconti Venosta that Italy's foreign policy should be one of 'wise inertia'; of the remark of Depretis, 'When I see an international question on the horizon, I open my umbrella and wait till it has passed', and the statement of Cairoli, 'We shall not be clever: but we wish above all to be honest'. It is indeed small wonder that he returned with his hands unsoiled but his pockets empty. When the Congress assembled the members had already divided the spoils in private, to which they now gave a joint sanction. England, with her usual blend of moral principle and realism, returned with 'Peace with Honour' plus Cyprus. Austria acquired rights over Bosnia and Herzegovina, while France made good her claim to have Tunis recognized as her 'sphere of influence'. Italy, as the newest and weakest member, was certainly in no position to dictate, but she would have gained much in prestige if she had boldly protested against Austria's new acquisitions or at least used them to claim the 'rectification' of her Tyrolese frontier. But Count Corti showed little spirit and less initiative. He signed everything on behalf of Italy and returned without having even succeeded in getting Italy's disinterested honesty recognized as something to her credit.

The Cabinet had to face a storm of abuse from the Press when Corti returned empty handed. The weakness and want of foresight of the Ministry and the feebleness of Italy's first appearance as a Great Power, roused intense indignation and deepened the sense of failure which brooded over the nation. The Ministry did not, however, immediately resign. In November, Cairoli accompanied the King and Queen on their first visit to Naples, where, as they drove through the streets, a fanatic, armed with a knife, attempted to assassinate King Humbert. With great courage and promptitude Cairoli flung himself in front of the King and deflected the blow, which wounded him in the thigh, and in so doing probably saved the King's life. Cairoli's brave action was greatly applauded but the blame was put upon

Zanardelli, as the firstfruits of his views of liberty, and the public indignation, in conjunction with the failure at Berlin, ruined the government, which resigned in December.

Cairoli's second Ministry began a year later after a confused interval in which Depretis was President of the Council. He found himself quickly involved in a tangle of cross interests with France in Tunis. After securing Algiers, France had begun the process of peaceful penetration across her eastern border. Before long she had control of the post and telegraphs, her officers were training the Bey's small army, and by grants in aid, she secured financial control of the country. During the same period, the area around Bizerta was being rapidly developed by Italian emigrants from Sicily. A fierce rivalry between the two energetic consuls ended with the purchase of the Goletta-Tunis railway by Italy, whose government found the exorbitant sum demanded for its purchase. This brought matters to a crisis. France, whose action had already the consent of the Powers given at the Congress of Berlin, at once sent troops, occupied the ports, including Bizerta, and by the Treaty of Bardo (May 1881) signed with the Bey, assumed a protectorate over the country. There was a furious outcry in Italy, but her position, unless prepared for war with France, was hopeless. A storm of questions and demands for explanation assailed Cairoli in the Chamber, and quite unable to meet them, he resigned. The loss of Tunis, or rather its occupation by France, was a severe blow to Italy. It seemed to put the seal on her sense of failure and impotence. But the methods of France laid up trouble for herself, for they flung Italy into the arms of the Central Powers, and weakened still further her position in Europe.

The soreness of Italy over Tunis gave Bismarck his opportunity, and it was not long after the return of Depretis to power, which he was to hold until his death in 1887, that Germany began to approach Italy to join the Austro-German alliance which was already in existence. Bismarck's aim to keep order in Europe had always been the alliance of the three Emperors, Germany, Austria and Russia. But after the Congress of Berlin Russia drew apart, and Bismarck now turned to Italy. Over an Italian alliance with Germany herself there was little difficulty, but to bring Austria and Italy together was not so easy. Yet except for the hereditary distrust of Austria, the only difficulty was the anti-Austrian agitation in the Tyrol. But Zanardelli's reversal of the old adage that prevention is better than cure, had been discredited after the attempted assassination of King Humbert, and a little firmness was all that was needed. Bismarck pressed his suit and in the autumn of 1881 the King and Queen went to Vienna and were very well received. After that there was no trouble and the next year, 1882, Italy joined the Central Powers and constituted the Triple Alliance.

On the whole, especially at the time of its first signature, to join the Alliance was probably a wise move on the part of Italy, for it gave her what she most needed for her development, a sense of security, but she had to pay dearly for it. France was by far her best customer, and the Commercial Treaty with her signed the year before was an important source of income. France did not repudiate it, but when it expired in 1886 she would not renew it, and a tariff war began from which Italy suffered severely. The withdrawal of French capital and the hostile attitude of the French bankers, did much to bring about the banking scandal which ended in the failure of the Banca Romana. It led also, through a false sense of pride, to an excessive expenditure on the army and navy, which absorbed at one time 25 per cent of the annual budget. Nor did Italy gain much from the Alliance in prestige. She was very much the junior partner, and too often for her liking she was treated as such, and though the Alliance was at least four times renewed and lasted until the Great War, neither of her allies placed much faith in her support and before 1914 she had become little more than an appendage.

During the last years of his Ministry Depretis carried through two important reforms. The grist tax was reduced by successive stages and finally abolished and the franchise was widened. The new electoral law raised the number of voters from six hundred thousand to well over two millions, but the educational standard required, though low enough, pressed unfairly on the south and the country districts, where schools were fewer, and excluded many rural voters. But in Italy the eligible number of voters was one thing on paper and another in practice, largely through the adverse attitude of the Church. From 1860 Rome had supported the general principle that 'neither electors nor elected' should be the attitude of Catholics, and it had greatly reduced the poll. In 1874 the Pope issued his *non expedit* that it was not expedient for Catholics to vote, and this too had its effect, so that the actual number of votes was always much smaller than it should have been, and still represented an inadequate expression of public opinion. The name of Depretis in Italian political history will not, however, be generally associated either with the franchise or even the Triple Alliance, but rather with the political system known as 'transformism'. A rigid party discipline had never commended itself to the Italians. It conflicted with their individualism, with their cherished ideals of freedom of thought and expression, and seemed to interfere with other personal or regional loyalties. The result had been that, from the first, the Chamber contained groups united by other bonds than that of party loyalty. With the advent of the Left, the position grew even more complicated. The tradition behind the Right had kept them together, but the Left had no such unifying principle, and the Chamber split into divisions whose classification was impossible. The solution of the problem as to how to get a working majority, as devised by Depretis, was the system of 'transformism'.

In theory, it was a national government, in which the men best qualified to take office were to be chosen without regard to parties, but in practice is was something very different. Depretis was a cynic who believed that most men had their price and did not hesitate to ask them to name it, and he adopted the simple principle of making it worth while for an individual or a group to vote for the government. As soon as any section of the Chamber became dangerous to the passage of a government measure, or an individual made himself sufficiently objectionable as to require suppression, they were bribed. If of sufficient merit or importance, a member might be offered a seat in the Cabinet, or a profitable post. He might be won over by a decoration or possibly inside information of financial value. Sometimes a member could be satisfied by the provision of a schoolhouse or a railway station in his constituency and thereby induced to vote the right way. There were various means but the end was the same. A good example of his method is afforded by the sugar tax. In a speech at Stradella, Depretis had stressed the inequality between the heavy tax on salt, a prime necessity of the poorest classes, and that on sugar, 'the salt of the rich', which was light, and expressed his intention of correcting it. The general expectation was that the salt tax would be lightened, instead of which Depretis merely increased the sugar tax. It was an exceedingly unpopular measure and strong opposition was anticipated when the Bill was brought in, instead of which, it was passed with but little opposition. The explanation came a few days later, when in the Official Gazette a list of no less than sixty Deputies who had supported the Bill were given the rank of *Commendatore*.

The effect of 'transformism' on parliamentary life was disastrous. The post of Deputy became the recognized road to social or financial advancement. The Chamber itself became a hotbed of intrigue and life at Montecitorio became a thing to itself, cut off from the nation, representing personal and sectional interests, in the midst of which the wider needs of the nation were neglected, if not ignored. In his last year of office Depretis brought Crispi back into the Cabinet, which he quickly dominated, and when Depretis resigned shortly before his death Crispi took over the presidency (1887).

When Crispi assumed office, the morale of Italy was at its lowest ebb. To the failure at Berlin and the occupation of Tunis by France was now added the unpopular Triple Alliance, by which Italy found herself an ally of her hereditary enemy Austria, against whom, even then, as the unjustified possessor of the Tyrol and Trentino, the patriotic elements were raising the banner of irredentism. From the Congress of Vienna, a Parliament had been too often regarded in Italy as a self-acting panacea, which once established, would bring in the millennium. The idea that they would have to learn to work it, a long and difficult process, seems not to have occurred to any one. Now, after fifty years of struggle to obtain it, the reality proved a cruel disillusion. Ten years of Depretis completed the process, for Depretis was a pessimist who never believed in the greatness of Italy but in her weakness, and his policy was to run the country on the lowest common denominator and to avoid difficulties in Parliament by inertia and judicious corruption. While Parliament thus conducted robbed Italy of any feeling of pride in her new political system, its hand fell heavily on every aspect of life. Italy was a poor country. It was calculated that the income per head of the population was under £8 a year, compared with £31 in England and £26 in France. Having as yet no extensive manufactures, taxation fell on all the prime necessities of life, flour, meat, oil, wine, salt, sugar, and much else. Everything was taxed, and being an agricultural country with innumerable villages and small towns the collection of the revenue necessitated an expensive army of officials. In Crispi's day they had already reached a hundred thousand. Not a peasant could drive his little cart into town or village without its contents being examined, weighed and taxed. Thus taxation was not only heavy but vexatious. Salaries and wages were low. The highest state functionaries seldom drew £800 a year. Sella calculated that no more than thirty-three thousand of the twenty-five millions in the country had an income exceeding £400 a year. A village doctor might earn £100 a year: a schoolmaster half that sum: few agricultural labourers could earn ten shillings a week. There were compensations in cheap cottages, gardens and grazing: living was cheap and luxuries few. But life was hard and hours of work long, and the whole standard of life was scaled down to a level of simplicity which bordered on indigence. But Italy would have borne her poverty, if not with cheerfulness at least with resignation, if she could have held her head high before Europe, if she could have felt proud of her government and known that she was respected abroad and not pitied. It was just this that Crispi set himself to do.

Crispi was a Sicilian by birth. He had been a conspirator throughout the Risorgimento. A republican by conviction, he had changed when Italy had decided on monarchy, and had quarrelled with Mazzini's republican obsession with his dictum, 'The Monarchy unites us, the Republic divides us'. He had been the directing brain behind Garibaldi and the Thousand in 1860 and had acted as his pro-dictator. Since 1870 he had kept himself aloof from parties, assuming the attitude of a *solitario*, as his reply to the question as to what party he belonged indicates. 'I', he said, 'am Crispi'. In character, he was by nature authoritarian with a tendency to dictatorial methods, born of his immense self-confidence and belief in his own ability. In the Chamber he revealed a good deal of *fortiter in re* with a corresponding lack of *suaviter in modo*. His weak point was his impulsiveness and readiness to act on insufficient evidence. He carried this almost to the point of want of balance, rushing to extremes and then reversing with equal violence. His motto was 'energy' and he was determined not only to galvanize Parliament into activity, but to make the country feel it had a real government which would hold its own in Europe and bring Italy out of the slough of despond.

Almost his first action was to dash off to Friedrichsruhe to consult Bismarck. The visit was wrapped in profound mystery. Critics said that its purpose was to increase his self-importance and to raise Italian prestige by provoking discussion. Its real reason was probably to find out how far the policy of the Triple Alliance, in relation to France, was defensive or offensive. His first measures were excellent. A Bill on Provincial and Communal Administration, giving them regional control and freedom from government interference. An admirable Law on National Hygiene and Sanitation, which lessened the death rate and improved the health of the people. The publication a little later of Zanardelli's penal code, revealing a praiseworthy liberal spirit, enhanced the government's reputation still further. People began to feel the country was being actively governed and self-confidence came back. The other side of Crispi's character came out, however, in a Bill on Public Order, giving the authorities power to prohibit meetings and processions and requiring notice of such to be given beforehand. This was probably aimed at the irredentist movement in the Tyrol, which Crispi was determined to suppress out of loyalty to the Triple Alliance, whose support he felt was necessary owing to the delicate relations with France. Naturally this irritated the Left and in conjunction with other factors, such as his retention of both the Foreign Office and that for Internal Affairs, and his overriding manner in the Chamber, provoked a good deal of personal opposition. Crispi, however, took small notice, justifying his action on the ground that exceptional times demanded exceptional measures and continued as before.

Crispi's premiership coincided with the expiration of Italy's Commercial Treaty with France. Realizing the serious loss which Italy would suffer, for France took fully one-third of all her exports, he at once opened secret negotiations for a fresh treaty. Though prolonged, they were quite futile, and the real reason was bluntly expressed by the French commissary when he told the Italian representative 'as long as you remain in the Triple Alliance no commercial treaty with France will be possible'. A wave of protectionism was at this time sweeping over Europe and a tariff war began. France imposed a prohibitive tariff on Italian exports and Italy responded in kind. Italy was the chief sufferer. Her oil and wines, especially from the south and Sicily, became almost unsaleable and great hardship resulted. Germany, however, increased her imports from Italy and the economic position was gradually restored. Less dependence on the French market was, in any case, desirable. The continued hostility of the French Press, which seemed as if its purpose was to drive Italy out of the Triple Alliance, produced a violent reaction in Crispi. He became suddenly convinced, on the quite unreliable reports of spies and secret agents, that France was preparing an immediate attack on Italy. He was always haunted by fear of a Franco-Papal alliance to break up Italian unity. He urged his War Minister to get ready for all eventualities and represented the danger with such vehemence to England that the government despatched the Mediterranean fleet to Genoa. There was no basis for the alarm and Crispi quickly recovered his poise, but the incident was typical of the man.

The same want of steady purpose, based on a well-thought-out policy, was conspicuous in Crispi's dealings with the Vatican. As a lifelong anti-clerical and a free thinker, he was thoroughly unsuited to initiate negotiations of this kind. Nor was the moment propitious, for the opposition of Germany and Austria to Pope Leo's feelers on behalf of the restoration of the Temporal Power, made Papal enthusiasm unlikely. His intermediary was the old Neo-Guelf of 1848, Father Tosti, but the opposition of Jesuits on one side and Freemasons on the other, quickly brought the negotiations to an abrupt conclusion. Crispi at once went to the other extreme and revealed himself as a determined anti-clerical, introducing clauses dealing with clerical abuses into the new Penal Code, removing schools in the Near East from the Religious Orders and putting them under lay control: making religious education in the primary schools optional, and, finally, adding insult to injury by sanctioning the erection of a statue of the philosopher Giordano Bruno in the Campo di Fiori, on the site where the Church had burnt him as a heretic in the year 1600 A.D.

Crispi had a passionate love of his country, 'my Italy' as he always called her. He longed to see her strong and flourishing, and amongst his visions for her future was a great colonial empire. Italian explorers, travellers and traders, were already active in Africa, but the history of Italian colonial enterprise began in 1882, when England, shortly after the bombardment of Alexandria, invited Italy, on the withdrawal of French collaboration, to take her place in the pacification of Egypt. Mancini, the Foreign Secretary in the Depretis Cabinet, refused, partly from fear of French annoyance, partly from financial reasons and partly from Italian sympathy with Arabi Pasha whom they regarded as a kind of Garibaldi. Two years later the murder of an Italian trader brought up the question of Italian colonial activity in Parliament. This time Mancini announced the despatch of a military force to protect Italian interests. Two further expeditions followed, and encouraged by England, jealous of French expansion, Italy occupied Massawa and a number of other places. But both in the country and in Parliament a forward colonial policy met with strong opposition on account of the cost, and the budget of 1885 was passed with so narrow a margin that the Cabinet resigned. Mancini was replaced by di Robilant, Italian ambassador at Vienna, who, occupied with the revision of the terms of the Triple Alliance previous to its renewal, neglected the colonial question altogether, until suddenly the country was horrified at the massacre of an Italian column under Colonel de Cristoforis at Dogali in January 1887. It was typical of Depretis that he regarded the disaster of Dogali, not as a challenge to Italian pride and self-respect, but as just one more proof of Italian feebleness, and he was all for withdrawal from Africa, and when this was stopped by the firm opposition of Crispi in the Chamber, he promptly brought him into the Cabinet to share the responsibility. Soon after Depretis died and Crispi succeeded him. The colonial policy of Crispi was one of consolidation: he drew together the scattered areas in Italian occupation and formed them into a colony which he called Eritrea. He made friends with the treacherous Menelik, King of Shoa, who, on the death of the Abyssinian Negus John, became Emperor. With him he signed the Treaty of Uccialli (1889) and in 1890 announced to Europe that Abyssinia was an Italian protectorate. Such was the position when Crispi resigned his first Ministry in 1891.

Throughout all his first Ministry Crispi's cardinal preoccupation was neither with colonies nor Papacy, but with France, and for the hostility between them French pride was chiefly to blame. Throughout the Risorgimento the influence of France over Italy was supreme, and she could not now reconcile herself to a non-dependent Italy. Italian unity galled her, and the alliance with Germany intensified French ill feeling, which Crispi did nothing to soften. In 1888, and again the next year, he ostentatiously visited Bismarck, and the more he flaunted his friendship with the all-powerful Chancellor the angrier France became. Bismarck was only too pleased, for it took France's mind off *revanche*. Moreover, Crispi's attitude achieved the very purpose he had set himself, for the Italy that was flattered in the German Press, invited to co-operate with England, and treated with respect by Austria, took a very different position in Europe to that which she occupied after the Congress of Berlin, when the contemptuous diminutive 'Italietta' was heard in the land. It was something very new for Italy to have a Premier who stood up to France, even though it was the German bayonets behind him that gave him the necessary assurance. Crispi's fall in 1891, over which France rejoiced, was unexpected. It was, in fact, more a personal than a political question. The Chamber was tired and irritated by his energy and his egotism. Supremely confident that his presence at the head of the government was recognized as essential, he turned a criticism of his financial policy into a demand for a vote of confidence, and lost it, and forthwith resigned.

His successor, di Rudinì, only lasted a year and his tenure of power was uneventful. In May 1892 he made way for Giovanni Giolitti, who throughout the next twenty years exercised a more thorough influence over Italy's political life than any Premier since Cavour, though its quality was of a very inferior calibre. Giolitti was called upon to face what is generally known as the 'Bank Scandal'. It was the climax of a financial irregularity which had its source in the removal of the capital from Turin to Florence in 1865. The new importance of Florence as the seat of government led to widespread speculation in building. The banks, the more important of whom had the right of issuing paper money, regardless of any fixed gold cover, issued so freely that, when four years later the capital was again removed to Rome, they found themselves in difficulties. The same vicious process was thereupon repeated even more extensively in Rome, and the result was a bad financial crisis. While Crispi was still in power the position was causing great anxiety. Bankruptcies had doubled, several banks had failed, and an acute financial depression followed. It came to a head when rumours began to circulate as to the position of the Bank of Rome. A Commission of Inquiry was appointed, whose report the Ministry, then under Giolitti, hushed up. Whereupon the Chamber opened up the whole matter, insisting on a new inquiry and the publication of its Report. The subsequent revelation of fraudulent methods, though no worse than similar revelations in other countries, shook public confidence in the Ministry which was forced to resign and make room once more for Francesco Crispi.[22]

It was not, however, the bank scandal which gave rise to the public demand for the return of the strong man Crispi, but the simultaneous agrarian trouble in Sicily: and here we meet for the first time in its militant aspect the new Socialist movement which was to prove a very potent force in Italian life and development.

The earliest form of Socialism in Italy was the Anarchist teaching of the Russian Bakounin, who was in Naples for two years in the latter half of the sixties. But though the anarchists got some hold, especially on the congenial soil of the Romagna with its long tradition of violence, it gained little ground generally amongst the masses. It inspired, however, the extreme element, even when its creed was generally rejected. In the seventies the industrial movement in the north started, and Labour began to adopt the Socialist tenets against capitalism. The widening of the franchise in 1882 spread it still further, and about 1885 there was a 'working men's party' at Milan with forty thousand members. In 1891 the first Socialist newspaper, the *Critica Sociale*, appeared, with a definitely anti-anarchist programme. In this year the first Socialist Congress was held, in which a hundred and fifty working men's societies were represented. About the same time Socialist ideas reached Sicily where they were adopted as an agrarian policy. The movement was directed by men of the middle class, for the ignorant Sicilian peasant was quite incapable of so doing. It began by being educational and co-operative, with schools and libraries and co-operative societies. It had a religious and patriotic side as well. The network of unions (*fasci*) was soon strong enough to make terms with the landowners, known as the Pact of Corleone. But the ruling classes grew frightened, clashes between peasants and police occurred and the landowners appealed to the government for protection. Violence begets violence and the movement spread. Giolitti, then in power, sent troops, but resigned before any decision had been reached. In December 1893 there were riots and bloodshed and the call came for Crispi. With his usual impulsiveness Crispi went to extremes. The reports of spies and police officials convinced him that Italy was in serious danger. He believed as true tales of the peasants selling Sicily to Russia or England: that French gold was supporting the movement. Forty thousand troops were despatched to overawe the island: martial law was proclaimed and military courts set up, and once again the unfortunate peasantry went through the process of fines and imprisonment and expulsion to the penal islands, made only too familiar in the past by the hated Bourbons of Naples. When a little later the marble workers of Carrara revolted, the same process was repeated. The revolt, as in Sicily, was effectively stamped out, and Crispi preserved once more his reputation as the man for a crisis.

When the Sicilian trouble was suppressed and Crispi turned to foreign policy, his work revealed the same two-sided qualities as before. He made approaches to France and then held them up. He adopted a conciliatory attitude to the Vatican, solving awkward questions regarding the appointment of Bishops, in a manner which pleased the Pope, who, moreover, tended to be himself conciliatory, for Crispi's attitude to Socialism met with decided approval in clerical circles. But his other side came out when he unveiled the statue to Garibaldi on the Janiculum and organized a *festa* to commemorate the entry of Italy into Rome. His most valuable piece of work, however, at this time, was the balancing of the Budget, which he carried out with the help of a clever financier, destined to be well known later, Sidney Sonnino. Crispi's changed attitude to France, though of small significance, was an indication, nevertheless, of a wider movement in European politics. The vain and restless young German Emperor William II having got rid of Bismarck, was beginning the process of alienating both Russia and England, and though his wholesome respect for his august grandmother made any breach with England unlikely during her lifetime, it reacted on the significance of the Triple Alliance, from which any hostility to England had been excluded from the first, for Italy at that time would not consider war with England.

The common ground upon which Crispi and the Vatican, together with the industrial and propertied classes in Italy, met, was the dread of Socialism. The success which had attended coercion, both in Sicily and the Lunigiana, emboldened Crispi to attempt its eradication by force throughout the country; so in the autumn of 1894 he began a deliberate campaign to suppress the movement. Anarchist outrages in Europe, and the special measures enacted in France, justified to some extent his procedure, though the state of Italy herself gave no cause for his severity. In October 1894 he dissolved all the Socialist societies and associations. He extended the hated *domicilio coatto* (enforced domicile on the penal islands) to all citizens found guilty of inciting to disturbance, which included such charges as singing the 'Labourers' Hymn'. Men were tried, fined and imprisoned all over Italy, and harmless associations such as the Agricultural Labourers' Union were broken up. Newspapers were prosecuted, and some Socialist Deputies, of whom there were only eight, were arrested at the close of the Session. As usual, he veered round after a time, finding the immediate danger illusory and that his severity merely strengthened public sympathy with Socialism. The imprisoned Deputies were promptly re-elected at the 1895 elections, at which the seats held by the Socialists were increased to twelve, in addition to the substantial percentage of votes given to their candidates in many other constituencies. The net results of his efforts, far from suppressing Socialism, revealed how deeply their aims had penetrated into the public mind and gave one more illustration of the failure of coercion to suppress ideas. Crispi's popularity waned quickly in public opinion, but his position was still very strong, backed as he was by the landowners, business men and the Church, and had he not sealed his fate by his headstrong colonial policy, he might still have retained power for a considerable time. It was this which proved his undoing.

Crispi deserves full credit as the one Italian statesman of his period who revealed a sense of vision regarding the value of colonies. He had travelled and talked with foreign statesmen and business men who already realized, that if world trade continued to expand much further, the problems of raw materials and new markets would soon become a vital question in the commercial world. But these ideas were 'caviare to the general' in Italy. The tendency in Parliament was to restrict all activities to the *status quo*, and to involve the country in no further commitments. As to the general public, the pressure of home necessities, finance, reform and a wider social programme, made adventures on the Red Sea coast appear an ill-timed adventure of no value and of great expense. Crispi had, however, one eloquent and fervid writer behind him; for in 1889 Alfredo Oriani had published his volume of essays *Fino a Dogali* with its vivid picture of the heroism of Colonel Cristoforis and his five hundred troops, and since then (1892) his *Lotta Politica in Italia* had appeared, in which the call of Africa to Italy was stressed with the same insistence. But Oriani was in advance of public opinion and was little read, and his imperial vision was marred by a remorseless doctrine of subjugation which shocked his humanitarian contemporaries.

On his return to power in 1893, Crispi was greeted by the news of the signal victory of Colonel Arimondi in Abyssinia, and this whetted his appetite for a realization of his imperial vision. In spite of his other activities, he kept continually in touch with the colonial situation, of whose real difficulties he had, perhaps, small appreciation, and, in consequence, he was largely responsible for the ultimate disaster. The danger centre of the whole situation was the crafty and treacherous Menelik, now Emperor, who, while he rallied his chieftains round him, for his ultimate purpose of attacking the Italians, sent a deputation to Rome to thank the King for his 'high protection' and blandly assented to Italy representing his country at the anti-slavery congress held at Brussels. Unfortunately for Italy, the two men on the spot, the civilian governor Count Antonelli and General Baldissera, differed widely in their estimates of the situation; the former trusting Menelik and agreeing with the policy of intriguing with the regional chieftains or Rasses, while Baldissera, with fuller knowledge and experience of the country, warned Crispi not to trust the Emperor. Crispi encouraged expansion. Local successes led to the annexation of the Tigre; a new governor, General Baratieri, replaced Baldissera, and a forward movement was prepared. In the summer of 1895, the new governor returned to consult Crispi, and on his return to Abyssinia found the situation greatly deteriorated. Menelik, whose policy had all along been to find fault with the Treaty of Uccialli, and so keep open an excuse for aggression, suddenly attacked the fort of Makalle with a large army. On receipt of this news Crispi despatched reinforcements under General Baldissera, the former military governor, who was, moreover, senior to Baratieri and would supersede him. Unaware of the odds against him, and actuated by his habitual impulsiveness, Crispi urged General Baratieri to action, writing contemptuously of 'military paralysis'. Prudent restraint in the face of official impetuosity was no part of Baratieri's mental equipment, and without waiting for the reinforcements—and the senior commander—he attacked. The result was the disaster of Adowa. Four thousand five hundred men and two generals were killed, two thousand wounded and fifteen hundred taken prisoners. It was the end of Crispi. Unable to face the wave of national grief and anger that swept the country, he forthwith resigned, not only from power but from political life, to end his days in poverty and futile bitterness at the ingratitude of the nation to whom his name had once been so dear. Two years later he suffered the added cruelty of a vote of censure passed upon him by the Chamber of Deputies. He lingered five years, dying in 1901 in his eighty-second year.

Crispi was the most striking political personality the new Italy produced; the only Premier who caught the national imagination. His energy was a great tonic after Depretis, but too violent in its action. Eloquent, forcible and dominating in Parliament, he roused the Chamber to an unaccustomed activity and gave Italy a feeling of confidence in the government which she had not felt for many years. But Crispi's energy was neither informed by knowledge nor controlled by a sound judgement. He was ignorant of the true aims of Socialism, and acted on a class judgement. He tried to make Italy run before she could walk, and she stumbled. The word 'megalomania' coined for him by Count Jacini, was not inappropriate. His ideas were grandiose beyond the resources of the country, and he tried to build before the foundations had properly settled. He was a great patriot but ill-balanced.

CHAPTER TWELVE

FIN-DE-SIÈCLE, 1896-1900

THROUGHOUT the half century of the Risorgimento which culminated in the occupation of Rome, the Italian people had lived at high tension. The great struggle for liberty and independence, unity and freedom, which had inspired them, was a noble but exhausting ideal, and as action and reaction are equal and opposite, it was scarcely surprising that the period which followed should be characterized by a feeling of apathy and a sense of disappointment. The twenty years from 1870 to 1890 were, in fact, an inevitable reaction. Italy had struggled up that purgatorial mountain with all its setbacks and sufferings, buoyed up by the belief that on the summit stood the Earthly Paradise, and when at long last they reached it, they found, not an Earthly Paradise—but a building site. In other words, with fulfilment the poetry of the movement had vanished. Ideals had become realities and all the beauty and colour lent by distance had faded.

In the last decade of the century, however, a new spirit is to be observed in Italy and its inspiration comes from Socialism. We have seen how the movement began, emerging from the violent doctrines of anarchism, which did not appeal in general to the Italians, though an extreme party existed in their ranks. For some years the Socialists kept rigidly apart from the other Left groups, the Radicals and Republicans, but the pressure of Crispi's coercive measures in 1894 forced them together, until they formed a somewhat unstable alliance, though politically united as an opposition in the Chamber. By 1902 they had shaken off anarchism, and numbered some 250,000 adherents, mostly in Piedmont and Lombardy. Three years later they held twelve seats in Parliament, and with the renewal of restrictive legislation under Rudini and Pelloux, they became a solid 'extreme Left' of Socialists, Radicals and Republicans, controlling a hundred votes and thus of sufficient strength to form a menace to any government.

The power of Socialism was not, however, to be gauged simply by the number of seats held in Parliament, but by its influence in the country. Very early in its career it had developed an intellectual side. Its first newspaper, Turati's fortnightly *Critica Sociale*, was well written and economically sound. It was followed by the *Lotta di Classe*

(The Class Struggle) and then by a daily paper, *Avanti!* all of them rivalling the best of the periodical Press. The adhesion to the movement of Antonio Labriola, a brilliant young Professor at the University of Rome, who became a keen Marxian, lecturing on Historical Materialism, translating the Communist Manifesto, and publishing Letters on Philosophy and Socialism, gave a *cachet* to the whole movement. But it was not the academic discussion of Marxian dialectic, though it helped, which was the true centre of Socialist influence but its clear cut, progressive and practical Social Programme. This was what the nation had been demanding from the government for years and what it had utterly failed to produce. The absence of organized political parties with definite programmes based on the needs of the country, had reduced parliamentary life to an unseemly scramble for votes on isolated measures, in which groups of every colour sold their support for ribbons and offices or railway stations and schoolhouses, regardless of the wider needs which a rapidly increasing industrial life was rendering urgent. As has been well said, Deputies came 'moins pour servir que pour se servir'. When, therefore, the Socialist Party produced their Minimum Programme in 1895, and three years later published it in a revised and improved form, it was hailed with widespread approval and formed a rallying point for general support of the movement. It demanded adult suffrage for both sexes, payment of deputies, neutrality of the government in disputes between capital and labour, religious equality, a national militia instead of a standing army and a more humane Penal Code. Its economic demands included nationalization of mines and railways, an eight-hour-day, old age pensions, accident insurance, feeding of school children, and many other proposals which have since then become integral parts of the social structure.

Perhaps the best summary of the influence of Socialism in the final decades of the century is that of a distinguished contemporary, still an ornament of Italian life, Benedetto Croce, whose verdict is given in these words, 'Socialism won over all, or almost all, the flower of the younger generation: and that to remain uninfluenced by and indifferent to it, or to assume, as some did, an attitude of unreasoned hostility to it, was a sure sign of inferiority. . . . Socialism produced a whole complex of results, correcting, restoring, renewing, deepening, and giving a new content to Italian culture. It raised Italy from the depths into which she had sunk when the spiritual force of her heroic age had spent itself.'

The relation between Church and State since 1870 had been one of armed neutrality. Socially, Rome was divided into two circles, with centres at the Vatican and the Quirinale, between which there was no communication. But Papal hopes of a Catholic movement in favour of the restoration of the Temporal Power had received small satisfaction. The dogma of Infallibility following the Syllabus had done nothing to promote enthusiasm on the part of the Catholic sovereigns to forward the Papal wishes, and the question was now generally regarded as one to be settled between the Vatican and the Italian government. Both, however, recognized the necessity of finding a *modus vivendi*, since neither had any intention of leaving Rome, and below the surface many matters were quietly settled without any overt display of reconciliation. The Papal attitude and the political *non expedit* were, in fact, a help rather than a hindrance, since they enabled the government to settle the country without the complicating factor of a Catholic Parliamentary Party. Church and State met on common ground in their hostility to Socialism, yet here again the Church found it impossible to ignore the support given by Catholics to the socialistic programme and before long found it necessary to revise her attitude. The non-expedit was allowed to lapse and the Encyclical *Rerum Novarum* gave an opening to Catholics to take their part in social activities. The influence of the Catholic Socialist Movement in France and Germany had its effects in Italy. From 1875 Catholic Congresses had been held, and after 1891 they adopted a social programme. But the most advanced branch of Catholic social thought came from the Christian Democrats, who demanded a minimum wage and a maximum day's work, a reduction in the army estimates, and financial reform, herein coinciding with the Socialist aims. It is not a little curious that from the Catholic ranks came ideas which, under Fascism, were adopted and developed. Professor Okey, writing before 1900 in his volume, *Italy To-day*, mentions their keenness in promoting 'Corporations' both of employers and employed, and in dealing with their political ideas refers to their 'strange political conception of parliaments representative not of localities but of trades and professions'. We must now consider how this great Socialist movement fared at the hands of the governments that succeeded the fall of Crispi.

The Marquis di Rudini who formed the next Cabinet faced a difficult task. The country was angry and humiliated over the disaster of Adowa. Although there were some who in the name of national honour demanded the continuation of the war on an enlarged scale, the opinion of the military experts put it out of the question, for Italy would have had to send half her army and be prepared to spend hundreds of millions on its maintenance. Some local Italian successes inclined the Negus towards peace, and negotiations were opened. The Tigre was evacuated, Kassala was returned to Egypt, and Italy withdrew behind the Massawa triangle of Eritrea. The prisoners were restored and peace was signed in November 1896. This reversal of Crispi's policy was repeated in Italy's attitude to France, which was now friendly. Two conventions were signed, one dealing with the Mercantile Marine, the other safeguarding the rights of the Italian nationals in Tunis, and later a new commercial treaty was drawn up. Rudini, moreover, inherited a tense political situation as the result of Crispi's attempt to crush the Socialist movement by force. The policy still had its supporters in the parliamentary Right, backed by the Court circle and the clericals, nor was the position eased by the attitude of the Socialists themselves, who, exasperated and defiant, made themselves thoroughly objectionable. Croce's laudatory estimate of Socialism may be true, but there is no doubt that the rank and file of the party showed a dangerous tendency to the use of force. The views they expressed and the language they used were ill calculated to pour oil on troubled waters. True to their Marxian creed they talked loudly and incessantly of the class struggle and professed an unlimited contempt for the despised 'bourgeois'. Nor was their attitude to Italy's Abyssinian disaster creditable, for though the best members of the party deplored it, there were plenty who regarded it with ill-concealed satisfaction as the well-deserved result of bourgeois militarism.

Rudini, a well meaning man, but by no means a strong character capable of taking an independent line, was swayed by both parties. He published an amnesty, lightened taxation in Sicily and regulated the sulphur industry, without, however, touching the fundamental trouble between capital and labour, which was the root of the evil. In his institution of a National Fund for the provision of old age pensions and sick benefit, we can trace Socialist influence, as in his laws making workers' insurance compulsory. But the Socialist agitation and demonstrations continued, and pressure from the conservative elements induced him to dissolve the Socialist clubs and Chambers of Labour and even extend the government veto to the now active Catholic associations. His use of the military to suppress strikes and the prosecution of strike leaders recalled only too vividly the provocative methods of Crispi. But Italy's troubles were not only political, and in the autumn of 1897 a wave of revolt broke out in the south which had nothing to do with politics. The peasantry and lower classes lived habitually so close to the bleak realm of hunger, that the least disturbance of prices brought a crisis. This year the harvest was bad and the Spanish-American War interfered with the normal imports of cereals and doubled the price of bread. The government, as usual, were late with remedial measures, and misery and hunger led to outrage. Shops were sacked, followed by acts of violence and bloodshed, until troops had to be sent to restore order. General Pelloux, the officer in command, wisely avoided extreme measures and handled the situation with tact. The government suspended the corn duty, an iniquitous tax which made bread artifically dear, though even this was a mere recognition of a *fait accompli*, for the people had refused to pay it and the authorities were too frightened to attempt to collect it. In the spring the revolt spread to the north. At Ravenna, Parma and Piacenza and Bologna, there were extensive strikes of agricultural labourers, clashes with the police, and loss of life. The unrest spread to Tuscany, there was some trouble at Florence, and all over the country there was disturbance and often violence. But the climax came when the movement reached Milan, where it coincided with acute political tension within the municipality itself.

The local trouble was over the extension of the city boundary to include new areas, which meant the imposition of the heavier city rates. It had created much feeling, for the inhabitants of the new districts were amongst the roughest of the city, drawn into the new factories from the country and unused to town life. There was municipal agitation as well between the Moderates who ruled the city and Republicans and Clericals. All the elements for trouble, in short, were present, but the accusations put forward by the government of a deep laid plot for a 'revolution' had no basis in fact. The immediate cause was the shooting of the son of the Syndic of Milan in a *fracas* with the police at Pavia, which roused intense feeling in Milan. Crowds gathered and workmen came out in protest. Then followed arrests by the police, attempts at rescue and the killing of civilians. Cavalry charged the mob, who retaliated with barricades. Then the authorities lost their heads. Troops were called in, and convinced that they were facing a revolution, shot down the unarmed populace without mercy. For three days the firing continued. A hundred citizens were killed and three times that number wounded. Military law was proclaimed at Milan, Florence and Naples, hundreds were arrested and imprisoned. Military courts were set up, newspapers suppressed and the city handed over to the mercy of a badly scared general and his satellites. Though the evidence before the military tribunals made it clear that the trouble was unpremeditated, the government insisted on linking up the disturbances of the last six months with the events at Milan, and regarding the whole as a vast Socialist plot to overturn the government of the country. Their attitude revealed in a flash the panic created in the upper classes by the Socialist movement, the dread of a class war and fear of a reign of terror. The military court at Milan, presided over by General Bava-Beccaris, commanding the troops in the city, covered itself with ignominy by the savage sentences inflicted upon the flimsiest evidence. Two Deputies, one of them Signor Turati, the editor of the Socialist paper *Critica Sociale*, received a sentence of twelve years' imprisonment for 'stirring up class hatred', two others, six and four years on a similar charge. The convictions ran into thousands and the whole conduct of the authorities was a travesty of justice and a mockery of legal procedure. The panic of the government became grotesque, however, when the King was induced to bestow the Grand Cross of the Military Order of Savoy on General Bava-Beccaris, 'the Butcher of Milan', for his 'great services to the State in the suppression of the revolution'.

When the Chamber met in June Rudini at once resigned, and the state of mind prevalent in the government majority was clearly revealed in the nomination of General Pelloux as his successor, who, with a bevy of other generals, immediately took office. The new Premier, who had held office in the previous Cabinet, was a Piedmontese, and Piedmontese generals had not the best of reputations. Though no doubt there were plenty of exceptions, as a class they were strait-laced, narrow, strict disciplinarians and too often redolent of the barrack square. They were fanatically loyal to the House of Savoy, but statesmanship was hardly to be expected from them. Pelloux had shown restraint and humanity in dealing with the outbreak in the south and he now promised reforms and moderation. When the May Disorders were over, petitions rained upon the government for pardon and before the close of the year an amnesty which released two thousand seven hundred (which gives some idea of the repression, for it was only partial) was granted. But the trial of strength between the Socialists and the reactionaries was not over, it was merely transferred from the piazza to the floor of the Chamber, and in February 1899 Pelloux belied his promises by the introduction of a series of 'Exceptional Provisions' which produced the gravest constitutional crisis which the new Italy had had to face.

The released Socialists returned to civil life to find a great change in public opinion. Not only were they now supported by their own partisans but both their conduct and their programme had won wide approval in the ranks of the despised bourgeois. The action and severity of the authorities was strongly condemned and the Socialists were quick to make it clear that the charge of inciting a revolution was a fantastic invention of a badly frightened government. The general sympathy with which they were met changed their attitude to the bourgeois. The artificial barrier, which adherence to strict Marxian principles had erected between the two sections, began to break down and socialism and liberalism commenced to merge together. In the elections following the resignation of Rudini, not only were the Socialist Deputies at once re-elected but thirty more seats were won, and the Extreme Left now became a formidable element in the Chamber. Pelloux was blind to the change in the political atmosphere, and urged on by the conservative extremists and reactionaries, introduced his new measures in February 1899. These new provisions put into legal form powers which the government had intermittently exercised without scruple, but which were a doubtful interpretation of the law as it stood. They gave power to the Prefects to prohibit public meetings, a point unmentioned in the Albertine Statuto: allowed magistrates to dissolve associations which in their opinion were of a nature 'whose object was to subvert by overt acts social order or the constitution of the State'; they reintroduced the practice of sending political offenders to the penal settlements: established a severe control of the Press and put the public services under almost military discipline.

On the first reading, while meeting with warm approval from the Right, the Bill met with strong opposition on the general ground that now the country was quiet it was a mistake to rouse uneasiness by so provocative a measure. However, the general tone of qualified approval enabled the Bill to be dealt with in detail. Numerous amendments modifying its actions were moved, and at first the tone of the government seemed to favour their acceptance. The Bill was then sent to Committee, and the matter dropped for the time being. In the interval Pelloux reconstituted the Ministry, discarding the elements drawn from the Left and replacing them with uncompromising supporters of the measure drawn from the Right. This roused the suspicion of the Socialists and their temporary allies, Republicans and Radicals, and when the Bill returned from Committee, with the amendments deleted and the repressive clauses strengthened, the

Extreme Left, now supported by the Moderates, headed by Zanardelli and Giolitti, initiated a determined opposition. Deliberate obstructionism had not hitherto been a recognized element in Italian parliamentary tactics, but now, faced with the assured passage of the Bill if it came to the vote, the Left bent itself to a calculated and sustained policy of obstruction, and by interminable speeches and interpellations effectively prevented any decision being arrived at, until in June the session was prorogued.

Pelloux, with true Piedmontese obstinacy, refused to be beaten, and with the Chamber now safely *en vacance*, proceeded to publish the Bill by Royal Decree (Decreto-Legge). But again he was foiled, for the Court of Cassation, for once asserting its independence, pronounced his action as unconstitutional and annulled the Decree. Pelloux was thus obliged to bring the measure again before the Chamber when it met for the autumn session, and obstruction at once began again more furiously than ever. The government then moved an alteration in the Standing Orders, which would enable them to deal with obstruction by naming and removing members and limiting the length of speeches. The proposal was not unreasonable, and had a precedent in the English Parliament where the Speaker has authority to name members and order their removal when he deems it necessary; but in the Italian Chamber it met with violent opposition because the President was a party nominee whose impartiality was not to be relied on, for he was subject to official pressure. To suspend a disorderly member for eight days or to apply the closure to an unduly prolonged debate, were not excessive demands, but the Left considered full freedom of speech vital. The attempt to pass the new Standing Orders reduced the Chamber to chaos, members shouting and singing until the sitting broke up in confusion. Nevertheless, the President by a snap vote succeeded in getting them accepted, and while the Left in protest withdrew from the Chamber, Pelloux, content with his technical success, withdrew the Decreto-Legge. The Cabinet then decided to dissolve Parliament, hoping that in a general election the defeat of the Left would enable them to carry out their programme.

The directing mind behind Pelloux was Sidney Sonnino, whose influence in the Right was paramount. He had already, in a widely discussed article, advocated what he termed a 'Return to the Statuto', which meant the nomination of Ministers by the Crown, which thereby rendered them independent of the Chamber. He hoped, perhaps, for the reversion of the premiership with a strong Right party in the Chamber which would enable him to carry out his ideas. But the result of the general election confounded any such hopes, for the Right returned with so small a majority that their retention of power became precarious. An attempt to revise the Standing Orders in a manner to suit both parties was frustrated by a sudden revolt of the Right, who refused all compromise. This rendered Pelloux' position impossible and he resigned. A whole year had been wasted in the parliamentary struggle, and the King, determined not to prolong it, chose as Premier, Saracco, a moderate Deputy of the Right, over eighty years of age. He formed a Cabinet of conciliation, a formula satisfying all parties was devised for the Standing Orders, and parliamentary life returned to the normal (June 1900).

These four years (1896–1900), which separated the dominance of Crispi from that of Giolitti, were of critical importance in the political history of modern Italy. Though the old nomenclature of Left and Right was still maintained, their original content had completely changed. The Right, born after the Revolution of 1848, with its ideals of liberty and independence, had, of necessity, disappeared with the occupation of Rome; and the same event robbed the Left equally of its meaning, for its enthusiastic support of Garibaldi, its creed of revolution and extra-legal methods, evaporated with unity. Fragments of it remained in irredentism and anti-clericalism but its substance had gone. In the closing years of the century the struggle lay between a Right which, in reality, was clinging to Piedmontism, and a Left which was looking to industrialism. From another angle it was a conflict between force and reform as the basic principle of the State. The Right, intensely loyal, clung to the House of Savoy with its long aristocratic and military tradition, and the Pelloux Ministry was the last effort to dominate elements considered subversive to the well-being of the State by the familiar methods of the past, penal laws and, if necessary, military force. The Left, on the other hand, was middle class, pacific if not anti-military, bent on reform based on the social problems arising from a rapidly growing industrialism. In its ranks were business men, lawyers and professors, those in close touch with modern social conditions. Between the two parties a conflict was inevitable and the defeat of the authoritarian methods of Pelloux and his group of generals, was to lead to a type of government which, without adopting the principles of Socialism, was to emasculate it as a party by incorporating most of its programme in current legislation.

But the century was not to close without one final tragedy to be added to the sorrows of Italy, when in July 1900, a few weeks after the formation of the Saracco Ministry, King Humbert when on a visit to Monza, was assassinated by a foreign anarchist. Destined to reign in a time of peace and in the afterglow of his great father, King Humbert appears as a smaller figure; nevertheless he was a good King. A keen soldier, intensely jealous of the good name of the army, he allowed himself, perhaps, to be too much influenced by the traditional policy of the Court circle. His support of Crispi's colonial ventures was unpopular, and he was taxed with imperialist ideas, which for a time after Adowa went against him. But his public conduct more than merited the nation's gratitude. In times of distress he was the first to help. His energy and sympathy during the inundations in Venetia and the earthquake at Ischia, his courage in the cholera epidemic at Naples, were exemplary. His generosity both in his public gifts and in his private assistance to those in need, was princely. He was firm in his attitude to the Vatican and loyal to the Triple Alliance, paying frequent visits to Vienna and Berlin. This, however, did not blind him to the need for a naval understanding with Great Britain of which he was always a warm advocate. His assassination was the third attempt on his life. The first was at Naples when Cairoli saved him, which wrung from the Queen the words 'they have destroyed the poetry of the House of Savoy' for such an attempt had never before been made in all its long history. The second was at Rome in 1897. All were the work of anarchists from abroad. There may well have been heartburning amongst the military clique which surrounded him, when they learnt that the anarchist who killed him, confessed that it was the letter which they had induced the King to write to General Bava-Beccaris, congratulating him on his great services to the State by the slaughter of the unarmed populace of Milan, which had been the motive of his atrocious act. In spite, however, of his good qualities, it cannot be said that King Humbert did much to strengthen the hold of the House of Savoy on the throne of Italy. He was too much under the sway of the Court *camarilla*: he failed to give a lead to the country: and his want of sympathy towards the prevailing social tendencies neutralized the good qualities he showed in other directions. The throne passed without incident to his only son, Victor Emanuel III, the present King.

CHAPTER THIRTEEN

1900-1915, GIOLITTI AND THE NEW NATIONALISM

A FEW months after King Humbert's death, the transitional Ministry of Saracco fell, and the young King Victor Emanuel invited Zanardelli to form a government. His choice reveals very clearly the anomalous and immature condition of Italian politics. The Right under Sonnino, who was the obvious selection, had a majority in the Chamber, but they had been the supporters of Pelloux and the 'Exceptional Provisions' and though it might reasonably have been expected that, aware of the unpopularity of their previous programme, Sonnino would now moderate it, the King thought it wise to nominate a more 'popular' Ministry and chose Zanardelli, a staunch liberal of the old school. Zanardelli should either have refused or demanded a general election in the hope of obtaining a working majority; as it was, he accepted, and tried to carry through a liberal programme with a reactionary majority in opposition. He had, moreover, to submit to conditions, the retention of the Ministers for War and Marine, and a continuation of foreign policy on the lines of Visconti Venosta. His position, in consequence, was hopeless from the first.

Zanardelli struggled on for two years seeing his Bills on the flour tax and divorce thrown out, and his whole position weakened by an outbreak of strikes, culminating in one by the railwaymen which for some days threw the country into chaos. During the previous decade, trade had steadily expanded, but the benefits had fallen to the capitalists, for there had been no corresponding rise in wages. Strikes were the new weapon used by Labour to improve its conditions. In the ten years before 1890 they had numbered some seven hundred, since then they had risen to seventeen hundred. The Right suppressed them by force, using the military to replace labour, but the Left held firmly to the principle of government neutrality in all trade disputes. A railway strike, however, was a different proposition, for they were government employees. The demands of the men were just and Zanardelli promised redress and the government found the money and ended the strike. The principle was bad. For the companies should have paid, if they had had the money. Unfortunately

212

they had not, unless the shareholders suffered. In 1903 ill health compelled Zanardelli to resign and three months later he died. He was one of the best of the leaders of the Left, honest, high principled and cultured, with a real sympathy for the poorer classes and a hatred of intrigue and corruption.

The fall of Zanardelli made way for Giovanni Giolitti, his late Minister of the Interior, who, highly endowed with the happy gift of leaving the sinking ship, had already resigned some months before the government fell. Giolitti was the most remarkable politician of the new Italy. For some years now he had been the power behind the throne and henceforth until his final resignation early in 1914, he controlled the political life of Italy.[23] During this period there were other Premiers, but it is nevertheless true to say that throughout he remained in power though not always in office, for he invariably left his successors dependent on a majority controlled by himself so that he could displace them whenever he wished to return to power in person. Giolitti had entered the civil service as a junior clerk and by sheer ability and hard work had reached the highest grades. He then became a Deputy and in May 1892 had succeeded Di Rudini as Premier, inheriting the Bank crisis. His connection with the irregularities was so equivocal that he resigned, and for some time lived abroad until the matter was forgotten. He now began his second Ministry after two years as Minister of the Interior. A widespread and prolonged movement eventually throws up an individual who embodies, more or less in perfection, the virtues or vices inherent in it, and Giolitti was the fine product of 'transformism'. From the first his conduct was actuated by two principles. The first was to collect as large a number of Deputies as possible, personally attached to himself. For this his position as Minister of the Interior had given him unexampled opportunities of which he had made the fullest use, bestowing favours and offices with the one idea always in mind. His second principle was to retain power at all costs and by all methods. A political calculator, treating parties and groups as mathematical quantities rather than as human beings, he was prepared to accept any party, Right, Left or Centre, if they helped to secure his majority. He feared crises or dangerous political situations, and when they arose withdrew from power, leaving a puppet-Premier to face the music, until such time as he thought well to return. How unassailable his position became may be gathered from the words of a Deputy who before his final retirement could say with truth, 'The Hon. Giolitti in his long career has nominated nearly all the Senators, nearly all the

Councillors of State, all the Prefects and all the other high officials in the administrative, judicial, political and military hierarchy of our country'.

Giolitti's ascendancy coincided with a remarkable expansion of trade and industry. Italy had turned the corner and began to feel the refreshing effects of a credit balance at the Treasury. Between 1890 and 1907 Italian foreign trade increased by 118 per cent, more than double that of England during the period. The use of electricity multiplied fivefold after 1900. Coal imports doubled. In 1900 Italy made six motor cars, in 1907 the number was 1,283 and in a few years it was a great industry. The population rose from thirty-two millions in 1901 to thirty-five ten years later, in spite of the extensive emigration, which reached its high-water mark in 1905 with 726,000. Though this depopulation of the poorer parts of Italy was viewed as a loss to the country, financially it was a gain, for in Italy their contribution to the national wealth was small, but from America or the Argentine these expatriated Italians sent back sums of money which in their totality made a welcome addition to the wealth of the country. In 1906 the conversion of the national debt and the reduction of interest from 4 to $3\frac{1}{2}$ per cent was not only a great financial operation but a relief to the Exchequer. The revenue increased by hundreds of millions of lire and at last showed a steady surplus, which, however, ended abruptly with the Libyan war of 1912. In silks and textiles, electrical machinery and motors, as well as in other branches Italy bid fair to become a serious competitor in the markets of the world and she had not then developed her most promising and extensive industry, agriculture.[24]

All this advance had its effect on Parliament. The Right, which included the upper strata of society, content with better dividends saw less reason to quarrel with the Ministry and provided the army and navy were not stinted, and Giolitti wisely saw to it that they were not, proved less difficult for a liberal Premier to handle. It was the same with the Left, for labour unrest quietens down with full employment. Besides, the Socialist party split and after 1900 their influence began to lessen as Giolitti gradually absorbed their programme in his social legislation. There was no official Catholic party in the Chamber. In 1904, when Giolitti's majority was in danger, the Vatican supported the Liberals against the Socialists and the following year the *non expedit* was officially raised. The result was a small Catholic group, who, provided their special interests were not attacked, were prepared to support the government when help was needed.

In general, it might be said that though each party retained a nucleus of diehards, who held rigidly to their creed and refused to co-operate when they felt their principles involved, the Chamber as a whole was a liberal pot-pourri, faded but still redolent of a more vigorous past, from which Giolitti picked his Ministers as he thought best.

Giolitti's first Cabinet, the usual *rimpasto* of Left and Right, was not as democratic as he had hoped, for he failed to induce Turati, the Socialist leader, to join it. A new figure was Tittoni, Prefect of Naples, who without any previous experience was hoisted into the Foreign Office. The attitude of successive Premiers since 1876 towards Foreign Affairs must strike an English reader as extraordinary, for to us the Foreign Office has a peculiar importance and the Foreign Secretary a special sanctity of his own. But in Italy, except when Visconti Venosta was in charge, no one of special knowledge was looked for, any one seemed to be suitable, and when Giolitti was once reproved for appointing an unsuitable member he replied, 'But, after all, I have only given him the Foreign Office!' Tittoni and his successors had, in fact, a delicate and thankless part to play; tied to Germany and Austria by the Triple Alliance, the real sympathies of Italy were towards France and England, and in a lesser degree towards Russia, despite the pronounced hostility of the Socialist party to the Czar, which had brusquely stopped the visit of the Russian Monarch to Italy during Zanardelli's term of office. In October 1903 the King and Queen went to Paris and in the following April President Loubet visited Rome. He received a triumphal reception and the enthusiasm shown over the visit revealed unmistakably where Italian sympathies lay. Germany, Austria and the Pope (whom the French President did not visit) were all equally annoyed but found difficulty in producing good reasons why Italy should not be friendly to others besides themselves.

The measures introduced by Giolitti in his first Ministry were not exciting or provocative. There were two commercial treaties, with Switzerland and Germany, a scheme for the systematic introduction of industry to Naples for the benefit of the working classes, and a number of measures dealing with Prison Reform, Charity, Public Health, and the salaries of school teachers and certain categories of public servants. In September 1904, however, there were outbreaks in Sicily and Sardinia whose suppression cost the lives of a number of civilians. The more extreme branch of the Socialists at once declared a general strike which after four days of disturbance, collapsed. To restore their prestige they violently attacked the government for 'repression' in the hope of overturning it. Giolitti countered their action by dissolving Parliament and ordering a general election, by which he hoped to break their power in the Chamber. The move was only partially successful, and afraid of his majority, he appealed to the Clericals. The Vatican raised the *non expedit* and sent priests and monks to the poll and saved the situation. A few months later, in February 1905, the railwaymen struck and to avoid another crisis Giolitti resigned, naming Fortis as his successor. Fortis settled the dispute ingeniously, for without forbidding their right to strike, which was the point at issue, he classified railwaymen as civil servants liable to dismissal if they ceased work. Fortis held office for a year and then Sonnino and the Right replaced him. Sonnino was an able man, a hard worker and full of ideas, but his manner was against him. Aloof and self-centred, with no gift of oratory, he could not handle the Chamber. He fell out with the Socialists who ruined his majority and he resigned in disgust, and Giolitti came back.

Giolitti's policy of interpolating his tenure of office with short periods of power by other Premiers, had several advantages. It disguised his own supremacy, put the burden of solving crises, which might damage his prestige or split his docile majority, on the shoulders of others, and had the further advantage that, if his temporary successor devised useful measures which they had not time to carry through, such might be appropriated and the credit transferred to himself. Two Bills of this kind he took over from Sonnino. The first was a Railway Bill for the acquisition by the State of those parts of the system still controlled by private companies. It was a difficult and intricate measure to which Sonnino had given much thought and labour. It was now introduced by Giolitti and passed with acclamation. The second, a Bill for the Conversion of the National Debt and a reduction of interest from 4 to $3\frac{1}{2}$ per cent, was the work of Luzzatti, Sonnino's able Finance Minister. Its introduction in 1906 was a great occasion and its author's history of the long financial struggle which the country had faced so bravely, moved the Chamber to an unusual display of patriotic emotion.

Apart from the laurels gathered from these two purloined measures, the second spell of power by Giolitti from 1906 to 1909 is not of great interest. His dominance was so undisputed, his methods so effective and his majority so docile, that he reigned supreme. Measures of general utility continued to be passed without much opposition. Ministers died or resigned and new ones were selected. Within the charmed circle of Montecitorio, presided over by the corrosive political genius of Giolitti, life went on as usual. Parliament worked in a vacuum, isolated from the national life, creating little interest, doing little harm and some good, and steadily losing its power to lead or stimulate the country. It was no novel condition for Italians, who long since under absolutism had learnt to live their lives and continue their work apart from the official circle at the summit, and Italy was doing that now. On all sides there were signs of industrial and social activity. Business was increasing, new factories were being built, and modern ideas of association and co-operation were taking hold of industry. Co-operative societies were springing up, People's Banks, a speciality of the Clericals, ran into many hundreds of branches. Industrial and Art Exhibitions were being organized, such as the biennial International Exhibition of Pictures at Venice, where each country exhibited its art in separate pavilions. Italy's own slender resources were being supplemented by foreign capital, in fact, before long the hold of German capital upon industry through the Banks, was to be a source of vigorous protest and not a little uneasiness.[25]

Italy too was taking her proper place amongst the Powers of Europe. Her fleet and army, reorganized under Giolitti, inspired respect, and she was receiving her quota of international courtesies. In 1907 King Edward VII met Victor Emanuel at Gaeta, not for the first time, for Victor Emanuel had been Italy's delegate at the Diamond Jubilee ten years before. Two years later the Czar paid his postponed visit to the King at Racconigi, the Royal Palace near Turin. These visits, however, following that of President Loubet, had political significance and were the fruit of years of quiet and successful diplomacy. For Italy's foreign policy guided by Visconti Venosta and followed by Tittoni, had at last developed purpose and continuity. Support for her increased influence in the Balkans, in opposition or rather competition with Austria, and acquiescence in her claims upon Tripolitania were her objectives; and following the precedent of Lanza in obtaining the consent of Europe before moving upon Rome, Italy made use of these royal visits to achieve her ends. Loubet had brought his Foreign Minister Delcassé with him and the Czar was similarly accompanied by Isvolsky. Edward VII was his country's best diplomat. Consent was obtained for Italy's reversionary rights on Tripoli and in return Italy supported France and England against German claims at Algeciras where Visconti Venosta represented Italy. In 1909 the threat to Italy, increased by Austria's absorption of Bosnia and Herzegovina in the Empire, and a simultaneous difficulty over a new Convention affecting the Mercantile

Marine, brought about Giolitti's resignation in favour of his nominee Sonnino, who formed his second Cabinet.

It would be a mistake to suppose that the dominance of Giolitti was not beneficial to the country. He kept Italy quiet, enabled her to go forward with her material advance, and carried through a long programme of valuable social and economic legislation. But there was neither magnetism nor moral elevation about Giolitti. He gave no lead to the country. He was more negative than positive, and his liberalism, sincere as it was, was a creed rapidly falling out of date. It was the misfortune of Italy that just as her unity and independence was won, the basis of liberalism upon which it rested, was crumbling throughout Europe. In its place came a double movement from Germany which was steadily changing the basis of European thought. The first of these was Marxism with its advocacy of the class struggle and its doctine of economic materialism, the one inciting to revolution, the other to imperialism, as the logical solution of the need for raw materials and fresh markets. In Italy, as we have seen, Marxism was toned down into a Socialist programme to be promoted by legal methods through Parliament. The second movement was the doctrine of force or Bismarckism, with which Germany, as the result of three successful wars, had become inoculated. Around this developed a medley of ideas all alike hostile to liberalism. Racialism, first put forward by the Frenchman Count Gobineau in 1853 in his *Essay on the Inequality of Human Races*, which at the close of the century found its fullest expression in the work of Houston Chamberlain. Aryanism with its sequel in anti-Semitism; Nietzsche and the superman; the Prussian doctrine of the super-state. All of these tended in the same direction, towards a rabid nationalism and an imperialistic creed of dominion. Nationalism raised its head in France in the teaching of Barrès and Maurras. In England the two Jubilees of Queen Victoria aroused a display of imperial power, which, if unprovocative, was at least an impressive display of strength, though the Boer War acted as a sedative to 'jingoism'. All of these ideas percolated through to Italy and though slow to germinate, eventually led to a nationalist creed which was to dominate the State.

Italy was not an aggressive nation nor had she any natural tendency towards militarism. Her attitude towards her government, which she regarded more as a necessary evil than an idol, offered no promising field for state collectivism. Divided for centuries into little states, she was not even yet, after thirty years of unity, fully conscious of her function as a single people, and the idea of mass movement was completely alien to her deep-rooted individualism. Yet, to change all this and convert Italy into an aggressive military power under an all-pervading state control, was precisely the purpose of the new nationalism. The general advance in Italy, the increase in quantity and improvement in quality of newspapers, magazines and books, together with the marked decline in illiteracy, which had fallen to 38 per cent, gave a wider scope than before to literary controversy or propaganda. Socialism was on the wane. It no longer attracted the youth of the country and the severe criticism to which it had been subjected by Benedetto Croce and the idealistic school of philosophy had robbed it of much of its influence. With these new conditions in its favour nationalism started with a propitious wind behind it.

The origin of the movement was primarily dissatisfaction with the moral and spiritual condition of Italy revealed by the deterioration of political life, the poorness of ideals, the growing materialism and the 'quietism' which seemed to have fallen on the country. To the majority of Italians, the occupation of Rome had closed a definite period in their history. To most of them the wider life of the present, the growing material prosperity and the rising standard of life, were all to the good, and the struggle and suffering of the Risorgimento a condition of things to which they would not willingly return. But there were some who looked on it very differently. To these the completion of unity was not an end but a beginning, which was to usher in the period of *grandezza*: the revival of the imperial greatness of the distant past. In support of this idea they appealed not only to ancient but to modern history. They quoted Mazzini's vision of the 'Terza Roma' and Gioberti's 'Italian Primacy', despite the fact that Mazzini's conception was of a spiritual and Gioberti's a civil and moral supremacy, and no thought of imperial greatness in the Roman sense, was claimed by either of them as Italy's destiny. So too they eulogized Francesco Crispi as the one survival of the 'heroic' age of Garibaldi and Mazzini, with his colonial vision, his belief in Italy's greatness and faith in her future. Alfredo Oriani had already laid the foundation and written the device, 'Greatness as the end and heroism as the means', as he had likewise indicated the imperial sphere of action—Africa— where Italy had 'conquered Hannibal, imprisoned Jugurtha, suppressed the Ptolemies and discomfited the Saracens,' and must therefore repeat her former triumphs.

The leaders of the movement, however, saw clearly enough that the mere advocacy of imperialism was insufficient: that, for any measure of success for so audacious a programme for Italy's future, not only would the parliamentary system have to be radically re-formed, suffering as it was from vicious political anaemia, but that the very mentality of the nation must be reversed. It was here that German thought was grafted on to imperialism. The movement soon produced a Press, *Il Regno* and the *Pagine Nationaliste* of Sighele being the first, but its full programme only became apparent with the publication of Corradini's *Idea Nazionale*. Corradini was the father of Nationalism. Already an author and journalist of standing, he left journalism for politics and to express his views founded and edited the *Idea Nazionale*, which became an important daily paper. He set himself to re-educate the people in the classical tradition: to make them conscious of being the heirs of Rome. To create a new political class capable of founding a new constitutional order, and to inoculate the nation with what he called a war-morale, in opposition to the *morale umanitaria* of the Socialists, which would instil within them a sense of the true nobility of sacrificing all for the greatness of their country. The rising generation must be brought up to realize that they be-longed to a nation which 'aspires to conquer for itself the largest share in the rule of the world'. They must no longer be educated in the old ideals of liberalism but rather in the 'morality of men that do things'. He advocated state control, militarism and colonial expansion to absorb emigration. In opposition to individualism, he emphasized the collectivism of modern industry, maintaining that in comparison with the needs or safety of the country the individual was of no more importance than the fall of a leaf in relation to the forest. It was the full programme of power-politics.

Nationalism found a powerful propagandist in the poet Gabriele D'Annunzio. Poetry has always been a great influence in Italian thought and in the hands of so great an artist as D'Annunzio it was a weapon of no mean calibre. He was the fine flower of the school of minor poets known as the Veristi or Realists who sprang up after 1870. Unity had killed the old patriotic idealism in poetry which had been the staple ingredient of the poets of the Risorgimento. The new school was materialistic and practical, dealing with the poverty and suffering around them, treating love as a physical enjoyment, and clothing their ideas in a simplicity of language and form which varied little from prose. D'Annunzio was a great master of words, with a fine dramatic sense and an exquisite lyrical touch, and a prolific writer both in prose and verse. But his work is tainted. A voluptuary and hedonist, his cult of the physical senses, his streak of morbid cruelty, his love of bloodshed and destruction, vitiates the value of his work.

He was the poet of speed and power, hymning the motor car and the aeroplane. His gospel of daring and adventure blended with the glory of the conqueror triumphant amid the ruins of his victims, stirred the pulses of the rising generation. He was the poet of the sea and Italy's young navy, and in the Libyan war he sang the glories of destruction and bloodshed with all the intensity of his nature. But his influence was bad. He appealed to the restless and the dissatisfied, setting before his readers an ideal devoid of loftiness or purity, based on a gospel of force. But he was a great asset to Nationalism.

Nationalism found support in very varied quarters. Its colonial policy appealed to business men in need of raw materials and fresh markets. Catholic circles looked with favour on its authoritarianism. The call to a life of daring and adventure appealed to the young, and the vistas opened by D'Annunzio in the glories of love and war attracted the restless element tired of the materialistic ideals of Socialism, and its creed of international pacifism. Its central theme of national greatness was quickly followed up. Magazines came into being whose names alone are sufficient to indicate their programme, *La grande Italia, Il Carroccio, Il Tricolore*, echoing the words of Oriani, 'Imperialism is a dream only with the weak: it becomes vice only in the hands of those incapable of command: what will the future of Italy be, confined to her narrow limits? The future of Europe lies in other continents where alone will it prove the greatness of its soul. War is racial'. Pacifism and the inviolability of human life, declared Corradini, must be relegated to the realm of fable, the patrimony of the sentimental idealists of the past. It was necessary to remember that contempt for death was the greatest factor in life, and stressing the collectivist tendency of the modern world, he added, 'human life loses its value immediately man passes from a state of individualism to that of collectivism, and the morality of its sanctity becomes a true and proper immorality, for it gives value to that which has none. It is the individual egotism which betrays collective altruism'. It is hardly necessary to point out how these ideas coincided at a later date with Fascism. Under Mussolini, Corradini and Oriani became the textbooks for the young. Oriani died in 1909 but Corradini lived to be a Senator under the new gospel of power and a fervent Fascist.

Nationalism was strenuously opposed in the journals and reviews of the period. Croce, in *La Critica*, Salvemini, in *L'Unità*, never tired of stressing the dangers and falsities lying beneath the German doctrines of Race and State, while the Nationalists glorified war and power and denounced the pacifism of the Socialists and their anti-patriotic internationalism. But the evil was deep-seated and the efforts of a few enlightened thinkers were powerless to stop a trend of thought which rested on genuine motives and profound convictions. Besides, liberalism was a new tradition in Italy, it had no long history behind it, it lacked the support of religion, and had not yet realized the limits beyond which it sinks into licence and anarchy.

The rival political programmes which were occupying the thought of Italy found no echo in the work of Parliament. Sonnino succeeded Giolitti in 1909 with a wide programme of reforms including elementary education and local taxation. But his unsympathetic personality and disregard for the susceptibilities of the Chamber rendered the members hostile and he withdrew in disgust. Then came Luzzatti, 'kindly supplied with a majority', as one Deputy remarked, by Giolitti. He suggested that the Senate should be reformed, or rather, if they would reform themselves the Lower Chamber would assist. The Senate had never been of much value to the State. Its composition needed overhauling, for it tended to become more and more of a political lumber-room. It was nominated in theory by the King but in practice by a list supplied by the Premier. There was no limit to the number of Senators, in consequence, defeated Deputies, ambitious nonentities, tiresome secretary-generals as well as worthy ones, were periodically transferred to the Upper Chambers in batches. The Senate was a life appointment but not hereditary. In fact, the appointment of Senators had become a political manoeuvre, for the purpose either of removing opponents or of making room for those on whom it was desirable to bestow favours. Luzzatti's proposal was received without enthusiasm, no one knew quite what to do, and the idea was dropped.

One of the fundamental weaknesses of parliamentary life in Italy, as has been already mentioned, was its isolation; that it did not reflect the national thought. The result of this failing in practice, was that the electorate would not take the trouble to vote. It was not really interested in what happened at Montecitorio. Luzzatti now brought in a Bill for the reform of the franchise. He rejected universal suffrage and proposed instead a moderate extension, by admitting a literacy test to those at present excluded, and to make voting compulsory under penalty of a fine. The Left supported him in its firm belief that the wider the franchise the more votes they would secure. But the Chamber was unenthusiastic and critical. The result of this compulsory freedom would certainly have been interesting, for its effect upon an unorganized and uninterested electorate was incalculable. But the temper of the Chamber convinced Luzzatti that the Bill would not be passed and he determined to shelve it quietly until a more propitious moment. He reckoned, however, without Giolitti, who after nearly two years of absence from office had decided to return to power. He rose during the debate and after denouncing Luzzatti's measure as unsatisfactory declared that the only solution of the franchise question was universal suffrage. The position of Luzzatti was unenviable. He was already mortgaged to Giolitti by the loan of his majority, and when on the motion before the Chamber Giolitti suddenly foreclosed, he found himself deserted and defeated. As he had openly rejected universal suffrage, which Giolitti now declared essential, he had no option but to resign and Giolitti returned to power. The third Giolitti Cabinet came into office, in April 1911. With cynical indifference to their political principles, Giolitti took over Luzzatti's Cabinet with very few changes, and brought in a Bill for universal suffrage, which they had opposed under Luzzatti, but were now to support under Giolitti; it was, however, held up by the outbreak of the Libyan war, and it was not until 1912, when the war was over, that it found its way to the Statute Book.

The eventual occupation of Tripolitania by Italy had for some years been tacitly accepted by the European Powers. Under an energetic Premier, such as Crispi had been, it might, indeed, have been carried out earlier, once an understanding with France had been arrived at, such as took place in 1904. But Giolitti was essentially a bureaucrat not a war minister, more interested in internal than foreign affairs and in peace than war. The Italian Foreign Office had been slow and cautious, careful to obtain, in advance, the sanction not only of France but of England, Russia and Austria. Italy had, moreover, when the Triple Alliance had been renewed in 1902, endeavoured to get her claim to Tripoli formally acknowledged by her two allies. This was refused, but Austria signed a separate agreement by which she undertook not to oppose Italy's designs in North Africa. But the question of occupation was inextricably mixed up with the wider problems of Turkey, to whom it belonged, and this complicated the whole matter. The maintenance of Turkish sovereignty in order to prevent her absorption by Russia was an axiom in European politics. But Turkey was the sick man of Europe, who had much to bequeath, and Austria and Germany as well as Russia, were most assiduous in their attentions, as prospective heirs of her patrimony. No one more so than Germany, who had already extracted the Baghdad railway concession and who considered Turkey as a sleeping partner in the Triple Alliance. An attack, therefore, on Tripoli would be unwelcome at Berlin. The attitude of Italy, in her support of France and England at Algeciras, made Germany's acquiescence in the occupation of Tripoli by Italy still less probable, especially as Italy had some reason to believe that Berlin already had her eyes on Tripoli herself. Matters in the Balkans came to a crisis in 1908, an unfortunate moment for Italy, who, having barely recovered from the disastrous eruption of Vesuvius in 1906, was again plunged into national mourning over the thousands killed in the terrible Sicilian earthquake which destroyed Messina. First came the revolt of the Young Turks, bringing a new and incalculable element into Turkish politics, followed by the abrupt and unexpected annexation of Bosnia and Herzegovina by Austria. The threat to Turkey implicit in the action of Aerenthal alarmed both Berlin and London, while Serbia, now surrounded on both north and west by Austria, clamoured for war, looking confidently to Russia for support. The Bosnian annexation was scarcely less a threat to Italy than Serbia, bringing Austria to the verge of Dalmatia and jeopardizing Italian preponderance in the Adriatic. Europe seemed on the edge of war, but Russia, not yet recovered from the struggle with Japan, was forced to draw back from support of Serbia when Germany came openly to the side of Austria. War was postponed, but Germany had made an irreconcilable enemy of Russia and Austria of Italy, though in response to Italian protests Vienna agreed to withdraw from the Sanjak of Novi Bazar, which gratified Servia and helped to reconcile her to the inevitable.

One of the first fruits of the new situation had been the Czar's visit to the King of Italy and the signature of the Racconigi Agreement by which Italy undertook to support Russian policy in the Straits in return for her consent to Italian action in Africa. There were already considerable Italian interests in Tripolitania where Sicilian emigrants were established as well as others who had moved eastwards from Tunisia after its annexation by France. In 1909, the Turkish Sultan, Abdul Hamid, abdicated, and the Young Turks came into power. The change of government was soon felt in Tripoli. No aggressive opposition to Italian penetration had hitherto disturbed the relations between the two countries, but Italian merchants, once the Young Turks were in the ascendant, were quickly made aware of a new spirit of dislike and arrogance. Rumours to this effect soon reached the Italian Press and fed the Nationalist demand for war, and the government was vigorously urged to take action; but the decision of the Ministers was determined by far more important issues than the clamour of the Press. In 1911 came the Agadir incident; the occupation of Fez by the French troops with its threat to Morocco; the *riposte* of Germany in the despatch of the *Panther*, the open support of France by England, and after three months of acute international tension, the recognition of France's position in Morocco by Germany, in return for a vast area of the French Congo in compensation. Agadir threw the question of Tripoli into high relief. As the only section of the North African coastline as yet unoccupied by one or other of the Great Powers, its possession became a vital interest to Italy. She dare not allow herself to be deprived of every foothold on the southern shore of the Mediterranean, and if she hesitated she was lost, for Germany, though she had not yet developed her technique of 'tourists', was already displaying great interest in Tripoli through the suspicious activity of geologists and archaeologists. Her trade interests, too, were pressing upon those of Italy, and when it became known that the Bank of Rome, the chief financial backing of Italian merchants in Tripoli, was so hard pressed that it was contemplating selling its interests to a German combine, the situation became acute. It was necessary to act on Napoleon's advice to Cavour in the crisis of 1860, 'Bonne Chance et faites vite'.

Without alarming Europe, an expeditionary force was prepared and in October Italy suddenly delivered an ultimatum to Turkey, demanding immediate consent to the occupation of Tripoli, following it at once with the despatch of troops and a declaration of war. The occupation of Tripoli, Benghazi and Derna, was effected without much trouble, but the subjugation of the hinterland proved a long and difficult undertaking. Italy was, moreover, hampered by the attitude of the Powers who had previously recognized her claims to Tripolitania. There were unpleasant incidents with France; Austria and Germany, not only resented Italy's prompt reaction to the situation arising after Agadir, without even a previous request for permission from Vienna and Berlin, but objected to any further weakening of Turkey, for as Giolitti acutely remarked Turkey was 'armed with her foreign debts'. They vetoed any direct attack on the Straits and thus robbed Italy of the advantage of her sea power. The war dragged on for twelve months and might have lasted still longer if the Balkan States had not seized the opportunity for a joint attack on Turkey in the first Balkan war. This necessitated a prompt Peace with Italy, which was signed at Lausanne in October 1912. Turkey withdrew from Tripolitania which passed to Italy, the failure of Turkey to recall her troops, however, which was the condition upon which Italy was to restore the Aegean islands, led to their retention in Italian hands, Italy assumed responsibility for Tripoli's share of the Turkish national debt, and the authority of the Sultan over the natives in Tripoli was to be recognized.

The effects of the war on Italy fulfilled for a short time the prophecies of the Nationalists, for it drew Italy together in a manner which no event since the Risorgimento had succeeded in doing, providing a national cause transcending sectional differences and party programmes, in which all Italians had an equal interest. The Nationalists went wild with excitement, claiming it as the result of their propaganda and the first step in the fulfilment of their ideal. D'Annunzio, from his voluntary exile in France, flung himself into the orgy of applause, and with his Songs Overseas and Naval Odes hymned the brave deeds of Italy's army and navy. The war gave birth to the most fantastic hopes. Hundreds of thousands of Italians were to find a prosperous living in the new colony. Tripoli was to become what Egypt had been to Rome, the granary of the Empire. But the war went on too long. After the first phase of successful occupation the nature of the desert warfare (there were no armoured divisions in those days) lent itself but indifferently to a record of spectacular feats of arms, and the public interest waned. The truth as to the commercial possibilities began to emerge. The cost of maintenance of an army of occupation did not increase the enthusiasm, and the peace terms met with criticism. Nevertheless, it offered a great opportunity to lift the nation towards a real forward movement and it was almost a tragedy that Italy was in the hands of so utterly uninspiring a leader as Giolitti, who, the war over, went back at once to his parliamentary scheming without thought or perception of the great chance that was passing by.

When normal parliamentary work began again, Giolitti brought in a Bill for the State monopoly of insurance, designed to safeguard the small investor from fraudulent speculators and weak companies promising too advantageous terms. The Bill was duly passed, but the necessary process of absorbing the existing companies delayed its practical application for some years. He then brought forward the suspended measure for universal suffrage, which the Chamber accepted and passed without very strenuous opposition. It was followed by the dissolution of Parliament and a general election. The election of 1913 was of unusual interest, for no one could foresee the results of the increased franchise which had raised the numbers of the electorate from $3\frac{1}{2}$ to 8 millions. Confronted with this expansion of voting power the chief preoccupation of Giolitti was how best to preserve his majority. Surveying the political terrain he decided that the party most amenable to a satisfactory arrangement and whose support would be of the greatest help to him, was the Clerical Party. Although strong in certain areas, notably Venetia, there were not many constituencies in which the Clericals could carry an election by their own unaided voting power: but in a great many constituencies they were strong enough, if they voted solidly for one of the other parties, to turn the election in favour of their chosen candidate. Their general policy was not so much the advocacy of a special programme as to hold a watching brief to prevent the success of·any measure inimical to Catholic principles or susceptibilities. Perfectly aware of this, Giolitti opened negotiations with Count Gentiloni, the leader of the Clerical Party, and came to a satisfactory arrangement by which he guaranteed that no measure hostile to clerical interests should be introduced provided that the Clericals voted for his supporters in all constituencies where no Catholic candidate was being put forward or where his chances of success were obviously remote. This pact was to be kept secret. Not yet content with this safeguard, Giolitti went further and promised support to all and sundry, Radicals, Socialists and Freemasons, who undertook, if elected, to support him in the Chamber. The result of these manoeuvres was successful and when the elections were over Giolitti found himself with a comfortable majority. He had this time, however, overreached himself, for Count Gentiloni gave away the secret in an interview with a Press representative at which he estimated that no less than two hundred members of the government owed their seats to the Catholic vote. But the worst aspect of the bargain was the fact that Giolitti had undertaken to vote for the Catholic candidates in the constituencies they contested, which was a betrayal of his own party by the deliberate support of their most convinced and determined opponents.

The hold of Giolitti over the Chamber was really remarkable, for notwithstanding the publication of the terms of the Gentiloni Pact and the subsequent sarcastic criticisms of his conduct in the Chamber, the members gave him a substantial vote of confidence. But the composition of the Chamber, thanks to Giolitti's general support of other parties than his own, proved his undoing. The Radicals broke away, and the opposition became formidable. There were other difficulties as well. The Libyan war had depleted the Exchequer and there was a deficit at the Treasury of twenty-five millions. The railwaymen were again on the verge of a general strike and altogether the horizon was threatening. Giolitti could no longer rely on his majority, he held on until March 1914 and then resigned, hoping, as before, to return when the gathering clouds had dispersed. This time, however, he miscalculated, for seven years were to pass before, in the extremity of parliamentary failure, he was recalled to power as an old man, to face a situation which was completely beyond him.

The legacy of unrest and difficulty which Giolitti left behind him did not take long to mature. The Chamber, filled with conflicting elements, received a new leader in Salandra, for Sonnino, indicated as his successor by Giolitti, was not to be beguiled a third time into trying to govern with a Giolittian majority in the Chamber. Perhaps the new parliament's most noticeable feature was the decay of the Socialists, now almost non-existent as a national party, and comprising no more than a *congerie* of local groups. Salandra settled the railway strike by calling up two classes of reservists, but this was only one aspect of the unrest. The Socialists had lately found a valuable new recruit in one, Benito Mussolini, at this time a wholehearted revolutionary, going back to pure Marxism and the class struggle. He was now editor of *Avanti* and his energy both literary and oratorical brought new life into the party's propaganda, and he had been officially thanked for his work. Partly as the result of his firebrand methods, in May and early June, violent disturbances broke out in Emilia and the Romagna. Peasant leagues started boycotts and sabotage, threats and outrages terrified the countryside, and for a short while anarchy prevailed everywhere. Republics were set up, the soldiers besieged in their barracks and prominent citizens seized as hostages. Fortunately, there was no organization behind it and the whole movement was quickly repressed. The disorders of 'Red Week', however, gave the editor of *Avanti* and his supporters intense satisfaction. But the local troubles of Italy faded into insignificance when on June 28th the Archduke Franz Ferdinand and his wife were assassinated when on a tour in Bosnia. In the ghastly pause that followed the pistol shots at Sarajevo, the world looked into the abyss. On July 23rd came the Austrian ultimatum to Serbia. What followed is too well known to need repetition. Germany stood behind Austria, Russia behind Serbia. The first week in August the first World War broke out.

On August 13, 1913, a year before the outbreak of the World War, on the eve of the Treaty of Bucharest which closed the War of

Partition in the Balkans, ending in the crushing defeat of Bulgaria, Austria had informed her two allies that she intended to take action against Serbia, describing it as 'defensive' in the hope that by so doing she would obtain the support of both Germany and Italy. But neither responded as she expected. Italy refused point blank to regard an Austrian attack on Serbia as defensive, Germany also exercised a restraining influence at Vienna, and their joint efforts delayed the attack for twelve months. After the murder of Franz Ferdinand, Austria would wait no longer. In 1914 Italy again refused to recognize the attack on Serbia as a *casus foederis* and on August 2nd formally announced her neutrality. Her action was received with genuine gratitude by France and as obviously correct by England. As to her nominal allies, had there been any doubt as to their real opinion regarding Italy's value as the third partner in the alliance, it was made abundantly clear by the attack on Serbia. It came as a rude shock to Italy, for it flouted contemptuously the terms of the alliance. Italy had been neither informed nor consulted, and she was, in consequence, perfectly at liberty to act as she did and proclaim her neutrality, for the *casus foederis* simply did not arise.

The attack on Serbia had, moreover, another aspect for it brought up the whole question of irredentism. Italy was still a member of the Triple Alliance and its provisions continued to apply in her relations with Austria. Amongst these was a clause which stipulated that any acquisition of territory by Austria was to involve a corresponding compensation to Italy, and this meant the Trentino. Italy's claims on Austria were not all of the same validity. In regard to Istria and Dalmatia, she could claim them as having belonged to Venice for four centuries, but the Trentino and Trieste were never hers, and her claim had, perforce, to be based on the predominance of Italian inhabitants. Austria, on the other hand, regarded her Italian subjects as just part of the empire and was determined to treat them as she chose. The question was brought up diplomatically by the Italian Foreign Secretary, the Marquis San Giuliano, who on the invasion of Serbia wrote to Vienna claiming that the compensation clause vii now came into operation, adding that the only territory Italy would accept was the Trentino. Austria curtly refused to discuss the matter, and there for the time being the matter ended. The intransigence of Vienna's attitude, despite its solid basis in international law, fanned the flame of Italian anger and made any chance of her implementing her alliance by action on the side of her allies more remote than ever.

In the meantime the whole country was discussing the fate of Italy. Naturally the great majority were in favour of keeping out of the struggle, if possible. But to those in authority such a happy solution appeared increasingly impossible, even undesirable, for if Germany and Austria won, there would be small consideration for Italy, nor would she get much from the Entente if she stood aside in their hour of need. From the moral standpoint Italy was with France and England, and in this she had the full support of the Press. The attitude of the various parties inevitably brought confusion into public opinion. The Nationalists, for example, with their belief in the virtues of war *per se*, and the great purifying power of national sacrifice, portrayed so eloquently by D'Annunzio in his poems and romances and sustained by Corradini and Oriani, were almost indifferent as to the side on which they fought, and at first were eager to join Germany and Austria, until, finding no support, they changed over to become warm supporters of the Entente. On the other hand, the Socialists, with their creed of internationalism, were anti-patriotic, refusing to recognize the war as a true national issue. The irredentists were of course for immediate intervention and their attitude carried weight with the members of the government who could not disguise from themselves the opportunity offered to recover the coveted provinces and secure for Italy a defensible frontier. Before long the terms 'Neutralists' and 'Interventionists' came into vogue, but they were scarcely accurate, for very few held to an absolute neutrality and the difference between them was rather one of opportunity and means, than of fighting or not fighting. The Conservatives, for instance, regarded most generally as the stronghold of neutrality, were no pacifists, but demanded the utmost prudence and the exploration of every channel for a peaceful solution before having recourse to war. In any case immediate intervention was impossible, for apart from the serious deficiencies revealed by the Libyan war, the army had no equipment for a winter campaign in the Alps. Nothing could be done before the early summer of 1915.

This delay, while it was of the utmost value for the material preparation of the nation, made the spiritual preparation even more difficult. The revelation of the appalling cost of life, the cruel suffering of Belgium and northern France, the pictures of the horrors of war, deepened the revulsion against throwing the country into the struggle. Yet even this had its reverse side, for to stand aside in the hope of material gain, to shrink from sharing the sacrifices demanded of so many, was no creed for a great nation. The racial sympathy with France, the appeal of England's battle against tyranny and her agelong love of freedom, sentiments long revered in Italy, moved the nation to take her stand beside them, as the memory of the brutal Croats and Hungarians and the long years of oppression under Austrian bayonets made all thought of fighting for the Habsburg an outrage on decent feeling. So too the Church, though it did not for a moment forego its love of peace on earth, showed its wisdom by restraint, leaving Italy to win her own salvation even in fear and trembling.

While public opinion was in this state of flux the government was negotiating with both sides. Italy, however, could get no satisfaction from Austria. No concessions such as were considered essential were forthcoming, and Salandra turned to the Entente.[26] The *pourparlers* had not yet begun when a crisis developed in the Ministry. The demands of the Minister for War for the sum deemed necessary for the needs of the army was so large, that the Cabinet resigned in a body, and Salandra had to reconstruct it. Sonnino was brought to the Foreign Office, not a very happy choice for all his ability, and V. E. Orlando, an honest and able man, took the portfolio of Justice. Negotiations were now opened with England. Italy found the Entente ready and willing to grant generous terms for an alliance. All she asked for was conceded and on April 25th the secret treaty was signed. Documents of this kind made in the middle of war, when the concessions had yet to be won by force of arms, are not very reliable, as Italy was to discover later. It was at this moment that a second ministerial crisis developed. The trend of public opinion was clearly hardening for intervention on the side of the Entente, and before the position became past recall Giolitti decided to throw his influence against immediate action.

Giolitti came up to Rome in the first days of May and his advent created a sensation in Parliamentary circles. Regarded as the embodiment of political wisdom and experience, the Deputies flocked to his house in the Via Cavour, literally by hundreds. Always the calculator and always pessimistic, distrusting the army, and fully aware of the country's financial weakness and the limitation of her resources, his advice was a blend of prudence and depreciation. After laying his views before the King he put them before the Deputies. The result was a stiffening of opinion in the Chamber against active participation in the war. The position of the Ministry was critical, having already a signed agreement with the Entente not yet communicated to the country. The prospect of an adverse vote decided Salandra on an extreme step and he resigned. It chanced, however, that while Giolitti was preaching his programme of prudence and delay to the Deputies, a rival and no less influential voice was declaiming an entirely different gospel. For just at this time Gabriele D'Annunzio had left France and returned to Italy to rouse her to war and greatness. Disdaining practical difficulties D'Annunzio appealed not to reason but to sentiment, to the heart not to the head. In a series of fervent speeches at Genoa, at Quarto on the anniversary of the departure of Garibaldi and the Thousand, and later at Rome, he roused huge audiences to wild demonstrations of patriotic ardour and the youth of Italy to a half-mystical craving for self-sacrifice. Under the influence of D'Annunzio's burning oratory, the sudden announcement of Salandra's resignation roused an angry note of protest, for the hand of Giolitti was quickly perceived. While the nation waited in suspense, the King consulted the oracle as to forming a Ministry, but Giolitti refused. To displace Salandra and nominate a successor amenable to direction from behind, might be desirable, but to face the situation in person was not at all to his liking, and the King, without waiting to hear his further proposals, recalled Salandra.

While the country, driven on by its destiny, wrestled in the last throes of its conversion to war; too often, alas, marred by violent party spirit and bitter denunciation, as if Italy was unconsciously working herself up to accept the desperate sacrifice of her manhood, Salandra laid before the Chamber the results of the government's negotiations with Austria and the terms of the secret treaty with the Entente. There could be no hesitation in their choice. The die was cast. Full powers were given to the government: on May 20th Italy's withdrawal from the Triple Alliance was communicated to Vienna and Berlin. Three days later mobilization was ordered and on May 24th war was declared on Austria, later to be extended to Germany, Turkey and Bulgaria.

CHAPTER FOURTEEN

THE WAR AND THE PEACE

THE outbreak of the European War in August 1914 found Italy quite unprepared. Although she had had her army and navy on a war footing more recently than any other of the Great Powers, demobilizing after the war in Tripoli only at the end of 1912, the serious deficiencies then revealed had not been made good. Parliament had always grudged the military and naval expenditure which in proportion to the needs of the country were already considered as extravagant, and when in 1914 the War Minister demanded twenty-four millions to equip the armed forces it was indignantly refused and reduced to one third. Nevertheless, the war with Turkey had value. The navy had learnt the realities of escort and transport work; there had been one naval action, though of small value; the staffs of both services had been tested, and a proportion of the troops had been in action, though the conditions of desert warfare were peculiarly unsuitable as a preparation for warfare in the Alps. The war in Tripoli had been on a relatively small scale, some eighty thousand troops had been mobilized, whereas now the staff had to think in hundreds of thousands and, before long, in millions. Fortunately, the Commander-in-Chief, General Cadorna, the son of General Raffaele Cadorna who had commanded the troops which occupied Rome in 1870, was a fine organizer.

The deficiencies in the army were chiefly in munitions and artillery. There was no siege train: there were no heavy guns, and only sixty-four of medium calibre to each army corps, compared with the hundred and forty-four in the German army, and only some six hundred machine guns altogether. Their own need for armaments made it impossible for the nations from whom Italy was accustomed to buy, to satisfy her wants, and her own resources, until expansion took place, were inadequate for her needs, and she opened the war very poorly equipped. As to the personnel, there was a plethora of senior officers, due to the fact that the pay was so meagre that every kind of influence was freely used to reach the higher ranks, where an officer could live in decent comfort. For a similar reason there was a shortage of junior officers for almost any civilian employment was more remunerative than the army. Nevertheless in the ten months of neutrality much was done to put the army on a fighting basis but the want of artillery could not be improvised, and the lack of adequate artillery preparation caused exceptionally heavy casualties. The task, moreover, of Cadorna was not only in material equipment. He had to restore the fighting morale of the army. Numbers of officers owing their positions to favour and political wire-pulling rather than ability, had to be removed and replaced by capable subordinates. It was the same with the rank and file. They had been used far too much in the suppression of civil disturbance—in putting down strikes, shepherding crowds and replacing strikers in essential services—to have an offensive spirit, for the uncongenial work of handling unarmed mobs was a poor preparation for war with Austria. All this added to the difficulties of the regimental commands and bred doubt as to the reliability of the army when faced with a determined enemy.

When Italy announced her neutrality on August 2nd there was considerable uneasiness as to whether Austria would respect it. Marshal Conrad von Hotzendorf, the Austrian Commander-in-Chief, was an old and unscrupulous enemy of Italy. In 1908, when Italy was temporarily paralysed by the Messina disaster, he had strongly urged a 'preventive' attack upon her, and during the Libyan campaign he had been removed from his post for a time owing to his insistent advocacy of the same line of action. But the war with Russia saved Italy from the danger, for all Austria's efforts were needed to repel invasion from the east. Nevertheless, to meet this possible contingency Cadorna ordered a secret mobilization, and as early as October troops were being drafted to their war stations from the depots, so that when mobilization was officially announced on May 23rd there were already nearly four hundred thousand men under arms. There were four hundred miles of Alpine frontier to be defended, in shape like the letter S laid upon its side. The western loop represented the boundary stretching from Switzerland across Lake Garda and round the Trentino, whilst the northern edge after circling under the Carnic and Julian Alps descended south along the valley of the Isonzo to form the eastern boundary. Throughout its entire length the dominating positions were in the hands of Austria as settled by the Delimitation Commission after the war of 1866. On the lower Isonzo she held both banks and her position opened to her a double line of attack on Italy, from east and west. She could either advance from the Isonzo towards the Venetian plain, or on the west, through the screen of mountains protecting the Trentino, follow the valleys of the Adige and the Brenta upon Vicenza and Verona and the valley of the Po. Italy, on the other hand, had but one effective area for an offensive, across the Isonzo, fringed on either side by precipitous mountains, which, once penetrated, would lead to Gorizia and Trieste and the main road system into Austria.

The months of Italy's neutrality were employed by Austria in strengthening her defences. Under the direction of General von Rühr, the area round Trent was transformed into a veritable fortress, and when that was complete he took in hand the Isonzo fortifications, especially those round the two bridgeheads of Tolmino and Gorizia. Miles of trenches were dug and barbed wire entanglements erected and hundreds of gun emplacements sited and prepared. Full use was made of all the latest methods developed by Germany in the West. For the first year of war Austria concentrated on defence. Although her man power was less than the Italians (there were only twenty-five Austrian divisions against thirty-five Italian in the west until the defeat of Russia), she had strongly fortified positions and a great superiority in gun power. When neutrality ended Italy had four armies in the field, the Trentino Army which stretched from Switzerland along the Trentino to the Val Cismon, the Army of the Cadore northward and eastwards to the Carnic Alps, the Army of the Carnia comprising sixteen Alpine battalions, and then the Army of the Isonzo, equal in size (fourteen divisions) to the other three combined, stretching southward to the Adriatic. Seven divisions were kept in reserve.

Cadorna's opening move was dictated by Italy's inferior defensive position along the frontier. The general mobilization was ordered on the 23rd May, the day before Italy declared war. Relying on the probability that Austria would not expect to be attacked before mobilization was complete at the end of June, Cadorna ordered a surprise offensive along the whole frontier immediately war was declared. It could not be a sustained effort, owing to lack of reinforcements until the completion of mobilization, but it was hoped that the element of surprise would enable Italy to seize and hold a better line of defence. Definite objectives were allocated to each army and on May 24th a simultaneous advance was made on all fronts. An attack before the Italian army was at full strength was quite unexpected by Austria and nearly everywhere she was pushed back. In the Trentino sector, Monte Baldo and Monte Altissimo were seized and further east Monte Pasubio, and the troops advanced as far as Ala. These positions were strongly held even during the Austrian offensive from

the Trentino in 1916. In the Cadore region the Italians crossed the Val
Sugana and occupied Borgo on the Upper Brenta. The nature of the
terrain in the Carnic Alps made any ·big advance impossible but
several passes were seized. Even more success was achieved by the
Isonzo army, in the middle sector they reached and crossed the river
near Plezza, occupying the surrounding heights and getting a foothold
on the massif of Monte Nero. Monte Colowrat opposite Tolmino was
occupied, as was Monte Corada further south. Between Gorizia and
the sea the Austrians withdrew across the river, and Cormons and

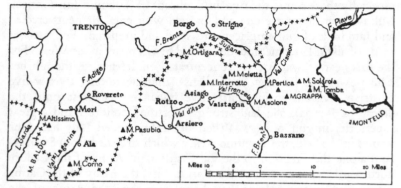

THE TRENTINO OFFENSIVE, 1916

Cervignano, amongst other places, were occupied without opposition.
They were now faced not only with the entrenched area surrounding
Gorizia, defended by every modern device and supported by a ring
of strongly held mountains, but by the great limestone plateau known
as the Carso, the scene of bitter fighting throughout the war. The
fighting lasted until the beginning of August, by which time the
Italian troops were nearly everywhere over the border: little real
impression had, however, been made on the southern half of the
Isonzo which was the key position to any advance into Austria or
the occupation of Trieste and Laibach.

Italy renewed the offensive in October, known as the second battle
of the Isonzo, there were twelve in all. With the army now fully
mobilized a greater force was employed, but the lack of adequate
artillery support was a terrible weakness, and even the guns they had
could only be used for short periods, for want of shells. To give the
troops cover the artillery was massed on a narrow front but this
proved terribly expensive, meeting as it did a converging fire from
a wider range of guns. This time not only was the element of surprise

absent but the Austrians had received substantial reinforcements from the Russian front. Some progress was made around Gorizia but the total gain was negligible compared to the cost. In these two offensives in 1915 Italy lost over a quarter of a million men. In November, winter put an end to the fighting and both sides prepared for a renewal of the struggle in the spring.

Whilst the army was in winter quarters in preparation for the spring campaign, the Italian navy carried out a difficult and exacting task in the Adriatic. Although Italy had fourteen battleships, including six Dreadnoughts, and Austria had four Dreadnoughts out of nine battleships, there were no fleet actions and the heavy ships on both sides remained mostly in harbour. The east coast of Italy had no suitable ports—Venice was an open anchorage, Ancona too small and Brindisi not yet properly equipped. The naval war, confined to the Adriatic, was one of mines and submarines and torpedo craft. Austria had in this type of warfare considerable advantages, for while the Italian coast was low and sandy, the fringe of Dalmatian islands was an ideal lurking place for submarines and small craft, and she had besides three first-class harbours at Cattaro, Pola and Trieste. Throughout the war there was an unceasing struggle between submarines, aircraft and light surface ships, mingled with minesweeping, raids and coast bombardments, with gains and losses on both sides.

In September 1915 the gallant Serbian army, after facing three attacks from Austria, began its desperate winter march through the Black Mountains to the Dalmatian coast, hunted by the Bulgarians on their flank, and from the north by an Austro-German army under Mackensen. Preceded by a tragic mass of destitute, homeless Serbians of all classes, the army, fighting desperate rearguard actions at every mountain pass, struggled slowly towards safety at Durazzo and Valona. These two ports, together with the small harbour of San Giovanni di Medua, were the only places for embarkation. Early in December Italy occupied all three, fifty thousand troops being transported across the Adriatic. Doctors and nurses, engineers and workmen, were brought over, camps laid out, hospitals and hutments built, and troops pushed up into the surrounding mountains forming a strong defensive area round both Durazzo and Valona. England and France landed medical supplies, stores and food at Brindisi to be transported across. Camps were prepared at Corfu and Cagliari in Sardinia and France prepared a large reception area at Biserta. Before the end of the year the stream of refugees, gaunt with hunger, verminous, exhausted and foul with wounds and disease, began to arrive, first in small groups, then in hundreds, finally in thousands. All who were fit were at once transferred to the waiting steamers, and evacuation began. All through January and February the work continued. Early in the year the Germans seized San Giovanni di Medua, but not before every one was evacuated, including King Peter of Montenegro and his son and Ministers, together with Admiral Troubridge our representative. When the enemy pressed on within artillery range of Durazzo there were still seven thousand refugees to be moved, including thirteen hundred hospital cases. All were safely got away. On February 26th the last Italian troops retiring slowly from the hills were embarked and Durazzo finally evacuated. A similar task was successfully accomplished at Valona where more thousands of sick and wounded were brought to safety. Altogether some two hundred thousand Serbians were thus rescued. Throughout the Italian navy played an effective part, bombarding the approaching enemy from the sea, guarding the transports, keeping the fifty mile passage to the mainland swept by minesweepers and helping in the evacuation. The whole operation was highly creditable to both the Italian army and navy and won high commendation from their allies.

The plan for the spring campaign of 1916 was again an offensive on the Isonzo. The munitions had improved both in quality and quantity during the winter and great efforts were made to increase the number of guns. The fortresses throughout Italy had been denuded to supply the army and even the navy had been put under contribution. The new offensive was to extend from Tolmino to the sea and the plans were well advanced when information began to come through of a big concentration of troops in the Trentino. At first the idea of an Austrian offensive from the west was discounted, the difficulties of transport and the great distance from the centres of supply, making it highly improbable. It had all along, however, been the favourite plan of Marshal Conrad and although it was said to have been coldly received by the German staff, who did not believe that Austria could accumulate the men and munitions which would be required, it was persisted in. The offensive was, in fact, inspired by sentimental no less than strategic reasons, for it was known as the *strafe expedition* and was meant as a punishment for Italy's desertion of the Triple Alliance. Convincing evidence of the seriousness of the effort was soon forthcoming and Cadorna moved three brigades, followed by two divisions, to the threatened area, so that when the offensive opened the Italians had 162 battalions against 177 Austrian.

Conrad had massed 150,000 men and 2,000 guns, many of heavy

calibre, between Mori on the Adige below Rovereto and the area round Strigno in the Val Sugana. On May 15th the attack was launched. A new technique was employed. Instead of the usual prolonged preliminary bombardment, the front line was subjected to a short but severe bombardment, followed immediately by an infantry attack. The two wings carried out an orderly withdrawal to their main defensive positions from which they were never ejected, but an effective breach was made in the centre. This success was due to overkeenness on the part of the Italian commanders. Cadorna's plan had envisaged a strict defensive on the Trentino front, but encouraged by the success of the opening offensive in May the previous year, the local commanders had pressed steadily forward without consolidating a main defensive position, and anticipating a further advance, had brought up their artillery to forward positions. In consequence many guns were lost in the opening attack. As the danger of a serious breakthrough by the valleys of the Adige and the Brenta became critical, the Supreme Command transferred the seven reserve divisions from the Isonzo to form the core of a fifth army based on Vicenza designed to meet the Austrians as they emerged from the mountains to the plain. But they did not get through. On June 3rd Cadorna wrote that the offensive was held on the whole front. By that date the Austrian line ran from Monte Pasubio, still held by the Italians, south of Arsiero and half-way between Asiago and Valstagna and thence due north. Further Austrian progress was held up completely by the new Russian offensive under Brussiloff which prevented reinforcements coming to Italy from the east where Brussiloff took 350,000 prisoners in ten weeks in the Lemberg offensive. He claimed to have saved Italy, but this was an overstatement since the Trentino offensive was held before Brussiloff attacked. The help was, in fact, mutual. The large concentration of men and guns in Italy made Brussiloff's success possible and that in turn held up further advance from the Trentino. A fortnight later on June 16th Cadorna counter-attacked, drove back the Austrians north of Arsiero and west of Asiago, roughly half-way between their original positions and the extreme limit of their advance. Here the line became stabilized.

All fear of the real danger from the Trentino offensive, an attack on the Isonzo army from the rear, was now past, and Cadorna, with a rapid appreciation of the possibilities of the new situation, for which he deserves full credit, decided at once to carry through the Isonzo offensive hitherto held up. He had, in fact, never dropped it, for even during the height of the Austrian offensive he had kept writing to the Duke of Aosta, commanding the third army opposite Gorizia, to make every preparation for an attack from Monte Sabotino to the sea, 'in the hope that by great rapidity of execution we shall take the enemy by surprise, for he will not expect an attack upon the Isonzo front when we have scarcely contained the offensive from the Trentino'. The Italian counter-attack, which began on June 16th, continued until the middle of July when the troops were ordered to consolidate their positions and remain on the defensive. Then, after a fortnight's rest, on July 29th Cadorna, knowing that he could transfer troops to the Isonzo far quicker than the Austrians could send reinforcements round the perimeter of the arc, switched back the fifth army, partly by rail and partly by road, to the Isonzo in support of the new offensive. The movement was completed before August 4th on which day the attack opened.

The terrain which barred the road to Trieste, and over which the Italians fought in the third and following battles of the Isonzo, presented greater difficulties than those of any other European theatre of war. Gorizia itself, in addition to all its elaborate field works, was protected by a ring of mountains converted with infinite labour into veritable fortresses. On the north was Monte Sabotino, on the east Monte San Marco, Monte San Daniele, Monte San Gabriele and Monte Hermada, four strongholds which defied capture to the end. To the south lay the plateau of the Carso, which rose steeply a thousand feet from the river. The summit was a wilderness of limestone, without trees, water or shelter, scorched by the August sun and swept in winter by the bitter wind, the Bora, which made it more dreaded by the troops than even the snow-clad eyries of the Carnic Alps. The problem of transport for supplies and munitions no less than the transfer of the sick and wounded, was an unceasing tax on the ingenuity and skill of the Italian engineers.

On August 4th to distract the enemy's attention from the real centre of attack and if possible to divert the reserves, a violent bombardment heralded an offensive in the neighbourhood of Monfalcone, near the mouth of the river. The feint was successful, and reserves were hastily sent south from Gorizia; then, on the 6th, the real attack began from Monte Sabotino to the Carso. Every available gun had been concentrated on this section of the front. After some hours of artillery preparation the infantry advanced. Monte Sabotino was captured, then Oslavia and Podgora. On the northern edge of the Carso Monte San Michele was seized, but at terrible cost. On the morning of the 9th Gorizia was occupied and the next day the heights in the immediate neighbourhood fell into Italian hands. The plateau of the Carso was reached and the Vallone, a deep dry river bed which crossed it. was passed and a line established beyond it. This was the limit of success. The great mountain strongholds defied attack and the road to Trieste was still effectively closed. The offensive died down in August but the Austrians were given no rest and in September and October battles continued until the winter made fighting impossible. The losses on both sides were again very heavy; the Isonzo offensive alone cost over a hundred thousand men without counting the losses in the Trentino.

Although Italy had entered the war on a great wave of popular enthusiasm the opponents of the national decision were by no means either converted or silenced. The 'internationalists' in the Socialist ranks, the Giolittians in the Chamber and their followers outside, the convinced neutralists, all alike held to their opinions and expressed them freely. Germany had plenty of friends in Italy if Austria had few, and her defeat meant disaster for many financial interests whose capital came from Berlin. Nor was any real effort made to mobilize national opinion nor to stiffen the country's morale, and for this the government were at fault. Salandra continued to carry on as before. He made no attempt to form a national Cabinet and thus identify sectional opinion with that of the government by finding room for their leaders in the inner circle of control. Too busy to pay the Chamber the attention it expected, with Sonnino at the Foreign Office as aloof and uncommunicative as ever, trouble in Parliament was left to ferment, until, forgetful of the war, a mere party issue, the interpretation of a phrase in a speech made by Salandra, consolidated the opposition, and in the middle of 1916 Salandra resigned, nominating Paolo Boselli as his successor with the task of forming a national government.

Boselli was a popular member rather than a national leader and he had stronger men than himself in the Cabinet. Sonnino remained at the Foreign Office, Orlando became Minister of the Interior, and room was found for Bissolati, the Socialist leader. They came into power with the halo of the capture of Gorizia round them, but the expensive failure of the autumn attacks on the mountain strongholds brought a renewal of discontent and bitterness which was vented on the Ministry. A diversion, however, came when the Allied leaders met in conference in Rome during the winter. Cadorna urged the view, consistently held by the Supreme Command in Italy, that to crush Austria by a large scale united Allied effort was the most hopeful method of defeating Germany. Although supported by Lloyd George, the problem of manpower on the Western Front was held to make any substantial assistance for Italy impossible, and the plan was turned down. Nor was Cadorna more successful in his demand for artillery. Guns were promised, but on condition of their return before the Allied summer offensive, which was to demand their withdrawal just when most needed, so no guns came. Italy was left to fight on her own resources. Unity of command was not yet a reality.

The atrocious winter of 1916 was a terrible trial to the Italian army. In the northern sectors, thousands of feet up in the intense cold of the Alpine snows, with a daily struggle for munitions and supplies, where landslides and avalanches too often took a grievous toll of life, the hardships were even more severe than those of the armies on the Western Front. In the Isonzo valley, incessant rain flooded the rivers and waterlogged the trenches, sweeping away the bridges and cutting off supplies, until the morale of the troops was strained almost to breaking point. While the armies on both fronts alike thus battled for existence with the elements as well as the enemy, the Supreme Command was mapping out the spring offensive. The year 1917 was destined to be desperately critical for the Allies, but to close with renewed hope. First came the unrestricted submarine campaign with its threat of starvation for England. Then the final collapse of Russia and the abdication of the Czar was followed by the entrance of America into the war. The first two of these events were added blows to Italy; the submarine menace still further restricted supplies both of food and munitions, and the collapse of Russia released the full resources of Austria for the Italian front. For Italy it was also a bad year. Her offensives gained little ground, and the success of the August effort was more than neutralized by the autumn disaster of Caporetto. Nevertheless by November they were holding their own on the Piave despite terrible losses.

The May offensive was the most ambitious and most extended effort that the Italians had yet made. Thirty-five divisions were employed, practically half the army, and the area attacked reached from Tolmino, the northern Austrian bridgehead, to the sea. For the first time in these operations we hear the note of weakening offensive spirit in the Italian troops. The home front was already affected. War weariness, increased shortage of food, the absolute liberty left to the public to spread their views, added to the terrible list of casualties and the slow progress made, all contributed. Soldiers on leave found a poor public spirit and a freely expressed desire to end the war by compromise, and returned to the front with their morale lowered. Orlando, the Minister of the Interior, let things be, quarrelled with Bissolati, who wanted urgent measures to repress 'defeatism', and finally resigned from the Cabinet. Nothing was done, and the insidious propaganda spread until it ended in Caporetto.

The offensive opened on May 12th with a violent bombardment from the Gorizia area. The infantry followed and some positions were taken, but it was, in reality, a diversion. On the 15th to the 22nd one of the main attacks was made by the second and seventh armies on the mountainous area facing Tolmino, for here the Austrians held both banks. It was a struggle for mountains, two, Monte Cucco and Monte Vodice, were captured, but the attack on Monte Santo failed. While this effort was in progress the third army struck on the Carso. The Austrians, now hard pressed, attempted to relieve the strain by a sudden attack on the Trentino sector. This failed and the third army after regrouping again attacked and reached the outskirts of Monte Hermada in the last days of May. The first week in June the Austrians counter-attacked and the third army was thrown back. The last phase of the offensive before the fighting died down, was an Italian counter-attack on the Asiago plateau, for two more mountains, Interrotto and Ortigara; it was again a failure and it was here that the lack of an offensive spirit was most marked, for both in fire power and in numbers the Italians had great superiority.

So marked was the failure of the offensive spirit in the troops during the May battles, that the Supreme Command was seriously disturbed, and three times in June Cadorna wrote on the matter to the President of the Council: 'If the defeatist spirit in the country', he said, 'was not checked, the results in the army would be disastrous'. His letters were not even answered, and nothing was done. The collapse of Russia added yet another cause of depression, and the cry, 'Not a man in the trenches next winter' was now raised by the peace advocates and the harm done by such propaganda was incalculable. In the meantime the Allied Conference in Paris was urging Italy to start another attack. Cadorna recognized that their operative balance was not fulfilled by the May offensive, and it was better that the men should be fighting than thinking, and a victory would restore confidence in Italy. Nothing could be done until August, by which time the expenditure of munitions would be made good. Throughout the war the length and intensity of every Italian offensive was conditioned by the supply of shells. It took three months to accumulate sufficient for a major operation and the allowance for each had to be strictly calculated.

THE ISONZO FRONT

Some miles north of Gorizia, bastioned on its southern edge by the mass of Monte San Gabriele and protected to the north by the formidable Austrian bridgehead of Tolmino, lay the Bainsizza plateau. It rose so abruptly and to such a height directly from the river that a frontal attack was deemed impractical. The plateau itself, whose summit was a mass of trenches and wire entanglements, stretched eastwards for some sixteen kilometres, rising in wide slopes to its highest point and then sharply descending into the valley of the river Idria, known as the Val Chiapovano. This was the collecting area for the whole Austrian front and its possession would not only dislocate the entire defence, but open the road to Laibach and Trieste behind the fortified zone facing the Isonzo. It was the capture of this vital area upon which the Italian staff now concentrated all its resources.

No less than fifty divisions were allocated to this operation, a force which reduced the rest of the front to a bare minimum. Over 5,000 guns, including 2,700 of large and medium calibre, with 1,700 mortars, were concentrated on a front of fifty kilometres. On August 18th the bombardment began and during the night fourteen bridges were flung across the river north of Bainsizza and the troops crossed and began a flank attack on the slopes leading to the plateau. At the same time an advance began from the position round Monte Cucco, resulting in the important capture of Monte Santo which had defied attack in May. But the most spectacular event was the assault of the twenty-fourth corps on the steep face of the plateau which they scaled behind a heavy barrage to the summit. This together with the advance on the northern flank determined the evacuation of the whole position facing the river, and the Italian troops advanced eight kilometres to the centre of the plateau and half-way to the valley of the Idria. Being now unsupported by their artillery, still across the river, they were obliged to stop. Elsewhere on the front small progress was made, neither around Gorizia nor on the Carso was the advance more than local gains, in spite of intense efforts. Until bridges and roads could be constructed to enable the artillery to be brought across the river and up to the plateau the action on the Bainsizza became mainly defensive, without either side having effective artillery support. Before the end of August the fighting on the plateau died down, to flare up again in a final attempt to overwhelm the defences of Monte San Gabriele by concentrated gunfire; but, though over seven hundred guns hurled nearly fifty thousand shells on the defences during three days' continued assault, it was quite useless, for the garrison, hidden in the caves and tunnels of the mountain, remained practically unharmed. In September the assault on the Bainsizza was definitely suspended. Orders were given to consolidate the positions won and return to the defensive, for the supply of shells was exhausted.[27]

The success achieved in the August offensive heartened Italy, but although the conduct of the majority of the troops had been admirable, the reports of the commanding officers again revealed a bad spirit prevalent in some sections of the army; so much so, that Cadorna again wrote strongly to the Premier, ending his despatch with the words, 'The Italian government is pursuing an internal policy ruinous to the discipline and morale of the army against which it is my duty to protest with all my strength'. It was a mistake on his part that he did not promptly send in his resignation which was probably the only means to force the government to act, but he did not. The casualties of the two 1917 offensives were again terribly heavy, amounting together to 270,000 men killed, wounded and missing. As usual the length of the offensive was determined by exhaustion of supplies. A million and a half of shells had been expended and the reserve limit reached, and until stocks were once again replenished no major operation could be considered.

Early in September the Supreme Command began to receive definite reports of an Austro-German concentration behind the Bainsizza front. Its origin is usually ascribed, partly to the severe strain inflicted on the Austrian army by the incessant Italian offensives, as the result of which the High Command now feared that under another such attack the front would give way: partly to the arrival of substantial new forces from the eastern front and partly also to the appreciation shown by the German staff for an attempt to crush Italy, as the weakest enemy; the policy, that is, which the Allies had rejected in regard to Austria at the Rome Conferences during the previous winter. This force consisted of picked Austrian divisions, strengthened by seven German divisions including the Alpine Corps. The spearhead of it was the fourteenth army under the German General von Below, divided into four groups, those of Krauss, Stein, Berrer and Scotti, placing them respectively from north to south. They took up their position between the northern army of Marshal Conrad and the southern army of Marshal Boroevic, on the front from Plezzo to Tolmino. The task of the two Austrian armies flanking von Below's spearhead was to engage the Italian forces opposite them and prevent help being sent to the threatened centre and if the attack here was successful, to widen the breach on either side.

The situation on the Italian front on the eve of Caporetto gave every reason for confidence in a successful defence. Not only were they holding positions of immense natural strength carefully fortified, but they were holding them with a force numerically superior to the attackers. Careful calculations show that 437 enemy battalions were facing 560 Italians. Moreover, behind the lines in the neighbourhood of Cividale lay seven reserve divisions and further south three more. All of these were within, at the most, forty-eight hours of the furthest part of the front line. Neither was there lack of artillery nor munitions, though, on the cessation of the Bainsizza offensive, the Allies had at once recalled the hundred cannon which had been loaned to Cadorna for that operation, refusing to believe in an Austro-German attack. The Supreme Command took all precautions, and the reports of the corps commanders on the morale of the troops were full of confidence in their fighting spirit. As events were quickly to prove they were completely deluded.

Von Below's plan was simple in conception but intricate in execution. They were to attack everywhere at once, with a view to confuse the defence and complicate the best use of the reserves. The troops were to keep to the valleys and mountain roads, avoiding frontal attacks, masking or if possible by-passing the mountain strongholds, and relying on speed to disrupt the defence. One of the clearest of the combined operations is that which led to the capture of Caporetto which gave its name to the whole battle. The morning of the 24th October was heavy with fog and rain. At 6 a.m. the general advance began, preceded by a demoralizing bombardment of gas shells and high explosive. On the extreme right, Krauss having broken the front at Fornace, drove out the troops on Monte Rambon and having thus blocked the passage for reinforcements from the northern Army of the Carnia, turned left and came down the valley of the Isonzo towards Caporetto. They were held up at Saga. But a simultaneous advance up the Isonzo had been commenced by Stein from Tolmino. This force should have been stopped at Gabrie, but the Italian troops laid down their arms without fighting and the enemy thus taking the troops at Saga in the rear, forced their retirement and the two Austro-German forces joined and then occupied Caporetto at 4 p.m. The next day (October 25th) having been reinforced, they crossed the Isonzo valley and began working west through the mountains. The seizure of Creda and Staroselo covering the mouth

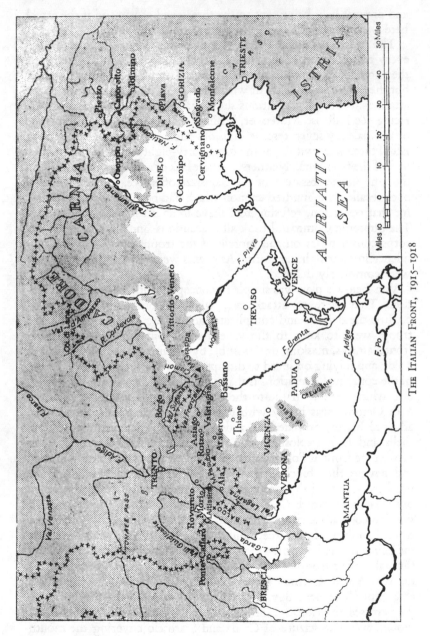

THE ITALIAN FRONT, 1915–1918

of the valley of the river Natisone, which flowing south behind the mountain bastion facing the Isonzo, opened the road to Cividale from where the railway to Udine, the army headquarters, began, brought them behind the Italian frontal positions. In the meanwhile the groups of Stein, Berrer and Scotti, were attacking the main defences everywhere. Their success was as thorough as it was unexpected. Here and there the Italians fought well as at Monte Jeza where the enemy were completely held up, but elsewhere the whole front crumbled. Some laid down their arms without fighting, others flung them away and ran; the most impregnable positions were overrun at the first attack and the speed of the advance completely demoralized the whole central front. Cadorna then attempted to stabilize a second front, pivoted on Monte Maggiore, west of Caporetto, through Monte Cavallo and Monte Purgessimo (covering Cividale) to Monte Santo, passing through Plava and Monte Cucco, but on the night of the 26th the capture of Monte Maggiore made the whole line untenable and it was decided to withdraw what remained of the original front behind the Tagliamento.

The collapse of the centre imperilled the armies north and south, and as early as the 26th the Duke of Aosta, commanding the Third Army at Gorizia, was warned to prepare to evacuate and withdraw across the Isonzo to the Tagliamento. At the same time the Army of the Carnia to the north was to fall back to the foothills, the Prealpi, while what remained of the Second Army was to take up the intermediate position. These orders were carried out, though with heavy losses of men and material, and by November 1st the Third Army was in position behind the Tagliamento from Codroipo to the sea, the Second Army north of it from Codroipo to Osoppo where it bent westward to meet the Army of the Carnia on the foothills. The Army of the Cadore, likewise withdrawn southward, now filled the gap between the First Army on the Asiago plateau and that of the Carnia on its right. By now there was an unarmed fleeing mass, estimated by Italian writers at four hundred thousand, streaming westward by every road and pass, behind them pressed the enemy so quickly that the line of Tagliamento was threatened with disruption at the critical point where the line bent west, and it was decided to withdraw to the Piave.

The retreat to the Piave was carried out between the 1st and 9th November. The hinge where the line turned west was now the massif of Monte Grappa, already fortified by the foresight of Cadorna in 1916. It was, nevertheless, a close call, for the last troops of the

Third Army crossed under fire from the Austrian guns behind them. The recovery of the Italian army on the Piave was as remarkable as its collapse on the Isonzo. There were twenty-nine Italian divisions against fifty Austro-Germans. Their line was scarcely formed and they were lamentably short of guns and equipment of all kinds. They were given no time to reorganize for they were attacked the very next day (November 10th). The battle lasted a fortnight. Every attempt to cross the river was frustrated and the small bridgeheads the enemy succeeded in forming were contained and wiped out. But the centre of the struggle was the desperate battle for Monte Grappa and the neighbouring keypoint known as the Montello. The fighting was bitter: crucial positions were lost and retaken and the battle swayed to and fro without either side being able to gain the mastery. Further west the Austrians attacked on the Asiago plateau but without success. The Italians fought with ferocious courage and the utmost efforts of the German Alpine Corps failed to wrest the vital positions from the defenders and on the 25th the victory was won. Four days later, Allied divisions of French and English took over the Montello and Monte Tomba and relieved the exhausted Italians. The first battle of the Piave was the turning point of the war. It was fought and won by Italy alone and revealed a courage and tenacity as praiseworthy as her previous state of panic had been lamentable.

In the withdrawal from the Isonzo to the Piave the navy had played a notable part: supported by aircraft and some English monitors, they had carried out effective bombardments of enemy troops and positions and their work in transporting troops and supplies as well as guns and equipment, had been of great value. They had had their own triumphs as well. To support the attack on the Piave, the Austrians had used two of their older battleships stationed at Trieste, the *Wien* and the *Buda-Pesth*. On December 9th an Italian torpedo boat under Lieut. Rizzo forced its way into Trieste harbour, sank the *Wien* and so seriously damaged the *Buda-Pesth* that it was unfit for further service. Later the same officer sank the Dreadnought *Svent Istvan* and damaged a second.

The Allies had been quick to help: five British and six French divisions were hurried into Italy and Marshal Foch was at Treviso on November 30th. Two days before Christmas another violent attack was opened on Monte Grappa; it nearly succeeded, until the Italians restored the positions at the point of the bayonet. All through January fighting continued but no change was made in the position. By the end of the year the army was again at strength despite the enormous losses, well over a quarter of a million prisoners and 7,000 guns having fallen into enemy hands. Even so, the narrower front, now guarded by 638 battalions and 5,000 guns, proved more than an effective barrier to any further Austro-German advance. For some months the Italian front was quiet. The great German attack on the Western Front in March recalled several of the Allied divisions but also the German divisions, and in April 1918 Italy sent an army corps of fifty thousand men to help France. They were there until the end of the war and won high praise, especially for their work on the Chemin des Dames in October.

The disaster of Caporetto was a terrible shock to Italy. It brought home with appalling force the meaning of defeat. The thousands of homeless refugees from the occupied areas, for whom shelter had to be found, carried the reality of war to the country as nothing else could have done. Italy shuddered at the tales they told. The Boselli Ministry fell at once, and Orlando of the golden tongue became Premier. He rose to the crisis and Italy rallied round him. His first speech in the Chamber gave the keynote to his policy. 'The situation', he said, 'will not be discussed, it will be faced', and he echoed all that was best in the country when he declared that there was but one watchword, 'Resist, resist, resist'. A change of temper as abrupt and salutary as that which took place in the army between Caporetto and the Piave swept over the country. They knew at last the value of their soldiers. For the first time the army was cared for and helped. The men were entertained, efforts of all kinds were made for their comfort and the nation worked as it had never done before. Defeatism disappeared: 'Caporetto', said a Minister, 'saved Italy from moral collapse'.

At the front both armies were preparing for a renewal of the struggle. Austria was beginning to be in need of victory, for ugly cracks were appearing in the fabric of the Dual Monarchy. Foch was holding the Germans in the west and though the full weight of the American army was barely felt as yet, it was there. So a great Austrian offensive garnished with grandiose names was planned for June. A full scale attack on the Piave, known as the 'Albrecht Operation', was to coincide with the 'Radetzky Offensive' by Conrad's army on the pivotal sector between Monte Grappa and Rotzo, west of Asiago. Finally the 'Avalanche Action' was to seize the Tonale Pass. Conrad's objective was to open the two diverging valleys, the Val d'Assa which led down to the plain at Thiene and so to Vicenza, and the Val Frenzela, which would open the road to Bassano and Padua. The attack began on June 15th. It was no surprise, for the Italian Intelligence knew all about it, even to the day and hour fixed for the opening barrage which they anticipated by an hour with disastrous results to the Austrian concentration. On the Piave such troops as got across the river were isolated and attacked from all sides. The river rose and swept away the bridges, supplies ran short, and on the 22nd Boroevic withdrew those that remained. The attempt to seize the Tonale Pass was likewise a complete failure. Once again there was a terrific struggle for the Monte Grappa sector. At fearful cost Conrad almost succeeded, but he could not hold his gains and ferocious counter-attacks drove him back to his starting point. For a fortnight Conrad fought on, until with the loss of 150,000 men he gave up. The defenders were far too exhausted to follow up their victory but they had broken Austria's offensive power and crushed her last bid for victory.

The Italian army fought the two battles of the Piave under a new commander for on November 8th Cadorna had been relieved of his command and General Armando Diaz, a corps commander from the third army, took his place. Cadorna had shown both organizing power and strategic ability. He had made the peacetime army into a fighting machine. The operation which had led to the capture of Gorizia was boldly conceived and brilliantly executed. Nor can he be held responsible for Caporetto, for he had foreseen the danger and warned the government. He had the traditional faults of the Piedmontese generals. He cared little for the welfare of the men, with whom he was never in touch. He was perhaps too severe on the mistakes of subordinates and too rigid a disciplinarian. His retirement was inevitable after Caporetto, but the army owed him a great debt. He was never popular, feared but not loved. Diaz was of a different type who looked after his men and made a personal appeal which Cadorna had never possessed.

Throughout July and August Diaz prepared for the final offensive. He was in command of an Allied force with the French Twelfth Army and Lord Cavan's Tenth Army both on the Piave. By the end of September his plans were matured but the attack was not delivered until October 24th the anniversary of Caporetto. In the meantime the enemy was slowly breaking. September saw the collapse of the Bulgarian front and Allenby's victory in Palestine. Though the Dual Monarchy was rapidly crumbling politically, the army was still full of fight and every effort was made to keep up their morale. A strict censorship kept them in ignorance of the real conditions in Austria and an isolation zone behind the lines made contact with the home front almost impossible. Only the High Command knew how badly things were going. But in spite of all precautions it is clear that the 'Caporetto spirit' was at work in the Austrian, as a year before it had been in the Italian, army. There was still a hard crust but if it broke, collapse would be complete.

The symbolism of a village name, Vittorio Veneto, gave the title to the crowning struggle. It was a repetition of the first battle of the Piave in reverse, with the Allies attacking and the Austrians defending, fought over the same ground. The strategic conception was a double offensive, first from the Monte Grappa area against the Austrian mountain positions on Asalone, Pertica and the Salarolo-Valderosa group, to break the hinge of the line and separate Conrad's Trentino-Asiago army from that of Boroevic on the Piave, and simultaneously to cross the Piave and drive a wedge between the Fifth and Sixth Austrian armies and destroy them in turn. In a fierce three day struggle from October 24th to 26th the army from the Grappa captured the Austrian positions, then lost them by counter-attack, then recovered them. By the third day both sides were so exhausted that the fighting died down while they regrouped. On the Piave the Tenth English, the Eighth Italian and the Twelfth French armies crossed on the 24th; by the 27th there were three bridgeheads firmly established, despite the fact that the river rose and swept away many of the bridges. Enlarged the next day, they joined on the 29th and by a rapid advance cut off the Sixth Austrian army from the 'Isonzo' army which held the lower reaches of the river. By the 30th both were hastily withdrawing. This was the beginning of the end. Equal success attended the army of the Grappa on renewing the offensive, which pressed quickly forward, cut off the Trentino army from the Piave as was planned, and broke the whole front. Once this was accomplished the Austrians fell to pieces and the Allies advanced almost unhindered north, east and west. On November 3rd the first Italian army occupied Trento while in the eastern sector, from Venice, a mixed force on steamers and warships crossed the Adriatic and occupied Trieste unopposed. On November 4th the armistice was signed. Caporetto was more than avenged. Six hundred thousand prisoners were taken and the whole equipment of the army, and Austria was opened for the passage of the Allies into southern Germany. It made her position hopeless. On November 11th came the Armistice on the Western Front and the final defeat of Germany.

The war for Italy was over, and she now looked forward to obtaining the rewards of her sacrifices at the Peace Conference. These, though not generally known in Italy, were embodied in the secret Treaty of London signed in 1915 by the Allied Powers, from which the only absent signature was that of America, an exception which was to make all the difference.

It is instructive to observe the contrast, both in methods and results, between the policy of Cavour in the Alliance with the Western Powers in 1855 during the Crimean War, and that of the Italian statesmen in the Alliance with the same Powers in 1915. In 1855, Cavour's Foreign Secretary, General Dabormida, was insistent on Secret Clauses in the terms of the Alliance. To these, England and France objected, and Cavour, fully realizing the difficulties his allies would meet in fulfilling them, dismissed his Foreign Secretary, took the portfolio himself, and cancelling the secret clauses joined the Alliance without conditions. The result was that he won their confidence, entered the Congress of Paris as an equal, and earned the esteem of all parties. Though he came away from Paris without any material gain, the willing support given later to Italy by both France and England is too well known to need comment. Cavour went into the war on the broad principle of fighting for liberty and constitutional government against absolutism. His position *vis-à-vis* Austria made it impossible to maintain a genuine neutrality, for, as an armed neutral, he was a potential complication to both sides. So he fought on the side of liberty and progress against absolutism and reaction.

There was no savour of the 'Cavourian tradition' about the Italian statesmen of 1915. They bargained with both sides and joined those from whom they got most. The unfortunate phrase of Orlando, *sacro egoismo*, was nearer the truth than Italian historians care to admit. They drove a hard bargain: they asked for the limit: and the Allies, pressed as they were, promised all they asked. There is no hint of fighting for the sanctity of treaties, or against unwarranted aggression or in defence of small powers, but only for Italian security and the rescue of their own minorities. They got their pound of flesh, but in so doing they lost the goodwill of their Allies, who felt that they had taken the utmost advantage of their position and were entering the war not on any broad moral principle but just for what they could get. By the secret Treaty of London Italy was to obtain the Brenner line to the north, Gradisca and Gorizia, Trieste and the whole Istrian peninsula, all Dalmatia with the islands to Cape Planka, Valona and the Dodecanese, and southern Dalmatia was to be neutralized. Fiume was to go to Croatia. If Asia Minor was divided Italy was to have a portion of Anatolia centred in Adalia, and similar claims in Africa were to be recognized in the repartition of German possessions. During the later stages of the war when the entrance of America made victory almost certain, the Allies became busy dividing the spoils. France and England settled the partition of the German colonies, ignoring Italy. The Sykes-Picot Treaty divided up Turkey, again leaving out Italy, so that when the terms were known Sonnino protested strongly, and in a meeting with Lloyd George and Clemenceau at St. Jean de Maurienne the map of Asia Minor was redrawn giving Italy her share of Anatolia.

Italy was unfortunate in her relations with America. There was little knowledge or understanding of her problems in the United States, where, moreover, she did not fit into the scheme of things; for she was not regarded as a Great Power, like France and England, nor could she be classed as an oppressed nationality of the small-nation type like Czechoslovakia or the Jugoslavs, but was something between the two. The Delegation which she sent to America in 1917 to make herself better known, failed to impress; for instead of appealing to the ideas then prevalent in America, the reconstruction of Europe on a new basis of nationality, she revealed only her own differences and divisions and a national policy obviously based on the old ideas of the 'balance of power' with its system of territorial compensations regardless of the human element, all of which was anathema to such as President Wilson. She made another mistake in omitting to inform the President of the terms of the Treaty of London before the publication of his 'Fourteen Points' in which her share was, in consequence, limited to a 'rectification of frontiers' and nothing more. This error was repeated in January 1919, when President Wilson visited Rome before the opening of the Peace Conference, for he was allowed to return to Paris still officially uninformed of the terms of the Treaty of London and without any discussion on Italy's peculiar problems, the visit being devoted to social functions, flattery and an exhibition of *grandezza*.

It was in 1917 that the component parts of the Austrian Empire first began to agitate for national independence. The Jugoslav leader Trumbic went to Paris and London, where sympathetic meetings were held. The outcome was the Manifesto of Corfu, published in July of that year over the signature of Pasič, the Serbian Premier. This was the first official declaration expressing the desire for union under the Karageorgevic dynasty of Serbs, Croats and Slovenes. In addition to the value of this movement towards Austrian disintegration, it offered to Italy a prospect of a new sphere of predominance. With the collapse of Russia and the disappearance of Austro-Hungary, Italy's influence in the Balkans might now become paramount and she lent a sympathetic ear to the movement. In April 1918 a meeting was held in Rome which issued what is known as the Pact of Rome in which Italians, Jugoslavs, Czechs, Poles and Rumanians mutually recognized their rights to achieve national unity and independence and the need for common action to that end. Orlando welcomed the meeting and approved its purpose and a general tone of friendly support pervaded the Italian Press. Whether Italy enhanced her position as a Great Power in thus identifying herself with the oppressed nationalities may be doubted, but, at least, it was a good augury for the settlement of impending problems in the Adriatic. In June came the Austrian offensive and its defeat and then Italy waited anxiously for the Allied *riposte*. This opened on the anniversary of Caporetto (October 24th) and the resounding victory of Vittorio Veneto followed.

The effect of Vittorio Veneto on Italy was electrifying. After the disaster of Caporetto, the desperate struggle on the Piave, and the hard won victory against the June offensive, the completeness of the triumph was overwhelming. Italy was speedily convinced that this was the decisive battle of the war, in which not only Austria but Germany had been defeated. She felt herself raised at once to the seats of the mighty, the dauntless equal of France and England. This new exaltation became quickly evident in the expansion of her claims, as reflected in the Press. It was no longer the minimum but the maximum to which she looked. Visions of a new Empire beginning with Balkan predominance, the cession of southern Asia Minor from Adalia to Alexandretta, even further east to a sphere of influence in Armenia, with corresponding expansion in North and East Africa, passed within her purview as the possible fruits of victory, and her delegates to the Peace Conference a few weeks later, left Italy in an aura of expectant triumph. The new feeling of greatness in Italy was pardonable, though the dreams of empire did more credit to the imagination of Italian journalism than to its grasp of realities; it had, however, an unfortunate effect on the national attitude towards the projected formation of Jugoslavia. Italy was in no mood now to be thwarted in her claims by these backward Slavs, and friendliness speedily changed to hostility as their rival claims to areas, considered vital to Italian security, were put forward, which became intensified when the Conference displayed a tendency to narrow the Italian boundaries in favour of Jugoslavia.

Orlando and his Foreign Secretary Sonnino were the leading Italian delegates to the Peace Conference. A fine speaker and naturally conciliatory, Orlando had the type of mind which sees all sides of a question but without, perhaps, the trained judicial power of weighing the evidence and coming to a clear decision. In consequence, he was apt to be indefinite and indecisive. He saw the force of Wilson's new nationalism based on self determination, yet he clung to Italy's conception of what was necessary for national security and he became a fanatic on the possession of Fiume. Sonnino pinned his faith to the Treaty of London, though it gave Fiume to Croatia, and from this he never varied: thus between the two there was a distinct divergence of opinion. The reception of the Italians was not encouraging. They found themselves in an atmosphere coloured by prejudice rather than knowledge. Ill-informed and therefore unappreciative of the extent and difficulty of the Italian war effort, irritated by the anti-Ally tone of the Italian Press, there was an open tendency to depreciate Italy's share in the victory, which was too often considered a mere secondary theatre in the struggle. Though the magnitude of her victory at Vittorio Veneto could not be gainsaid, it was regarded as the forcing of a door whose hinges were already broken, and the collapse of Caporetto, the only time—the Piave being overlooked—when Italy met German troops, being taken as the true gauge of the fighting value of the Italian army. How utterly different was Italy's own reading of her part in the war can be seen from the notice fixed on the walls of Fiume by the Nationalists, which may be taken as reflecting a wide area of opinion. It read:

August 1914. Italy saves France by declaring her neutrality—May 1915. Italy saves the Entente by her declaration of war—Winter 1915. Italy saves the Serbian army—October 1917. In her terrible hour Italy saves herself unaided—Spring 1918. On the French Front Italy stops the invasion at Bligny—October 1918. Italy at Vittorio Veneto gives the decisive blow to the German bloc—April 1919. The Entente refuses justice to Italy.

There were two underlying aims in the Italian diplomacy at the Conference, both connected with prestige. The first was to ensure that the Italian settlement with Austria was signed simultaneously with that of Germany, lest the country should feel a sense of inferiority if relegated to a secondary position. The second was to prevent Jugoslavia being treated on an equality with Italy; their case should be dealt with in Committee, but that of Italy must be dealt with only by the Council. There were numerous complications involved in these contentions. The German settlement was clearly the most important and should be got out of the way first: then, the Austria against whom Italy declared war in 1915 no longer existed, and the problem of her frontiers was in part a question between Italy and Jugoslavia: and finally, Jugoslavia, now an ally, had provided Italy's most determined opponents throughout the war as part of the Austrian army, and the very name of Croats was a term of loathing to Italians. Had not the Italian peasants of Lombardy in 1848 hung their crucifixes upside down because God had made the Croats?

At President Wilson's first meeting with Orlando he made his position quite clear. He was willing to give Italy the Brenner line in the north as drawn in the Treaty of London but he could not sanction her claims on her eastern border. Fiume was necessary to Jugoslavia, being the only port north of Spalato with a railway connected with the interior and therefore became a vital outlet for central European commerce. Dalmatia too belonged to the Jugoslavs by an overwhelming majority of race, and Italy would be safe with the neutralization of the coast and the possession of the necessary islands. Orlando replied that he would gladly accept the Brenner line but that the destiny of Fiume should be determined by her Italian majority in population and her expressed desire to be united to Italy. Dalmatia also was a strategic necessity. The President's experts on whom he relied for facts and figures, were far less generous to Italy than the President himself. They proposed a northern boundary of less strategic value but more racially just, involving the transfer of far fewer Germans to Italy. Their line of division in Istria cut it longitudinally in half, leaving the valley of the Idria with its valuable mercury mines to Jugoslavia. Fiume and Dalmatia were likewise to go to the new state. From these opposed positions neither Wilson nor Orlando would move. To obtain Fiume became an *idée fixe* with Orlando, though why was a mystery. Fiume was not reckoned among the original points of great importance and its value was magnified out of all proportion to its worth. Sonnino, holding to the Treaty of London, would presumably have let it go, but the cry of 'Fiume and Dalmatia' was taken up so strongly in Italy that Orlando became pledged not to recede. In the negotiations which followed no *via media* could be found. France and England, realizing the tenacity of the two principal contestants, while still agreeing to honour their signatures to the Treaty of London, took up their position on the sidelines, leaving the centre court to the President and Orlando. After a month of fruitless negotiations Wilson was recalled to America and Orlando returned to Rome to deal with internal difficulties. Both were back in Paris by the middle of March.

In January 1919 two members of Orlando's Cabinet had resigned, Bissolati the Socialist leader and Nitti the Minister of Finance. It created a great sensation, especially when Bissolati announced that he had resigned because he did not wish to be an 'accomplice of the imperialist policy of the Italian Cabinet'. He went further, and in an interview with the representative of the *Morning Post*, did not hesitate to affirm that the Dodecanese islands were Greek and should go back to Greece, that Dalmatia was Slav, but that Fiume was Italian and should come to Italy. Strategic reasons, he added, cannot outweigh the rights of nationalities. Bissolati was a convinced Wilsonian. Such an attitude enraged the Italian Press to whom imperialism, naked and unashamed, was the sole perquisite of France and England. Italy was suffering from a cruel disillusion. She believed, wrote a contemporary French writer, that having won the greatest victory in history justified all her claims: that no recompense could equal her triumph: that she had given to the common cause more of her sons than France, more of her wealth than England, and a greater idealism than America. This may well be an overstatement, but the coldness of her reception in Paris, the failure of her Allies to appreciate the greatness of her effort and the magnitude of her final victory, the rejection of her claims, seared her spirit and filled her with angry bitterness.

The Press campaign against America and England, Jugoslavia, and especially France, redoubled. The French support of the new nationalities; her obvious policy of security by alliance, against Germany; her frantic efforts for guarantees of assistance from England and America, were interpreted in Italy as directed against herself, at least in part. To what lengths she went can be gathered from the *Corriere della Sera* which wrote, 'It is necessary to tell Italy plainly that there exists a Power who seeks the hegemony of Europe. This Power is not and cannot be Italy. The day when the weight of her conquests becomes too heavy, it will be necessary to rise up once more, and Italy will rise anew. Let us not abandon ourselves to grave illusions: we have suffered too many already. Let us prepare for the approaching war.' The government did nothing to check these outbursts. Orlando filled the vacant posts, delivered a few non-committal speeches and returned to Paris, leaving Italy restless and angry, economically strained and politically feeble.

By the beginning of April the terms to be imposed on Germany were at last settled and on the 13th word was sent to Berlin to send her representatives to receive them, and then the Italian problem came to the fore. On the 19th the Italian question was discussed in the Council. A memorandum restating Wilson's position was handed to the Italians to which they replied. The discussion and those on the following days proved equally abortive, neither side giving way. No progress having been made, President Wilson decided to issue a Manifesto to the Italian people. Its appearance on the 23rd in the French Press was a severe shock to the Italian delegates. It was answered the next day by Orlando who then left the Conference for Rome, followed by Sonnino. To appeal to the Italian people over the heads of their chosen representatives was a most unusual divergence from accepted diplomatic procedure. It had, it is true, been applied in the case of enemy countries, but to use such a form of pressure towards an ally, not only suggested that their delegates did not represent the true feeling in the country but that there was a serious breach in the Conference itself. The Manifesto contained nothing new. It was a broad statement of the principles underlying the Fourteen Points and of the League of Nations which was built up upon them. It restated the main points at issue, the Brenner line, Fiume and Dalmatia, and the reasons for the rejection of the Italian claims, ending with a warm tribute to Italy and an appeal for understanding and acceptance. Orlando's reply stressed the unusual nature of an appeal to the nation over the heads of its representatives, which necessitated his return to Rome to clarify his position; welcomed the Brenner line for Italy, but insisted upon the danger of a weak eastern flank: repeated the historic claims to Fiume and Dalmatia, and implied that the claims of Italy were the subject of adverse discrimination for which there was no justification.

Wilson's Manifesto was a mistake. It failed to effect any abatement of Italy's claims, rallied the nation round Orlando and gave his government a new lease of life. Both he and Sonnino had an enthusiastic reception and the Chamber endorsed the policy of their Delegates. They did not, however, return to Paris as expected, and the idea germinated that Italy was about to break with the alliance. But such a result was impossible. Italy was dependent on Allied economic support and American credits in particular. On May 6th almost secretly, with no announcement to the Press until after their departure, they hurried back to Paris. It was said that difficulties over granting the essential American credits had suddenly arisen, not unconnected with the delay in their return. Negotiations recommenced and until the middle of June a series of suggested compromises were brought forward. There was the plan of the American delegate, Miller, known as The Definite Solution; the plan of De Celere, Italian ambassador to America. Then Colonel House had a scheme for bringing the Italians and Americans together and presenting a joint solution to the Jugoslavs, and Orlando made his attempt to deal directly with the Jugoslavs and present their decision for acceptance by President Wilson. All alike were discussed, modified and finally rejected. The last effort was the Tardieu Plan, based on the erection of an independent state of Fiume under the League of Nations, to be administered by five members, two named by Italy and one each by Fiume, Jugoslavia and the League. Fiume to be a free port and after fifteen years a plebiscite was to decide the future of the new state. All the interested parties demanded modifications and then rejected those made by the others, until Orlando rejected the whole plan. The Tardieu solution was an elaboration of much that had gone before. Fiume was part of a small area—a *corpus separatum*—allocated by Austria to Hungary. The town proper had a two-thirds majority of Italians but if the suburb of Susak was included, the majority was then Slav, while the inclusion of the whole *corpus separatum* restored the Italian predominance. The new state would once more have reversed the balance in favour of Jugoslavia.

On June 4th the Austrian Treaty giving the Brenner line to Italy was made public and though much satisfaction was expressed the uncertainty about Fiume still occupied the chief place. Orlando's position was being rapidly undermined. Nitti, assured of the succession, was supported by Giolitti, who was once more in evidence working for power and in May and early June Orlando had had hurried meetings with his Cabinet at Dulx. The Tardieu Plan was the last straw, for it split the Delegation and weakened Orlando's position still further. In the middle of June he returned to Rome for the opening of Parliament. His fall was already certain. His review of his work was vague and unconvincing, and on a motion for a secret session to discuss foreign policy he was defeated, and the government resigned.

The signature of the German and Austrian Treaties, the departure of President Wilson for the United States, and the fall of Orlando's government, mark the close of the more important work of the

Conference, though the problem of Italy's eastern frontier remained unsettled. The work of the Italian Delegation at the Peace Conference was not impressive. In the wider aspects of the settlement they seem to have taken small part and carried little weight, concentrating from the first on the single problem of their own frontiers. Even this narrow outlook was quickly restricted further to the question of Fiume, which they allowed to grow in importance until it became a national issue which impeded their own liberty of action. In the colonial questions they likewise appear to have been only partially interested, being absent from Paris when the Mandates were distributed and being out-manoeuvred by Venezelos in the matter of Smyrna, though the French and English refusal to recognize the clause in the Treaty of London, which gave Italy an area in Anatolia, because the signature of Russia was never obtained, was an unworthy piece of legalism. Eventually they received an impressive acreage of African desert in the hinterland of Libya, and a small extension of Italian Somaliland with the Port of Kismayu on the Juba river.

The final phase of the Italian settlement lasted another twelve months. Nitti, who succeeded Orlando, sent to Paris his Foreign Secretary Tittoni, who produced three successive plans, all of which suffered the same fate as their numerous predecessors, modifications and rejection. Tittoni was then followed by Scialoja, but the Nitti Cabinet fell in April 1920 and Giolitti came into power. Between the second and third Tittoni projects the position had been still further complicated by the occupation of Fiume by D'Annunzio. The international force withdrew to avoid a collision and the poet and his Arditi were left in possession. By now the question had been narrowed down to a direct issue between Italy and Jugoslavia. After an interval, negotiations were reopened in the autumn with Count Sforza, Giolitti's Foreign Secretary, in charge. The defeat of President Wilson in the American elections robbed the Jugoslavs of their principal supporter and they changed their tone towards Italy. France too was tired of their opposition and brought pressure to bear for a final settlement. On November 12th the Treaty of Rapallo was signed between the two countries. Italy obtained the whole Istrian peninsula while Dalmatia went to Jugoslavia. The islands were divided between them but Zara went to Italy. A new state of Fiume was created including the whole *corpus separatum* with a strip of coastline connecting it with Italian Istria. A mixed commission was to trace the boundaries of the new state and both countries recognized and undertook to respect in perpetuity the full liberty and independence of the state of Fiume.

The Treaty of Rapallo apparently brought the Italian claims advanced before the Peace Conference to a close (provisional settlement). D'Annunzio was ejected with small trouble from Fiume and the new state began its brief life of independence until three years later it passed definitely to Italy. The Treaty likewise marks the end of a period of Italian history, for Italy was already descending into the trough of revolution from which she was to emerge under Fascism. Throughout the year of Nitti's weak government the country had seethed with strikes and social disturbance culminating in the temporary seizure of the factories by the workmen. The Fascist movement was already in being and the reign of violence had begun. All this, however, belongs to a new page of Italian history, which cannot yet be written with full knowledge. The century through which we have passed is complete in itself, and might almost be termed a history of the rise and fall of parliamentary government in Italy. The attempt to govern a country, almost completely lacking in political education, by means of an alien constitution with no sound basis of organization, devoid of coherent divisions and party discipline, and, at the crucial moment, led by men nurtured in conspiracy and rising from a soil impregnated with political corruption, was a failure. The whole system was discredited, no effort was made to defend it, and Italy surrendered her hard-won democratic freedom to a new system of force and compulsion.

NOTES

[1] *p. 7.* Fuller information on the conditions in Italy at this period will be found in Tivaroni's *Storia critica del Risorgimento Italiano*, vol. i. 'L'Italia prima della Rivoluzione Francese', and Simioni's *Le origini del Risorgimento Politico dell'Italia Meridionale*.

[2] *p. 14.* Nelson's action has roused much controversy. V. Cuoco in his *Saggio Storico sulla Rivoluzione Napoletana del 1799* deals with it, as does Croce in *La Rivoluzione Napoletana del 1799*. An English work on the subject is *Naples in 1799* by Constance Giglioli (Murray 1903), also Badham's *Nelson at Naples* (Nutt. 1930), and Mahan's article in the *English Historical Review*, July 1899.

[3] *p. 19.* The Secret Treaty of Prague is seldom quoted. The C.M.H. merely says that 'the diplomatic hagglings dignified by the name of conferences in this period, Rastatt, Prague, Chatillon, had amounted to little more than pretences, even in the eyes of those who took part in them'. There is no copy in the F.O. nor is it on the files of Treaties in the Record Office. But Bianchi in his *Storia Documentata della Diplomazia Europea in Italia* in the Appendix (No. 1) to his first volume, quotes *in extenso* a letter from Metternich to Castlereagh dated Paris, May 26, 1814, which reveals the full scope of the Austrian claims upon Italy made by the Traité secret signé à Prague le 27 juillet 1813 entre les Puissances coalisées et ratifié à Londres le 23 aout même année.

[4] *p. 29.* We have two firsthand accounts of these events, the *Memorie del Generale Guglielmo Pepe* and the *Storia del reame di Napoli del Generale Pietro Colletta*. See also the two volumes *Guglielmo Pepe a cura di Ruggero Moscati* containing many of his letters.

[5] *p. 31.* Two volumes of the *Biblioteca di Storia Italiana Recente* (xi and xii) are devoted to the Revolution of 1821. See also Rodolico, *Carlo Alberto*, vol. i. In English, the first volume of *Italy in the Making* by G. F. H. Berkeley.

[6] *p. 32.* Besides Confalonieri, the poet Silvio Pellico and Piero Maroncelli were sent to the state prison of the Spielberg. Many others were condemned *in contumaciam*. Confalonieri's *Memoirs* and Silvio Pellico's *Le mie prigioni* record their sufferings. They are often alluded to as 'the Martyrs of the Spielberg'.

[7] *p. 36.* On Henry Misley see Guido Ruffini's *Le cospirazioni del 1831* (Bologna Zanichelli, 1931). Also Arrigo Solmi *Ciro Menotti e l'idea unitaria nell' insurrezione del 1831* (Modena, Società Tipografica Modenese, 1931).

[8] *p. 40.* A very interesting and full account of these events will be found in Passamonti's *Nuova Luce sui processi del 1833* in Piedmont. The document forwarded by Metternich is quoted in Luzio's *Carlo Alberto e Mazzini*. Carlo Alberto's letters to the Duke of Modena edited by Maria Rosati are useful.

[9] *p. 47.* On the flight of King Charles X from France in 1830, the legitimate heir to the throne was Henri, Duc de Bordeaux, born in 1820, son of the Duc de Berry and Caroline of Naples. His father was assassinated the year of his birth. After a vain attempt to procure his recognition as King of France (Louis Philippe was chosen), he took up his residence with his mother at Holyrood. In 1832 the Duchess landed in France and tried to raise La Vendée for the legitimate heir. She failed and was taken prisoner. Henri later took the title of Count de Chambord. He was always known as Henry V by Carlo Alberto. See *La Duchesse de Berry et les Monarchies Européennes* by Etienne Déjean.

[10] p. 56. Events in Rome in 1848 will be found exhaustively treated in G. F. H. and Joan Berkeley's *Italy in the Making*, vol. iii. The corresponding events in Piedmont are dealt with in Crosa's *La Concessione dello Statuto*, Colombo's *Dalle riforme allo statuto di Carlo Alberto*, and P. Rinieri's *Lo Statuto e il Giuramento del Re Carlo Alberto*.

[11] p. 68. For fuller information see Berkeley, *Italy in the Making*, vol. iii, ch. xviii.

[12] p. 77. Much of interest written by a contemporary will be found in *La vita e i tempi del Generale Giuseppe Dabormida*, including the Duke of Savoy's criticisms.

[13] p. 79. Ramorino was afterwards tried and shot.

[14] p. 80. Charles Albert should be better known. There is no good complete life yet published. The French biography by Vidal is not altogether satisfactory and much important matter has appeared since it was written. Rodolico's two volumes only extend to 1843. A small but useful volume is the life by Raffaele del Castillo (V. Bompiani, 1938). In English Mr. Berkeley's account in his first volume is the fullest available source. I hope to publish an English Life of Charles Albert, which is already in preparation.

[15] p. 90. This political combination was generally known as the Connubio, or Marriage. For fuller details on this and other points throughout this chapter see my volume on *The Political Life and Letters of Cavour* (Oxford Press).

[16] p. 110. This is literally true as is revealed in the latest biography of Cavour by Alberto Cappa (Laterza Bari, 1932) from documentary evidence in the possession of the Marquis Visconti-Venosta which it was not considered, however, desirable to publish.

[17] p. 132. England's help to Italy is not to be measured in armed support, which she never gave; but besides the great value of her moral support and encouragement in Italy's struggle for unity and independence, she thwarted on four occasions the plans of Napoleon to prevent unity, which he never wanted. First when England persuaded Napoleon to agree to non-intervention, which checked Austria and prevented armed interference from France herself: secondly, when the English Government condemned the Emperor's plan for central Italy which enabled Cavour to get Tuscany: then when England refused to join France in patrolling the Straits and stopping Garibaldi from crossing from Sicily to the mainland, and finally by Lord John Russell's despatch of October 27, 1860, which recognized Italian unity when there was a real danger of European interference at the last moment. Without England the events of 1860 would have been very different.

[18] p. 159. There was no reason for this beyond Austrian pride, refusal to admit she was defeated by Italy, which was true, and a desire to humiliate her. The same procedure was employed as in 1859 in the transfer of Lombardy to Italy.

[19] p. 162. These were the terms by which the civil power signified its assent to measures and appointments made by the Church. The government was very jealous of its rights of veto over ecclesiastical nominations and the promulgation of Papal Bulls, encyclicals and other Papal pronouncements. No act of the Holy See was legal without the *Exequatur* of the civil government and no act of the Bishops without the *placet*.

[20] p. 167. I have been unable to discover under what auspices this 'Congress of Peace' at Geneva was being held. Ottenfels, the chargé d'affaires of Austria at Rome, writes on September 7th to Beust, 'Garibaldi paid a flying visit to the Congress of Peace at Geneva, of which he was honorary president': and pronounced a most violent discourse (Sept. 9th) against the 'pestilential institution of the Papacy'; he returned suddenly and invited the Romans 'to break their chains on the cowls

of their oppressors'. Revel mentions his departure and return, adding that he was hissed, which seems likely.

[21] p. 179. To what lengths ignorance and superstition can be carried is revealed by Tavallini who records that, in some places, wisps of straw, said to be taken from the heap upon which the Pope lay in the horrible dungeon where he was imprisoned, were sold to the populace as pious relics.

[22] p. 197. Giolitti's reputation was badly tarnished over the bank scandals. He burked inquiry, was accused of concealing documents and may have been financially interested in so doing. He resigned and went abroad for some time until the scandal was forgotten.

[23] p. 213. The failure of parliamentary life under Giolitti was not so much due to the quality of legislation, much of which was admirable, but rather to the feeling that the system as carried out did not represent the country: that it could not be safely entrusted with its highest interests. Giolitti's primary preoccupation was the retention of power achieved by a policy of political manipulation. The corruption and jobbery within and without, Giolitti's refusal to face a difficult situation, left a feeling that in a crisis there would be danger of collapse. Faith in the parliamentary system was sapped.

[24] p. 214. On Italy's commercial and industrial development see *Italy To-day* (Bolton King and Okey), 1901.

[25] p. 217. The economist Mario Alberti founded the Credito Italiano in opposition to the Banca Commerciale financed by Germany. With the help of the editor Prezzolini he exposed the German financial penetration but was unable to get the authorities to move in the matter.

[26] p. 231. Germany sent von Bülow to Rome to try and satisfy Italy's claims on Austria but he failed. Austria offered the former lands of the archbishopric of Trento but refused the Brenner Line.

[27] p. 246. The cessation of the Bainsizza Plateau offensive was decided by the information regarding the forthcoming Austro-German 'Caporetto' offensive, in which the French and English did not believe.

BIBLIOGRAPHY

The following list of works on the period, mainly in my own possession or from the London Library, aims at giving further information on each chapter. More recent books have been included where possible. The fullest Bibliography up to 1926 is *Il Risorgimento*, edited by F. Lemmi in the Guide Bibliografiche series (Rome, Fondazione Leonardo). The list might be almost indefinitely extended and can be added to by perusal of the Bibliographies mentioned in separate volumes.

SOME GENERAL WORKS

ENGLISH

Cambridge Modern History. Vols. x-xii.
History of Europe. Fisher. Vol. iii.
History of Italian Unity (1815-1870). Bolton King.
The Making of Modern Italy (1815-1918). Maps and Bibliography. A. Solmi.
The Makers of Modern Italy (Napoleon to Mussolini). Marriott. 1931.

FRENCH

L'Europe du xixe siècle et l'idée de Nationalité. G. Weill. (Albin Michel, Paris.)
L'Eveil des Nationalités (1815-1848). Weill. (Alcan, Paris.)
Mémoires de Metternich (1773-1859).

ITALIAN

Il Risorgimento Italiano. E. Masi. (2 vols.)
Storia critica del Risg. Ital. C. Tivaroni. (7 vols.)
Biblioteca di storia Italiana Recente (1800-1870). (Bocca, Turin.) (B.S.I.R., 12 vols.)
Gli ultimi rivolgimenti Italiani 1831-1846. Gualterio. (Le Monnier, Florence.) (Documents.)
Pensiero politico Italiano (1700-1870). L. Salvatorelli. (Einaudi, Turin, 1935.)
Storia Contemporanea d'Italia. M. Rosi.
Storia d'Italia (1850-1866). Zini. Vol. ii. Documenti. Maps.

DIPLOMATIC

Histoire Diplomatique de l'Europe. Debidour. (Alcan, Paris.)
Cambridge History of Diplomacy.
Storia Documentata della Diplomazia Europea in Italia (1814-1861). N. Bianchi.

1715-1815

1. *Le origini del Risorgimento Italiano* (1748-1815). F. Lemmi. (Hoepli, Milan.)
2. *La preparazione intellettuale del Risorgimento Italiano* (1748-1789). Aldo Ferrari. (Treves, Milan.)
3. *L'Esplosione rivoluzionaria del Risorgimento* (1789-1815). A. Ferrari. (Edizioni Corbaccio, Milan.)
4. *L'Italia prima della rivoluzione francese* (1735-1789). Tivaroni. (1st vol. of *Storia Critica*).
   L'Italia durante il dominio Francese. Tivaroni. Vols. ii and iii.
5. *The Age of Reason*. R. B. Mowat. (Chapter x on Italy.) 1934.
   The Romantic Age. R. B. Mowat. 1937.

6. *Le origini del Risorgimento politico dell' Italia Meridionale.* (2 vols.) Attilio Simioni. (G. Principato, Roma 1925.)
7. *Storia di Napoli.* Colletta. Vols. i-iii. (English trans.)

1815-1831

Bianchi (*Storia Doc.*). Vols. i and ii, part of vol. iii.
Debidour (*Hist. Diplom.*). Vol. i, ch. iv-vi.
Naples. Pepe. *Memorie.* Ch. xxiv ff..
        Colletta. *Storia di Napoli.* Vol. iv. (English trans.)
Piedmont. *Carlo Alberto.* Rodolico. Vol. i.
        Carlo Alberto in attesa del Trono. A. Codignola. (1936.)
        Carlo Alberto: Lettere a F. Truchness. 1937.
        B.S.I.R. Vols. xi and xii.
        Memoriali di Carlo Alberto.
        Carlo Alberto. Raffaele di Castillo. 1938. (Bompiano.)
        Carlo Alberto e le perfidie Austriache. P. Vayra.
        Sul Ventuno in Piemonte. Manno.
        Gli ultimi reali de Savoia. D. Perrero.
        Italy in the Making. Berkeley. Vol. i. 1815-1846.
On the Revolution of July and the rising of Central Italy in 1831.
   Le Cospirazioni del 1831. G. Ruffini. (Zanichelli, Bologna.)
   Ciro Menotti e l'idea unitaria nell' insurrezione del 1831. A. Solmi. (Modena.)
   Carlo Rossi e i suoi 'Diari' sul 1831. G. Canevazzi.
   L'Epilogo della rivoluzione del 1831. A. Sorbelli. (Modena.)
   Louis-Philippe, Metternich et la crise Italienne de 1831-1832. C. Vidal. (De Boccard, Paris.) (1931.)
   Berkeley. *Italy in the Making.* Vol. i.

1831-1848

Bianchi (*Stor. Doc.*). Vols. iii-v.
Weill. *L'Europe du xixᵉ siècle.* Bk. i, ch. vi (Bibliography).
Gualterio. Vols. 1-4, 1831-1846 (Documents).

MAZZINI

Biographies: Bolton King.
        Griffith, G. O. (1932.)
        Salvemini (chiefly classified extracts from Mazzini's own works).
Bonomi, Ivanoe. *Mazzini Triumviro della Repubblica Romana.* (Einaudi, 1936.)
Pensiero Pol. Ital. Ch. vi.
Passamonti, E. *Nuova luce sui processi del 1833.* (La Monnier, Firenze, 1930.)
Carlo Alberto e Francesco IV d' Austria d'Este. Lettere.

CARLO ALBERTO

C. A. *Lettere a Thaon de Revel* (Ed. G. Gentile). (Treves, Milan.)
C. A. inedito. *Diario autografo.* (Mondadori, 1931.)
Memorie inedite del 1848 (War diary).
Rodolico. Vol. ii. (1831-1843.)
Fossati. *Saggi di politica economica C. Albertina.* (1930.)
Prato, G. *Fatti e dottrine economiche alla vigilia del 1848.* B.S.I.R. Vol. ix.
Della Margherita. *Memorandum storico-politico.*
Berkeley. G. F. H., Vol. i, 1815-1846; G. F. H. and J., Vol. ii, 1846-1848; Vol. iii, *The War of 1848.* (Full Bibliography.)

Silva, P. *La Monarchia di Luglio e l'Italia.*
Lovera e Rinieri, S.J. *Clemente Solaro della Margherita.* (3 vols.) (Bocca, Turin.) 1931.
Predari. *I primi vagiti della Libertà Italiana in Piemonte* (rare).
Lemmi. *La politica estera di Carlo Alberto.*
Della Rocca. *Memories of a Veteran.*
Crosa. *La Concessione dello statuto.* 1936.
Colombo, A. *Dalle Riforme allo Statuto di Carlo Alberto.*
Mameli, G. *La vita e gli scritti.* Vol. i. 'La Nuova Italia,' Editrice, Venezia.
Taylor, A. J. P. *The Italian Problem in European Diplomacy* (1847-1849). 1934.

The Literary Movement

Greenfield. *Economics and Liberalism in the Risorgimento, 1814-1848.* (Johns Hopkins Press, Baltimore.) 1934.
Ferrari, Aldo. *L'Italia durante la Restaurazione.* Ch. iii.
Stella, Maria. *I nostri romanzi.* (Rome 1926.)
De Sanctis. *History of Italian Literature.* Ch. xx.

Tuscany

Hancock, W. K. *Ricasoli and the Risorgimento in Tuscany.*
Tivaroni: Parte vi. *La Toscana.*

States of the Church

Tivaroni: Parte vii. *Lo stato Pontificio.*
Farini. *Lo Stato Romano.* English trans.: *The History of Rome* (1815-1850). Berkeley. Vols. i, ii and iii.

1849

Trevelyan. *Manin and the Venetian Revolution of 1848.*
Garibaldi's Defence of the Roman Republic.
Dabormida. *La Vita e i tempi del Generale Giuseppe Dabormida.*
Huch, R. *La difesa di Roma.* (Ital. trans.)
Bonomi. *Mazzini Triumviro della Repubblica Romana.* 1936.

1849-1861

Cavour

English. *Paléologue.* (English trans.)
Thayer. *Cavour.* (Bibliography.)
Whyte. *Early Life and Letters.*
Political Life and Letters. (Bibliography.) 1930.
Orsi. *Cavour.* (English trans.)
French. Matter. *Cavour.* (3 vols.)
Italian. Massari. *Cavour.*
Cappa. *Cavour.* (Laterza, Bari, 1932.)
German. Treitschke. *Cavour.* (Ital. trans.)
Artom e Blanc. *Cavour in Parlamento* (selected speeches).
Chiala. *Lettere.* (6 vols.)
Trevelyan. *Garibaldi and the Making of Italy.*
Chiala. *Le Gouvernement Représentatif en Piémont* (1849-1852).
Zanichelli: Studi. Part i. *Studi di storia costituzionale e politica del Risorgimento Italiano.*
B.S.I.R. Vol. iv. 1853-1856 (The War in the Crimea).

THE WAR OF 1859

Wylly, H. C. Magenta and Solferino.
Bazancourt. La Campagne. (2 vols.)
Urquhart D. On the Italian War.

1861-1866

ASPROMONTE

Luzio. Aspromonte e Mentana. (Documenti inediti.) 1935.

THE CONVENTION OF SEPTEMBER

Jacini, S. Il tramonto del Potere Temporale (1860-1870) nelle relazioni degli Ambascia-
tori Austriaci a Roma. (Laterza, Bari, 1931.)
Politica Segreta Italiana (1863-1870).
La Marmora. Un po' più di luce sugli eventi politici e militari dell'anno 1866.
Massari. Alfonso La Marmora. Ch. xxxi-xxxiii.

WAR OF 1866

Zini. Storia. Vol. v, ch. vii.
The O'Clery. The Making of Italy (1856-1870). The author was in the Papal
Zouaves and gives that point of view.

1866-1870

Luzio (op. cit. supra Mentana).
Jacini, S. (op. cit. supra).
Tavallini. La vita e i tempi di Giovanni Lanza. Vol. ii, ch. xix-xxi.
Genova di Revel. Sette mesi al Ministero.

THE ROMAN QUESTION

Commissione Reale Editrice de' Carteggi Cavouriani. (2 vols.)
Binchy. Church and State in Fascist Italy. Chapters i and ii give an excellent
summary of the problem and a full Bibliography. 1941.

1870-1896

Croce, B. A History of Italy from 1871 to 1915.
Hentze, M. Pre-Fascist Italy. (Bibliography and notes.) 1939.
Cilibrizzi, S. Storia parlamentare, politica e diplomatica d'Italia.
Petruccelli della Gattina. Storia d'Italia del 1866 al 1880.
Lemonon, E. De Cavour à Mussolini. 1938.
Rosi, M. Storia Contemporanea. Part iii. (For culture: economic progress.)
Bolton King and T. Okey. Italy To-day (1901). (Politics: Industry: Finance:
Education: Emigration, etc.)

1896-1900

See above.

1900-1914

Ercole, F. Pensatori e uomini d'azione. Ch. xi-xiii. 1935.
Croce (op. cit.)
Hentze (op. cit.)
Giolitti, G. Memorie.
Sprigge. The Development of Modern Italy. 1943.

1914-1918

THE WAR

Barone, E. *Storia militare della nostra guerra.*
Cadorna, L. *La Guerra alla Fronte Italiana.* (2 vols.)
Libro Verde. *Documenti diplomatici italiani.*

THE PEACE

Italy at the Paris Peace Conference. Réné Albrecht-Carrie. (Columbia University Press, 1938.) The fullest and most authoritative source.

Publications of the Regio Istituto per la storia del Risorgimento Italiano, a series of recent volumes classified under 'Sources', 'Memoirs' and 'Scientific'. The full list of publications appears in each volume. One of the latest obtainable, *Lettere di Luciano Manara* (1939), gives 38 volumes. They are of varied importance.

Collezione Storica del Ris. Ital. Soc. Tip. Modenese. Like the above, the list of volumes published appears in each publication. The list is too long to reproduce. *L'Epilogo della rivoluzione del 1831* of Sorbelli is one of the series (see under 1815-1831).

INDEX

Alfieri, Marquis: 19

Balbo, C.: 49; Prime Minister, 62
Bava-Beccaris, General: 206-7
Beauharnais: 15, 16
Beccaria, Marquis: 7, 8
Bissolati: 259
Bonaparte, Napoleon: defeats Sardinians, 11; creates Cisalpine Republic, 11; signs Treaty of Campoformio, 11; Marengo, 15; divides Italy into three areas, 15; enlarges Cisalpine; influence on Italy, 17-18

Cadorna, Carlo: Minister, 80
Cadorna, General: occupies Rome, 177
Cadorna, General Luigi: 233; first offensive, 235; Austria's Trentino offensive, 238-9; capture of Gorizia, 240; Bainsizza offensive, 245; Caporetto, 247; retired, 252.
Cairoli, B.: Premier, 187; Congress of Berlin, 188; saves the King, 189; resigns, 189; 2nd Ministry; France occupies Tunis; resigns, 189
Cavour: early career, 88; member for Turin; Minister of Commerce, 89; Minister of Finance; creates centre party, 90; the Great Ministry, 91; the policy; difficulty with Austria, 92; foreign policy; sends troops to the Crimea, 94; Law on the Convents, 96; Congress of Paris, 97-8; Austrian policy, 99; Plombières, 105; treaty with France, 106; the struggle for war, 108 ff.; the ultimatum, 110; Minister for

War, 123; Tuscan policy, 124; Villafranca, 126; resignation, 127; return to power, 129; surrenders Nice and Savoy for Tuscany and Emilia, 130; Garibaldi's expedition, 132; struggle with Garibaldi, 135; invasion of Papal States, 136; first Italian Parliament, 137; speeches on Rome, 138; death, 139; the Cavourian tradition, 141, 254
Charles III of Naples: conquers S. Italy, 2; his reforms, 6
Charles Albert: Regent in 1821, 30; exiled, 31; King of Sardinia, 37; his policy, 46-8, 51-4; his reforms, 55; grants a constitution, 56, 86; war on Austria, 57; battle of Pastrengo, 59; S. Lucia, 60; Goito, 61; Custoza, 64; retreat to Milan, 66; Armistice of Salasco, 71; battle of Novara, 79; abdicates, 80; death, 80
Charles Felix: King of Sardinia in 1821, 30; exiles Charles Albert, 31; proposes to disinherit him, 33; at Congress of Verona; death, 37
Clement XIII: crime in Papal States, 4
Comitato Cosmopolita: 34-6
Crispi, F.: persuades Garibaldi, 131; pro-dictator in Sicily, 133; Minister of the Interior, 185-6; resigns, 186; tour of Europe, 187; Prime Minister, 192-6; 2nd Ministry, 198-201

D'Annunzio, G.: 220, 226, 232; seizes Fiume, 262; expelled, 263
D'Azeglio, M.: his historical novels,